GUY VAN HERBRUGGEN
CHARLES KENNEDY

THE STORY OF THE MD-11

DESIGNED BY SIMON DE RUDDER

astral HORIZON

Acknowledgements & References

Following the retirement of the last McDonnell Douglas MD-11 from passenger service in 2014 it seems appropriate to pay tribute to McDonnell Douglas last tri-jet workhorse: the MD-11.

First of all, our thanks to Simon De Rudder for his hard work in the design of this book.

Unless indicated, all pictures are from Guy Van Herbruggen's collection. Many photos shown were bought or exchanged at slide conventions. If the photographer is unknown, we would like to apologise for using these slides without stating the photographer's name, location or date.

We would like to record our appreciation to the following persons particularly for supplying photographic material: Sam Chui for a great cover image shot in Phuket, Rainer Bexten, Freek Blokzijl, Alex Saffe, James Rowson, Felix Gottwald, Tim Bryan, Sébastien Charousset, Frank de Koster, Simon De Rudder, Benoît Denet, Marco Dotti, Jannik Femerling, Martin Fenner, Eddy J. Gual, Jacques Guillem, George Hamlin, Jean-Marie Hanon, Michel Huart, Kentaro Iemoto, Pawel Kierzkowski, Julian Klein, André Kuiper, Paolo Maggiolo, Michael S. Prophet, Pierre Rohr, Michel Saint Félix, Nicholas Scherrer, Frank Schuchardt, Robert Szymczak, Mark Tang, Wil Teunissen, Richard Vandervord, Guy Viselé, John Wegg and Chi Lam Wong.

We are especially indebted to Kevin Stokes, MD-11 enthusiast for sharing a comprehensive collection of MD-11 pictures, McDonnell Douglas technical brochures - mostly acquired before the takeover of McDonnell Douglas by Boeing. Kevin also keeps up-to-date latest MD-11 development on a well-documented web site at www.md-eleven.net.

We would also like to express our thanks to former Swissair MD-11 First Officer Pierre Rohr for his recollections of a memorable flight to India and Pakistan depicted in chapter 7; to André Kuiper for his technical support in chapter 3; to Centurion Air Cargo MD-11 Captain Carlos M. Rodriguez for sharing his Aircraft Operations Manual and his experience on the aircraft; Dan Dill for his invaluable insight into flying the MD-11; to Servaas Verbrugge for sharing the MD-11 production list from his airlinerlist.com web site.

At Astral Horizon Press, we would like to thank Bhavna Vadher, Steve Finnigan and Ed Richards and our fellow authors Sebastian Schmitz and Christiaan Van Heijst; thanks for being on our team.

Dino Carrara at Aviation News, Craig West, Barry Woods-Turner and Andy Martin at Airliner World, Andy Mason at Key Publishing, Enrique Perrella at Airways magazine; Brian Wiklem; MigBro Chris Belcher and Wing Commander Peter Shorter; Ian Rowell, Mick Plock, Paul Bradd, Adrian Potter; British Airways; Tony Boden.

McDonnell Douglas is one of the great names in the US and world aviation history. Since the 1997 takeover of McDonnell Douglas by Boeing, the Seattle manufacturer refers to aircraft such as the DC-10 and MD-11 as Boeing products. In this book, when talking about the majestic aircraft as the DC-10 and MD-11, we felt more appropriate to refer to the original manufacturer's McDonnell Douglas designation.

We recognize that some technical descriptions, aircraft and engine model names and designations mentioned herein are the property of the trademark holder. We use them for identification and historical purposes only. This is not an official publication.

The Story Of The MD-11
Guy Van Herbruggen and Charles Kennedy
ISBN 978-0-9932604-5-2

79 Wardour Street London W1D 6QB United Kingdom
www.theairlineboutique.com

Contents

Photo McDonnell Douglas

1 The road to the MD-11

I. THE GOLDEN AGE OF THE PROPLINER

Donald Wills Douglas was born in Brooklyn, New York, on April 6, 1892. His love of aviation started early, and as a teenager he travelled to Fort Myer in Arlington County, Virginia, to witness the 1908 exhibition flights performed by Orville Wright for the benefit of the US military establishment, the first-ever flights at a US military installation.

The following year Douglas joined the Naval Academy at Annapolis in Maryland, but left in 1912 to study the nascent science of flight, becoming in 1914 the first person to graduate from MIT (Massachusetts Institute of Technology) with a Bachelor of Science in Aeronautical Engineering.

After a brief stint working on dirigible design at the Connecticut Aircraft Company, Douglas joined the Glenn Martin Company in August 1915, making Chief Engineer at the age of 23. When the Glenn Martin Company merged with the Wright Brothers Company in 1916 to form Wright-Martin, Douglas left to become chief engineer for the US Army Signal Corps.

After another brief stint at the reformed Glenn L Martin Company, now in Cleveland Ohio, where he designed the MB-1 bomber, Douglas struck out for pastures fresh in California to form the Davis-Douglas Company with a $40,000 investment from financier David Davis. The intention of the partnership was to build the first aircraft to cross the USA nonstop but the Douglas Cloudster only made it as far as Fort Bliss Texas before it's journey was cut short due to engine failure. However, the aircraft did achieve two milestones — it was the first-ever aircraft lift a payload which was greater than its own empty weight, and set a local Pacific coast altitude record of 19,160 feet. Most significant of all, however: it was the first aircraft to bear the name Douglas.

Following the dissolution of the Davis-Douglas partnership, the Douglas Aircraft Company was formed on July 22, 1921 at the Santa Monica airfield, located at a picturesque spot on the Pacific coast to the northwest of downtown Los Angeles, California.

The company's first military contract resulted in the delivery of ninety DT (Douglas Torpedo) biplanes, forty-six of which were built at Santa Monica and delivered to the navies of the US, Norway and Peru; twenty more were built under licence by Lowe-Willard-Fowler in New York, six by the Naval Aircraft Factory in Philadelphia, eleven by the Dayton Wright Company, and seven by Marinens Flyvebåtfabrik in Horten, Norway.

The expanding team, which included future aerospace titan John Northrop, created the Douglas World Cruiser (DWC), building five to fly around the world. The four-ship expedition set off from Seattle on April 6, 1924, with two aircraft returning to Seattle joined by the prototype for the final stretch on September 28 after covering 23,942 nautical miles (44,342 km) and averaging seventy miles per hour (113 kmh) for 371 hours and eleven minutes in the air. The success of the DWC put the Douglas Aircraft Company firmly in the big leagues, with a new motto, First Around The World, Around The World First, and a new logo showing three aircraft encircling a globe. This logo would evolve over the decades to include a rocket, and remains Boeing's logo today.

It was the crash of TWA 599 on March 31, 1931 on the first leg of a flight from Kansas City to Los Angeles that stimulated Douglas Aircraft among others to make a great leap forward with airliner technology. The main cause was the failure of the Fokker F-10 Trimotor's wooden wing whose glue was weakened by moisture. The death toll of two crew and six passengers included beloved Knute Rockne, one of the greatest coaches in American football history. Inadequate hardware had killed before, but the loss of such a well-known figure made the accident a turning point and galvanised the aerospace industry into action.

Boeing were first to respond; the B-247 took to the air for the first time on February 8, 1933. Although TWA liked what they saw, their order was rejected because Boeing was also an airline and the first sixty all went into service with Boeing Air Transport, starting on May 22. (Boeing Air Transport later became United Airlines.) TWA turned instead to Douglas, who after initially doubting the market was big enough to justify the development cost, built a single DC-1 proof-of-concept prototype which first flew from Santa Monica on July 1, 1933 under the control of Captain Carl Cover. The all-metal, low-wing, twin-engined airliner was fully heated, insulated against noise, and was able to takeoff, fly and land on one engine; even in this embryonic form fully represented the leap forward the airline industry badly needed.

DC-2 • NC13717 • August 1979 Photo Collection Jacques Barbé

DC-3 • ET-AAP • Djibouti • March 1977 Photo Collection Jacques Barbé

After performing over two-hundred test flights including a cross-country trip in just thirteen hours and five minutes, the DC-1 was handed over to TWA on September 15. The cost of building the aircraft was $325,000 which was immediately justified when TWA placed an order for twenty production models, which were designated DC-2s.

The original DC-1 was sold to Scottish aristocrat Lord Forbes in May 1938, after which it went to Spain and flew for LAPE (Lineas Aereas Postales Espanolas), the Spanish Republican Air Force, and Iberia Airlines, until it force-landed near Malaga in December 1940 and was written off.

The first DC-2 flew on May 11, 1934, and went into service with TWA the following week, May 18, since all the test flying for the type had already been completed with the sole DC-1. TWA's initial commitment was followed up by orders from KLM, LOT Polish Airlines, Swissair and LAPE; five were built under licence in Japan by Nakajima Aircraft Co, and Douglas also sold sixty-two DC-2s to the US military, bringing production up to a total of one hundred and ninety-eight machines.

However, the DC-2 was merely a warm-up for the DC-3; after a marathon phone call between Donald Douglas and American Airlines CEO CR Smith, Douglas agreed to go ahead with a bigger airliner, based around Smith's desire to replace his fleet of Curtiss Condor IIs with a DC-2 category aircraft that would be wide enough to accommodate sleeping births. Led by engineer Arthur E. Raymond, the Douglas Sleeper Transport (DST) with berths for sixteen, or the DC-3 with seats for twenty-one, took to the skies over Santa Monica for the first time on December 17, 1935.

The number of DC-3s produced defies belief to this day — 16,079. The total unpacks as 607 civil DC-3s and 10,048 military C-47s produced either in Santa Monica, at a new plant down the Pacific coastline at Long Beach, or at a third production line in Oklahoma City; plus 4,937 in the Soviet Union as the Lisunov Li-2, initially at Aircraft Factory 84 in Khimki just northwest of Moscow, and after the evacuation of Moscow, at the factory of the Tashkent Aviation Production Association (TAPO) in the Uzbek Soviet Republic; and a further 487 under license as the L2D in Japan by two different airframers, the Nakajima Aircraft Co and the Showa Corporation.

American Airlines inaugurated service on June 26, 1936; the transformative impact of the DC-3 being so great that this could be considered the founding date of the modern airline industry. By the end of the year KLM was flying scheduled service from Amsterdam to Sydney, which even in 2017 would be one of the world's longest same-plane air routes.

Even before the DC-3 was in service, Douglas built a single DC-4E, a four-engined tricycle-undercarriage airliner with a triple tail that bore a resemblance to the Lockheed Constellation, in response to a request from United Airlines. First flying on June 7, 1938, the sole DC-4E was put into service by United but proved to be expensive to operate and performance was less than hoped for. The single aircraft was sold to Imperial Japanese Airways, who claimed the aircraft had crashed into Tokyo Bay shortly after delivery, but was in fact used by the Nakajima Aircraft Co to reverse-engineer into the unsuccessful G5N bomber.

However the DC-4E did lead to the better-known DC-4, which shared the four piston engines of its proof-of-concept predecessor

DC-4 • ZS-BMH • South African Airways • Rand • September 2014

but a simplified empennage. The first production aircraft took to the air on Valentine's Day 1942 and 1,163 were built as C-54 transports for the US military to fight World War 2; after the end of hostilities, despite many war-surplus C-54s now available at bargain basement prices, another seventy-nine civilian versions were delivered to airlines including Pan Am, Sabena, Cubana, Iberia, Swissair and Aerolineas Argentinas. In addition, Canadair built seventy-one under licence, known as the North Star, powered by Rolls-Royce Merlin engines and delivered to Trans-Canada Airlines (TCA), the Royal Canadian Air Force (RCAF), Canadian Pacific Airlines (later CP Air) and BOAC (who renamed the aircraft the Argonaut).

During 1940 Douglas built twelve examples of the little-known DC-5, a high-wing transport that was developed from the A-20 Havoc bomber / intruder / night-fighter but overtaken by the global war effort; only longtime Douglas fan KLM (the only airline to operate all Douglas Commercial types) received their machines before the production line was shut down to make more SBD Dauntless dive bombers. Interestingly, the prototype became the personal aircraft of William Boeing, who named it Rover. Other DC-5s had interesting lives, whether it was the damaged and abandoned KLM aircraft that was captured in Indonesia by Japanese forces and later used as a troop transport in Japan, or the three that flew for the USAAF in Australia during the war.

With World War 2 over, Douglas returned to civvie street along with the rest of the nation and launched the DC-6, an evolution of the DC-4 that started life as a military programme called the XC-112 and boasted a stretched fuselage, transatlantic range, and a pressurised passenger cabin. The DC-6 first flew on February 15, 1946 with first deliveries to both American Airlines and United Airlines on November 24. A fatal crash in Utah caused by an in-flight fire on a United flight on October 24 of the following year was followed by a similar conflagration on an American Airlines flight three weeks later; luckily the latter event ended safely with an emergency landing in Gallup, New Mexico. The type was grounded worldwide for four months until the cause was found to be venting fuel which was finding its way into a cabin heating air scoop; once the design flaw was rectified, the DC-6 went on to become the most successful post-war Douglas propliner, with 538 civilian examples delivered to commercial airlines, plus 101 C-118As for the US Air Force and sixty-five R6D-1s for the US Navy.

American Airlines led the way once more for the last Douglas propliner, the DC-7, essentially a stretched (by forty inches) DC-6 powered by Wright R-3350 turbo-compound engines. 105 standard DC-7s were delivered, all to US carriers, with a first flight of May 18 1953, and entry into service in November the same year. 112 DC-7Bs were built with increased gross weight and extended range, followed by 121 DC-7C Seven Seas, which, as the name suggests, had true long haul capability including nonstop transatlantic range in both directions.

The DC-7 was a sales hit, ordered in significant numbers by customers throughout the US (including fifty-eight for American Airlines and fifty-seven for United) and Europe (BOAC, Sabena,

DC-7C • OO-SFA • Sabena Photo Sabena

Swissair, SAS, and KLM among others) as well as further afield (Japan Air Lines, Mexicana, Persian Air Services; South African Airways used the DC-7B to fly all the way from Johannesburg to London with just a single stop), although the Wright R-3350s were troublesome, with diversions due to engine shutdowns. The joke about such-and-such four-engined aircraft being "the best three-engined aircraft ever built" has been applied to many different types but its true origin is the Wright-powered DC-7 and Super Connie, which would routinely end a trip, either at the destination or at some unplanned intermediate airfield, with a prop feathered.

II. THE JET AGE

The whine of the jet engine was not a novelty in the 1950s, as Maxime Guilliame had patented the idea of using a turbine to power an aircraft as early as 1921, and Alan Arnold Griffith published the ground-breaking An Aerodynamic Theory Of Turbine Design in 1926 for the Royal Aircraft Establishment. Fellow Brit Frank Whittle worked through the 1930s developing axial compressor designs, but the simultaneous efforts of Hans von Ohain in Germany meant the first jet aircraft to fly was the Heinkel He-178 on August 27, 1939. The Messerschmitt Me-262 followed it into the air on July 18, 1942 and entered service as the world's first operational jet-powered fighter in April 1944. The Brits were right behind, with the Gloster Meteor entering service with the Royal Air Force (RAF) in July of the same year.

With World War 2 still raging, the government of the United Kingdom formed the Brabazon Committee to determine the UK's civil airliner requirements in the post-war phase. Various jet-powered configurations were considered, from small airmail carriers to passenger jetliners, and in December 1945 BOAC ordered ten de Havilland DH 106 Comets. The world's first jet airliner flight was a thirty-one minute sortie in the evening summer sunshine of July 27, 1949 out of Hatfield in the northern suburbs of London, under the command of John "Cat's Eyes" Cunningham (a famous night fighter pilot in World War 2), along with co-pilot Harold "Tubby" Waters, and engineers John Wilson (electrics), Frank Reynolds (hydraulics), and test observer Tony Fairbrother. After two years of intense test flying, the first production aircraft, G-ALYP (known as "Yoke Peter" in the phonetic alphabet of the era) first flew on January 9, 1951 and was handed over to BOAC's Comet Unit for test flying, training, and route trials. The world's first jet-powered airline flight took place on May 2, 1952 from London to Johannesburg with five stops en route. By the summer of 1953 BOAC was operating eight jet departures a week out of London — three to Johannesburg, two to Tokyo, two to Singapore, and one to Colombo, all with many stops en route. Rome, Beirut, Basra, Karachi, Rangoon, Cairo, Hong Kong, Hargeisa, Nairobi, Blantyre… Global mass transit was on its way.

Boeing had made some inroads into the passenger airliner market with the B-377 Stratocruiser (another "best three-engined aircraft ever built") based on the B-29 Superfortress bomber, but only sold fifty-six (as well as 888 of the C-97 Stratofreigher military tanker / transport). The USAF Strategic Air Command (SAC) was in the market for a jet-powered aerial refueling tanker and transport, and Boeing already had significant jet experience with their B-47 Stratojet which had first flown on December 17, 1947. Consequently, as early as 1950, Boeing were seriously looking at building a jet transport called the Model 473-60C, and by early 1952 started custom-building a one-off proof-of-concept aircraft, which became the Model 367-80, registration N70700. The machine was unveiled in a public roll-out ceremony at the Renton plant on May 15, 1954, and America made a major leap towards the jet age when the "Dash Eighty" took to the air over Washington State on July 15, 1954.

Douglas had created a jet-propelled test aircraft, the XB-43 Jetmaster, as early as 1946, with a first flight date of May 17. The aircraft had stability issues but was an important first step into the jet age for what was then the world's dominant civil airframer. It was followed by another experimental design, the D-558-1 Skystreak. By 1948 Douglas was producing a successful jet fighter aircraft, the F3D Skyknight (265 built), which was eclipsed in 1951 by the supersonic F4D Skyray which sold even more (422) and marked the first time a carrier-based aircraft held the world's absolute speed record of 752.943 mph (1211.74 kph).

Douglas established an office at their Santa Monica plant to study a possible future jet-powered airliner. Chief Project Engineer Ivor Shogrun led a team of designers through the parameters to be massaged: range, payload, number of engines, and cost. Hundreds of configurations were considered, including a delta wing. By mid-1953, a swept-wing design with four podded underwing engines was decided upon, and a full-size wooden mock-up was built to show potential customers. Two versions were proposed: the DC-8A was a domestic machine with a maximum takeoff weight of 209,600 lbs (95,073 kgs) offered for delivery in 1956, while the DC-8B was an overwater variant with a maximum takeoff weight of 248,000 lbs (112,490 kgs) offered for delivery from 1958.

By September 1954, Douglas had committed over $3 million and 250,000 man-hours to the DC-8 project. However, despite the appearance of the 367-80 up in Seattle, Douglas felt the US military would turn to more than one manufacturer for their tanker / transport needs, so a military sale was assured.

However, in July 1955, General Curtis LeMay announced an order for twenty-one Boeing KC-135s, the production version of the 367-80. Despite personal appeals by Donald Douglas Sr, the availability of the KC-135 at least a year earlier than an equivalent Douglas product meant SAC had decided to go with an exclusive supplier. (Boeing's invention of the flying air-to-air refueling boom first deployed on the KC-97 Stratofreighter tanker variant of the B-377 Stratocruiser also helped.) Being the exclusive supplier to the US military in this niche proved to be incredibly lucrative for Boeing, as by the time production ended in 1965, 803 KC-135s had been delivered.

Losing the SAC order demonstrated to Douglas that being second in the race had serious commercial consequences. Since a hand-tooled flying prototype would consume valuable time, it was decided that Douglas would go straight to production from Ship One, and the first eight aircraft would be used for flight testing. To reduce surprises, in summer 1955 a complete mock-up was built at a cost of $7.5 million, to establish layout for major items such as ducting, wiring, fuel and hydraulic routing, even the best location for the "black boxes". Accommodating the request from United Airlines for a six-abreast seating layout meant a bigger wing and tail.

The earlier reluctance of Douglas to fully commit to a jet-powered transport seemed, prudent position to have taken, with the advent of the Lockheed L-188 Electra, Bristol Britannia and Vickers Viscount prop-jets all entering service while the pure jet de Havilland Comet remained grounded after a series of accidents caused by structural failure. The final decision to go ahead with a pure-jet airliner remained with Donald Douglas Sr himself, and it was made on June 7, 1955, with an allocated budget of $450 million, the most expensive privately-financed corporate venture ever, up to that time.

It was ironic that Boeing, by grasping the initiative with the 367-80, had been able to beat Douglas to the punch with the KC-135 order, but Douglas, having acquiesced to United's need for a six-abreast economy seating layout, was able to get the lion's share of the Pan Am order announced on October 13, 1955 — twenty-five DC-8s as opposed to twenty of the five-abreast 707. Because the Pan Am DC-8 order was for the overwater B variant, it was understood that Pan Am would not get the first aircraft built, which would all be domestic A machines, but with that order in the book, the DC-8 was in business.

Following the October 1955 IATA convention in New York, Donald Douglas Sr invited officials from twenty of the world's top airlines to Santa Monica where, on October 25, he and United Airlines president Pat Patterson jointly announced United's order for thirty DC-8As at a cost of $175 million with deliveries beginning in May 1959, the largest single order ever placed for commercial airliners.

June 1956 saw the important announcement that Douglas would build their jet age transports at their Long Beach plant, which had seen the creation of 4,285 C-47s (and over 3,000 B-17s under licence from Boeing) during World War 2. The production line would be on a new fifty-five acre plot alongside the existing factory, which by 1956 was being used for the production of the C-133 Cargomaster and B-66 Destroyer light bomber. Completion date for the plant was planned to be May 1957, but in the event, workers started moving into the sub-assembly area of the plant on February 18.

An important milestone in the preparation for flight took place on March 26, 1958, when four Pratt & Whitney JT3 engines were attached to Ship One, which was rolled out of the hangar into broad daylight before an invited audience including representatives of all seventeen customer airlines, with Donald Douglas Sr waving from the cockpit windows on one side, and his son, Donald Douglas Jr, now president of the company, waving from the other.

May 30 was the big day when DC-8 Ship One N8008D took to the air for the first time, with Arnold G. "Heimie" Heimerdinger at the controls, William "Bill" Magruder in the right seat and Paul Patten at the flight engineer's panel. Flight test engineer Bob Rizer was also onboard, monitoring the flight-data recorders in the main cabin. An escape chute was installed in the lower fuselage in case a rapid inflight evacuation by parachute was necessary, but the two-hour, seven-minute flight went up to 21,000 feet and 350 knots and back without a hitch, accompanied at times by a Cessna T-37 and a United Airlines DC-7 cameraship.

DC-8-51 • N8008D • Lufthansa • Brussels Photo Jacques Barbé

Ship Two N8108D first flew on November 29, followed by Ship Three N8208D on December 28 and Ship Four N8038D on January 2, 1959. The first DC-8B, registered N800PA and powered by Pratt & Whitney JT4A engines, joined the test programme on February 20 in full Pan Am livery, followed by two more Pan Am DC-8Bs shortly after. The first Rolls-Royce Conway-powered DC-8, N6577C, first flew on July 23, 1959.

One initial disappointment to come from the test programme was that parasitic drag, caused by friction between the airframe or wing and surrounding airstream, was higher than expected. While the guarantee was a cruising speed of 493 knots at 30,000 feet, only 469 knots was being achieved. Ship Two was grounded for a series of wing modifications; a revised wing tip and changes to the shape of the engine exhaust cones went some way to fixing the problem. However there was still a small shortfall and Donald Douglas Sr. reduced the price of affected aircraft.

As plans for more subtypes hit the drawing board, a new and definitive model identification system for the DC-8 was needed, and on February 4, 1960, Douglas vice president of commercial programmes Jackson R. McGowan announced that the domestic version previously known as the DC-8A and powered by JT3C-6 turbojets would become the DC-8-10 (with minor differences of engine power and weights creating the -11 and -12). Domestic DC-8As powered by more powerful JT4A powerplants would become the DC-8-20 (and -21), and the overwater DC-8B, also powered by JT4As, would become the DC-8-30 (and -31, -32, -33, -34). Finally, the DC-8 powered by Rolls-Royce Conways would become the DC-8-40. At the same time, a future variant powered by JT3D turbofans was announced, to become known as the DC-8-50.

June 3, 1959 saw the delivery of United's first DC-8-11, Ship Eight N8004U, at a ceremony at the factory in Long Beach. Delta's first DC-8-11 was handed over on July 21. Pilot training with the airlines' new toys took up the next couple of months, while Ship Seven N8068D made an important flight on August 31 from Long Beach to Baltimore to receive the DC-8-11's type certificate a whole month ahead of schedule. The certificate was presented to Donald Douglas Jr on the tarmac at Baltimore Friendship airport by Elwood R. Quesada, chief administrator of the FAA, before N8068D flew on to New York for a major press conference the next day with both United president Pat Patterson and Delta president C. E. Woolman. At the time of certification, the DC-8's order book contained commitments for 143 aircraft by eighteen airlines.

The era of Douglas commercial jets in service began on September 18, 1959. Delta were first into the air when DL923 left New York Idlewild (later JFK) at 0920, destination Atlanta; two hours and ten minutes later, United's first DC-8 flight blasted out of San Francisco, destination New York. By the end of 1959, twenty-one DC-8s had rolled off the line at Long Beach, all United or Delta DC-8-11s with the exception of two DC-8-41s for Trans Canada Airlines.

The first European airline to accept delivery of a DC-8 was, aptly, longtime Douglas champion KLM, on March 19, 1960. They began service on the Amsterdam to New York run on April 16, which became a daily service ten days later. SAS started Copenhagen to New York with their first DC-8-30 on May 1, and Alitalia's first DC-8-40 started Rome to New York via London on June 1.

The early jet age was beset by accidents related to the introduction of the new and demanding technology of jet-powered airliners, which ranged from hydraulic failures (in a single week in October 1960, two United DC-8s and a Western 720 made precautionary landings at Edwards AFB, and a Braniff 707-227 diverted to Carswell AFB near Fort Worth Texas, all due to hydraulic problems), to large-scale disasters such as the 1960 New York Midair Collision between a speeding United DC-8 and a TWA Super Constellation which killed 128 in the air and six on the ground. The first nine months of 1961 saw 995 people lose their lives in air disasters (316 in September alone) including sixty-one killed when a jointly operated KLM / Viasa DC-8 crashed into the Atlantic after leaving Lisbon, probably due to instrument failure; and seventeen were killed plus one on the ground in another United DC-8 crash in Denver caused by loss of directional control after landing due to a hydraulic fault.

On a more positive note, N9604Z, a DC-8-43 destined to become CF-CPG at Canadian Pacific, made history on August 21, 1961, by flying supersonic during a test flight over the Askania Tracking Range near Edwards AFB. This was the first time a commercial airliner exceeded Mach 1, and was not repeated until a Tupolev Tu-144 supersonic airliner broke the speed of sound for the first time on June 5, 1969 (Concorde's first trip through the sound barrier was on October 1 of the same year). The idea originated with Douglas test pilot Bill Magruder (who later became head of the FAA). The flight was carefully planned, with 5,000 lbs (2,268 kgs) of ballast in the rear cabin to provide an aft centre of gravity to assist with manoeuvrability during the pull-out. N9604Z was accompanied by a Lockheed F-104 Starfighter and a two-seat North American F-100 Super Sabre provided by the USAF Flight Test Centre to check speed and atmospheric data for accuracy, which was also corroborated by a weather balloon.

IV. THE DC-9 AND THE DC-8 STRETCH

For Douglas, the DC-8 was the all-important first step into the jet age, and connected the great cities of the world alongside the Boeing 707 and the British Vickers VC-10. The next step was to create a machine that could link smaller communities. In the early days of jet service, the big metal could be found on some of these routes, but a DC-8 was a lot of aeroplane to traverse the width of Michigan on a quick Detroit to Chicago run. Work on what would become the DC-9 began almost in parallel with the DC-8 in the form of the proposed Model 2067, a four-engined shrink of the DC-8 that was perhaps analogous to the Boeing 720 but for which there was little interest.

In France, Sud Aviation created the Caravelle, an eighty-seat rear-engined twin-jet which first flew on May 27, 1955 and entered service on April 26, 1959 on a multi-stop trip to Beirut in the service of Scandinavian Airlines. The Caravelle was an engineering and sales success – every national airline in western Europe deploying it as their shorthaul flagship with the exception of Ireland, Great Britain, Greece and Holland. The Caravelle was also a sales success in Africa, Asia and South America.

Douglas saw the Caravelle as an opportunity to steal a march on Boeing who were moving forward with the 727 trijet and in 1960 signed a two-year deal with Sud Aviation to build Caravelles in the USA under licence. An order for twenty such aircraft was solicited from TWA, but further sales did not materialise and indeed TWA's financial position in the final days of Howard Hughes' stewardship meant this order could not be consummated. Sud Aviation did a deal directly with United Airlines for twenty aircraft built in France which not only ended the Douglas-Sud deal but clarified the urgency of creating their own made-in-California shorthauler.

DC-8-62 • N801BN • Braniff • Brussels • June 1979 Photo Jacques Barbé

DC-8-61 • N8083U • United Airlines • San Francisco • January 1975
Photo Collection Jacques Barbé

Design work on the DC-9 began in earnest in 1962. Whereas Boeing prioritised commonality with the 707 on their 727 short haul product, Douglas went for a clean-sheet design featuring a small and highly efficient wing and high T-tail. FAA regulations at the time limited the maximum takeoff weight for a two-person cockpit to 36,300 kgs (80,000 lbs) which was where the DC-9 ended up, a weight which allowed for eighty passengers in a typical configuration.

As with the DC-8, Douglas dispensed with the building of prototypes; production airframe number one, N9DC, took to the air out of Long Beach airport for the first time on the morning of February 25, 1965. With the production line already up and running, the second airframe was airborne only weeks later and by July, five aircraft were hard at work in the test programme, meaning the type was able to be certified and ready for delivery to airline customers on November 23. The first flight of a DC-9 in revenue service was operated by Delta Airlines on December 8.

Meanwhile, to jump-start slumping DC-8 sales, a major stretch for trunk routes such as California to Hawaii and New York to Puerto Rico was embarked upon. The basic platform was much easier to stretch than the Boeing 707 which rode considerably closer to the runway; also, the DC-8's modest wing sweep meant engine pods would not risk scraping the ground during takeoff and landing. The DC-8-61 was the first stretched model, with a 200 inch (five metre) plug inserted ahead of the wing and another 240 inches (six metres) inserted behind the wing, resulting in a new fuselage length of 187 feet four inches (fifty-seven metres) and was able to accommodate 269 passengers in seating that was compatible with any other type

DC-9-34CF • 9Y-TFI • Long Beach • December 1977

Photo Collection Jacques Barbé

of airline seating using twin tracks along the floor (earlier DC-8s required bespoke seating that attached to the cabin wall). The cockpit instrumentation and lighting borrowed from the DC-9. The wing and engines were retained from the DC-8-55, making this, despite its impressive new dimensions, a "minimum change" upgrade.

A shorter stretch, the DC-8-62 had a new and upgraded wing, and the DC-8-63 married the new wing of the -62 to the stretched fuselage of the -62, create a true thoroughbred that could carry the biggest payloads of the early jet age across even the longest distances.

The three variants of the Series Sixty DC-8 were launched on April 4, 1965, with an initial order from SAS for four DC-8-62s with four options, followed by United Airlines for five DC-8-61s (and a top-up of various -50s) and Eastern Airlines for eight -61s. By the end of 1965, Douglas had orders for thirty-eight Series Sixtys as well as thirty-six -50s including twelve Jet Traders; and over 100 orders for the DC-9.

Cash flow problems that were a nuisance when orders were scarce was now a crisis with the boom in sales. The earlier decision to build both the DC-8 and DC-9 on the same production line had to be reversed as orders poured in, creating two separate production lines; this reorganisation alone ate up precious capital. Deliveries fell woefully behind schedule, with United asking Douglas to paint a test DC-8-61 in United livery so at least publicity photographs would give the illusion that the airline's new flagship was close to delivery even if reality was somewhat less appealing. The Vietnam War was adding to the difficulties of the commercial division, as the national war effort sucked up manpower and physical resources. With production lines going out of sync and parts having to be installed out of position, it was estimated that each aircraft delivery was costing Douglas half a million dollars.

V. MEET ME IN SAINT LOUIS

The state of distress at Douglas was widely known and merger partners circled, including North American, Martin Marietta, General Dynamics, Fairchild Aircraft and Signal Oil. The decision to merge with McDonnell Aircraft Corporation of Saint Louis, Missouri, was announced on January 13, 1967. The choice of savior wasn't a gigantic surprise as it was well known that chairman James D. McDonnell, chief design engineer on the Ford Tri-Motor, was keen to get back into the business of building airliners. Up to that point McDonnell were mostly famous for the F-4 Phantom fighter jet and the manned capsules for the Mercury and Gemini space programmes. The merger with Douglas created a powerhouse covering the full spectrum of manned flight – civil, military, space.

With the merger announcement still in the headlines, United finally received their first DC-8-61 on January 26, 1967 and inaugurated service on the busy Los Angeles to Honolulu run on February 25; Eastern Airlines opened DC-8-61PF service between New York and San Juan on March 3. The DC-9 was stretched to create the most popular single variant of DC jets, the -30 series, which ended up accounting for 662 of the 976 DC-9s produced; the first DC-9-30 was delivered to Eastern Airlines on February 27.

The first DC-8-63, N1503U, was rolled out on March 6 and first flew on April 10, another five hour sortie, this time with Cliff Stout and Harry Terrell flying. Meanwhile the DC-8-62 was certified on April 27, and the first example delivered to SAS on May 3. Entry into service followed on the Copenhagen to New York route on May 22. The DC-8-63 followed a similar pattern by being certified on June 29, the first machine delivered to KLM on July 15, and put into service on the North Atlantic on July 27.

The DC-8 was present on the airways with the early standard -10, -20, -30 and -40 series, in the early part of the jet age when flying was reserved for the megarich, movie stars, captains of industry, diplomats and spies, with hand-written paper tickets, boarding and deplaning by stairs, uncertain safety records even aboard household-name airline brands. The advent of the fan-powered -50 opened up the airways towards the end of the decade alongside the 707-320 with fares starting to come down. And although the Series Sixty machines were a product of the 1960s, it was in the 1970s they dominated, becoming trunk liners in an era when air travel started to look like it does today, with reservations handled by computer for the first time, boarding by airbridge, fares down and passenger numbers way up. No longer did every man wear a tie, and nor did every lady wear hat and gloves. The great human migration by air had begun in earnest.

IV. THE WIDEBODY AGE

Even as DC-8s were rolling off the line at Long Beach and the DC-9 was nearing readiness for airline service, Douglas, and their Advanced Design engineers in particular, was looking to the future. The US Department of Defense issued a request designated CX-HLS (Heavy Logistics System) for tenders to fulfil its need for a heavy lifter. The fuselage width was determined by the need to carry military vehicles in pairs, side-by-side. Douglas, Lockheed and Boeing were all asked to submit proposals.

The Lockheed entry was chosen, which became the C-5A Galaxy, and Boeing's research and development was used to create the Boeing 747 jumbo jet. Douglas looked at creating their own civilian jumbo, known internally as the D-918, with a proposed capacity of 900 passengers on two decks. However, this remained a paper aeroplane as Douglas was preoccupied with the possibilities of supersonic air travel, and it was widely thought at the time this was where the future lay. Even Boeing, fully immersed in the 747 programme, thought their jumbo was a stopgap, and that passenger airframes would be converted to cargo haulers as soon as the SSTs came online (led by, preferably, Boeing's own Mach 3+ swing-wing 2707).

Douglas took another look at widebody designs for their next civilian airliner, with the D-950 series of mostly double-bubble cross sections and the D-956 true double decker with dimensions approximately matching that of today's Airbus A380. However it was in May 1966 that the beginnings of what would become the DC-10 began to take shape, when the design team started to look at the development of a twin-engine "Airbus" intended to replace the Boeing 727, in response to an outline for a new airliner issued by American Airlines vice-president of engineering Frank Kolk.

Kolk could see that with lowering airfares and new liners such as the 727 and Douglas DC-9 arriving on the scene, runway and airspace congestion was becoming a major concern. The new airbus would carry 250 passengers (enjoying a generous 36 inches of seat pitch), be able to takeoff and land using La Guardia's postage-stamp 7,000 foot runways, and cruise at Mach .82 over a distance of 1,850 nautical miles with a full payload of 250,000 lbs. With a fuselage length of less than 150 feet to utilise existing parking, the passenger cabin would be a widebody with two aisles.

Led by senior configuration layout engineer Richard T. Cathers, various designs were considered including a V-tail design. The input of other carriers had slightly different expectations of the mission requirements: TWA felt that JFK, not little La Guardia, would be the main New York hub for domestic trunk routes (although, hedging their bets, still favoured low approach speeds), whereas United were more interested in a four-engined aircraft for New York to Los Angeles trips. European carriers felt their runways and airways faced a similar squeeze so had their own market for an airbus, but given the smaller size of the European continent, only required 750 to 1,000 miles of range.

While Boeing were fully committed to the 747, Lockheed had not built a civilian aircraft since the L-188 Electra and so began their own study on airbus designs, coming up with the CL-1011-28 twin engine widebody. The Lockheed entry was, even at this early stage, incorporating high tech solutions such as double-slotted Fowler flaps for high lift during takeoff approach and landing.

By August 1966, the latest designs under consideration at Douglas began to incorporate three or four engines for the first time, as the thrust needed to get the airbus off the ground at the start of its most demanding missions was in excess of 88,000 lbs, which was pretty much beyond the capability of any pair of powerplants available at the time or in the foreseeable future. The D-967-1 had an engine under each wing and one in the tail utilising an S-duct in the style of the Boeing 727, and the D-967-10 retained the centre engine but moved the outboards from under the wing to the side of the rear fuselage, in the style of a widebody 727. The -20 put two engines close to the fuselage under the left wing and one out on its own on the right wing, and the -30 had two engines rear mounted on the left side of the fuselage and one on the right. (Douglas engineers insisted that with a large rudder, the aircraft would remain perfectly flyable with the right engine shut down.) The D-968 was a four-engine version, with the -1 sporting two engines evenly spaced under each wing, and the -10 with rear mounted engines in pairs on either side of the fuselage in the style of the Ilyushin Il-62.

Another round of discussion with US domestic airlines at the end of 1966 saw that American Airlines was more philosophical about the number of engines, and was less married to the idea of a twin. Given that it would only operate to major hubs where self-sufficiency was not an issue, they did not see the need for an Auxiliary Power Unit (APU). TWA was keen on three engines but preferred the Rolls-Royce option to the General Electric engine that was being offered as standard, and asked that the high Mach .86 cruise speed of the 747 be matched. In case the forthcoming SSTs were unable to fly supersonically across the continental USA due to their sonic boom, transcontinental range was seen as essential. United sent mixed messages – their San Francisco engineering team wanted two engines and 1,850-mile range, while Chicago wanted four engines and true transcon range. Eastern joined TWA in asking for a three engine configuration. On November 22, 1966, a three-engined layout was chosen, with the outboard engines to be placed under the wing.

Other design elements were worked on, including establishing the size of the passenger main deck doors, by choosing three door sizes and placing each of them in the middle of a pedestrian tunnel that joined the two halves of the Long Beach facility during a shift change, to see which door sizes least impeded the progress of workers; two men could simultaneously pass through the 42-inch-wide aperture which was chosen for the new airbus. The landing gear had to support the weight of the machine and two four-wheel main gear bogies were chosen, with the possibility of adding an additional centreline two-wheel assembly for heavier variants.

The cockpit was still above the main deck in a hump similar to the 747 as nose-loading for cargo was still seen as an important function, but in late 1967 it was moved to the main deck in a more conventional layout. Four possibilities for the centre engine in the tail were considered, three with a straight pipe and one S-bend. By this point over 400 people were working on the programme under the leadership of Harold W. Adams who had led the DC-9 to a successful launch. He was instrumental in the fast development of the aircraft and specialised in systems design. After the costly debacle of the DC-8 and DC-9 delivery problems that had brought Douglas to its knees and necessitated the merger, major efforts were directed at forward planning including a new assembly building and engineering test centre.

Sales representatives from McDonnell Douglas began approaching airlines to lay the groundwork for soliciting orders, starting on September 11, 1967, when it was announced that the programme was open for orders. The internal estimate for sales was 900 machines by 1980 (Lockheed's estimate of the size of the market was 1,000). Cabin mock-ups and wind tunnel models were built and tested. The concept of a lower-deck galley was introduced.

In October 1967 the aircraft was formally named the DC-10. One final question remained – the engineering of the centre engine placement. The consensus was to place the engine behind the fin with a bifurcated intake, but after wind tunnel testing it was understood that the airflow into the engine would be distorted when the aircraft was in a yaw, so a straight-through duct was chosen. However the engineering challenge of building the tail fin around the engine without incurring an undue weight penalty remained. In the end four 'Banjo' spars were created using huge aluminium forgings. Since calculations established that using a straight-through duct would improve cruise thrust by 5.2%, the small weight penalty incurred by the heavy structure was easily worthwhile.

L-1011-1 • N303EA • Eastern • New York La Guardia • September 1977
Photo Collection Jacques Barbé

At the beginning of 1968 the sales effort began in earnest, led by vice-president in charge of sales David S. Lewis, senior vice-president of Long Beach aircraft operations Jackson R. McGowen, and vice president engineering John Brizendine. A crucial early customer was American Airlines, who, under president CR Smith, favoured the Rolls-Royce powered Lockheed L-1011; however when he left American Airlines to take up a cabinet post as Secretary of Commerce, the tables turned as his replacement, George Spater, was a big fan of all things Douglas.

On February 19, 1968, it was announced that American Airlines would buy twenty-five DC-10s with options on another twenty-five with deliveries to begin in late 1971, in a contract worth $800 million ($5 billion in 2016 money). Stung by the loss, Lockheed was able to quickly solicit orders from TWA and Eastern for a combined total of ninety-four L-1011s at a discount ($17 million per machine, versus $18 million paid by American for their DC-10s). United Airlines were ambivalent regarding the choice of airframe but had a strong preference for General Electric engines over the Rolls-Royce which was the L-1011's exclusive power plant, landing them in the McDonnell Douglas camp with an order for thirty firm and thirty options.

Northwest Orient was the next customer to come onboard with an order for fourteen firm orders and fourteen options, albeit powered by Pratt & Whitney JT9D engines (Northwest president Donald W Nyrop: "If I want a lightbulb I'll go to GE; if I want an engine, I'll go to Pratt & Whitney"). Although the JT9D was a few inches wider than the CF6, it was possible to accommodate it using the existing engine infrastructure although the centre engine had to be placed twenty inches further to the rear, and the inlet duct was enlarged to create a visibly flared signature engine intake to accommodate the fifteen percent increase in required airflow. The Pratt & Whitney powered variant was initially designated the

DC-10-20 • N141US • MDD • April 1972

DC-10-20 but Nyrop wanted something that clearly stated his airline operated the most up-to-date version, and the DC-10-40 was born.

Construction of the first DC-10 began on January 6, 1969 when the first cut-outs were made for the first windscreen forging at MDC's facility at Torrence, California; on June 23 assembly of the first cockpit window frame commenced at the Santa Monica factory, with a symbolic gold-plated rivet driven into the assembly by Jack McGowen and John Brizendine.

A group of European airlines operating DC-8s had formed the KSSU alliance to buy aircraft with a shared configuration and to share maintenance and parts – KLM (Netherlands), SAS (Scandinavia), Swissair and UTA (France); together they launched the first long range DC-10-30 variant with a combined order for thirty-six airframes on June 7, 1969. The Series -30 was to be powered by the uprated CF6-50A, which could deliver 49,000 lbs of thrust. This pushed the maximum takeoff weight up to 530,000 lbs with a maximum payload of 104,000 lbs and a range of 4,750 nautical miles with a 24F/229Y passenger configuration.

Ten days later, Overseas National Airways (ONA) launched the DC-10-30 Convertible Freighter (CF) with an order for three and an option for one. This order also put McDonnell Douglas back into the sales lead against Lockheed, who had 178 orders for the L-1011 (all series -1 domestic machines) compared to 183 for the DC-10 (in four versions).

The DC-10-30 specification was upgraded to meet the needs of Lufthansa, who wanted to operate from their Frankfurt hub to California and Brazil without penalty, and Alitalia for their Rome to Rio service, which was achieved by adding six feet to the wingspan

DC-10-10 • N1803U • MDD "Spirit of St. Louis - 1971" • Paris Le Bourget • June 1971

Photo Jacques Barbé

and two additional fuel tanks inside the fuselage. Further changes included a slight droop to the inboard ailerons and a revision to the flaps to improve airflow over the wing root, which combined to buy an extra 430 miles of range; to lift the extra fuel, GE created the CF6-50C engine which delivered 51,000 lbs of thrust.

Final assembly of DC-10 Ship One began on January 9, 1970 when the fifty-five foot long forward fuselage barrel arrived from subcontractor Convair aboard a Super Guppy air transporter, and within hours was being aligned with the first cockpit section that had been shipped in from MDC's in-house Santa Monica facility. The first wing set arrived from Canada on February 1 after a six-day journey by rail.

The historic roll out ceremony of Ship One took place on July 23, fifty years and a day after the founding of the Douglas Aircraft Company, in the presence of 1,000 invited VIPs including US vice president Spiro T. Agnew and California governor Ronald Reagan. In fact it was the spectators who were inside the hangar, while the DC-10 was parked around the corner out of sight. Vice president Agnew, James McDonnell and Donald Douglas Sr pushed a set of throttles up and the DC-10 then taxied into view past the hangar under its own power, led by fifty Scottish bagpipers. When the aircraft stopped in front of the hangar, stairs were positioned and the cabin crew of twelve launch customer airlines deplaned to form a guard of honour as the VIPs boarded for an inspection.

The following week at the Farnborough air show, McDonnell Douglas announced more orders – Finnair, Air New Zealand and Sabena, plus top-ups from Lufthansa, Continental Airlines and Air Afrique.

On August 29, weeks ahead of schedule and only twenty-eight months since the launch of the project, Ship One was ready for her maiden voyage. In front of 20,000 workers and their families as well as the world's media, N10DC got airborne after using just 5,000 feet of runway with DC-10 project chief pilot Cliff Stout in the left seat, Harris Van Valkenburg in the right seat, John Chamberlain on the flight engineer's panel, and technician Shojun Yukawa monitoring test data. The aircraft was carrying 25,000 lbs of instrumentation monitoring 2,300 sensors that recorded 360 million data points per hour. The information was broadcast via telemetry to antennae atop the 8,400-foot Frost Peak in the San Gabriel mountains then via ground link to the test headquarters at Long Beach.

After three hours and twenty-six minutes in the air which included a cruise at 30,000 feet and 300 knots, N10DC landed at Edwards Air Force base in the dry wastes of California north of Los Angeles. A second flight took place under the command of McDonnell

DC-10-30 • 9Q-CLI • Air Zaïre "Mont Ngaliema" via Nicholas Scherrer

Douglas chief test pilot Arnold G. "Heimie" Heimerdinger two days later, and within a week eighteen flights had taken place, logging eighteen hours and fifteen minutes of flight time.

By October, two more DC-10s were flying and Ship One had flown eighty-five hours, and by Christmas Eve the number of aircraft in the test programme had increased to four with 235 hours logged on 119 flights with the flight envelope pushed to Mach .95 and 42,000 feet. By mid-March 1971 the flight time logged by the programme had reached 550 hours and 300 flights, with up to ten flights a day operating including night flying out of the McDonnell Douglas test facility at Yuma, Arizona.

On May 24, the FAA issued a Provisional Type Certificate which allowed its inspectors to issue individual airframes with airworthiness certificates, permitting the delivery of DC-10s to customers for crew training and route-proving trips without passengers. The first ship to be certified under this regime was Ship Eight which flew via McDonnell's headquarters in Saint Louis to Paris Le Bourget for the 1971 Paris air show.

Eleven months after the first flight, the FAA issued the DC-10 with its type certificate and its production certificate, after 1,551 test flight hours logged on 929 sorties. At a ceremony at Long Beach on July 29, the first two machines were delivered to American Airlines and United Airlines. Bonus credit must be given to American Airlines for a PR coup, by flying in a DC-3 in original 1930s American Airlines livery, with former chairman CR Smith, Donald Douglas Sr, and Hollywood actress Gloria Swanson aboard. American Airlines flew the first DC-10 revenue service on August 5, operating American 184 from Los Angeles to Chicago, pushing back from the terminal at LAX at 0945 local time for its historic mission.

The sales success of the DC-10 continued into 1972 with orders from Iberia, Laker Skytrain, Martinair Holland, Viasa Venezuela, plus additional orders from existing customers such as United Airlines, Northwest Orient and Continental.

With the widebodies coming online, sales for the narrowbody DC-8, which had always come in volatile peaks and troughs, were winding down for the last time. 1969 had been the last year of DC-8 sales and unexpectedly included the wooing of four new customers — World Airways, American Flyers Airline, West German leisure carrier Air Atlantis, and Air Zaïre. Existing operators put their hat in the ring one last time — Airlift, Braniff, and Japan Airlines all placed top-up orders. The last order to be placed was by SAS in April 1971 for a final DC-8-63. Production was slowly reduced, from 1968's high watermark to eighty-five in 1969 to thirty-three in 1970, twelve in 1971 and a final four aircraft were built in 1972; SAS got their last -63 on May 17, and with it, production of the first Douglas jetliner came to an end.

VI. TROUBLE IN THE AIR

On June 13, 1972 came a premonition of disaster, when a major incident struck N103AA operating American 96 from Los Angeles to New York La Guardia via Detroit and Buffalo. Climbing through 11,750 feet at 260 knots five minutes after departing Detroit, the aircraft was struck by a hammer blow as the bulk cargo door at the rear on the left side blew open. The cargo hold depressurised, but with the weight of the air in the passenger cabin above not able to rapidly equalise, the differential caused the passenger cabin floor to partly collapse, jamming lines to the tail control surfaces and the centre engine.

Captain Bryce McCormick was able to stabilise the aircraft at 11,000 feet and 250 knots but with limited control – the rudder was fully deflected to the right, requiring forty-five degrees of left aileron to compensate, centre engine number two had shut down, and the elevators were partly unresponsive. The flight declared an emergency and turned back towards Detroit Metro airport. On final approach the sink rate reached an unsurvivable 1,500 feet a minute and only by pushing up wing-mounted engines one and three to a high power setting was it possible to reduce this to 700 feet a minute. American 96 landed heavily 580 metres (1,900 feet) deep into runway 03R and immediately veered onto the grass. Using asymmetrical power, the aircraft was steered back onto the tarmac where it rolled to a safe halt twenty-four minutes after taking off from the same airport.

DC-10-10 • N102AA • American • September 1974

Photo Collection Jacques Barbé

The culprit was immediately obvious as the door was missing, later recovered from a field outside Windsor Ontario, just over the US border. The underfloor cargo doors on the DC-10 were locked using five C-shaped latches mounted on a common torque shaft rotated around fixed latching pins fixed to the fuselage. Because of their shape, when the latches were in the proper position, pressure on the door actually further seated them on the pins.

Because of under-spec'd cabling powering the actuator motor, it was possible for the voltage delivered to the motor to be too low to drive it under high loads. In these cases, the motor would stop turning even if the latches had not rotated over the pins. Since the handling agents listened for the motors to stop as an indication of their complete rotation, a failure in the drive system during operation would erroneously indicate that the door was properly latched.

To ensure this rotation had completed and the latches were in the proper position, the door also included an additional locking mechanism, consisting of small pins that slid horizontally through holes on the back of the latches, between the latch and the frame of the aircraft. When the pins were in place, they mechanically prevented movement back into the open position, so even the actuator motor could no longer open them. If the latches were not in their correct positions, the pins could not enter the holes, and the operating handle on the outside of the door would remain open and visually indicate that there was a problem. Additionally, the handle moved a metal plug into a vent cut in the outer door panel; if the vent was not plugged the door would not retain pressure, eliminating any force on the door. Lastly, there was an indicator light in the cockpit that would remain on if the door was not correctly latched.

In theory, the motor failure could not present a problem because the locking lever would not be able to close. However, during the investigation a McDonnell Douglas test rig demonstrated that the entire locking pin operating system was too weak, allowing the handle to be forced closed even with the pins out of the locking holes. This occurred on American 96, when the handler forced the handle closed with his knee. In spite of the vent not closing completely, neither the handler nor the engineer considered this to be serious. Although the vent door remained partially open, it closed enough to cause it to blow shut once the flight began, and thereby allow pressurization of the cargo hold. Although the handle did not seat the pins entirely, the small amount of travel was enough to press on the warning indicator switch, deactivating the cockpit warning light. This was the combination of failures that allowed the accident to happen. Yet all of these indicators had a single common point of failure: the mechanical weakness of the locking pins that allowed the handle to be moved.

The rear cabin floor failure was also a matter of poor design. All of the other cargo holds had vents cut into the cabin floor above. In the case of a pressure loss either above or below the floor, the air would flow through the vents and equalize the pressure, thereby eliminating any force on the floor. However the rear cabin lacked these vents, and it was there that the failure occurred. Because the control cables ran through the floor for the entire length of the aircraft, a failure at any point on the floor would cut controls to the tail section and indeed this was what nearly doomed American 96.

The National Transportation Safety Board performed an in-depth investigation – the incident was deemed sufficiently serious to be investigated as though it was an actual crash – and the accident report determined that the changes must be made to the door's locking mechanism to ensure it could not be forced closed, and that venting must be carved into the floor of the rear passenger cabin to allow for pressure equalization in the event of any kind of structural damage.

The FAA, however, in charge of implanting the NTSB's recommendations, determined with McDonnell Douglas that adding venting would be difficult to install, and that improvements to the door mechanism, some of which were on the books even before American 96, would be sufficient to avoid a reoccurrence.

Shortly after the incident, Dan Applegate, director of product engineering at Convair, who made the door, wrote a memo to Convair management highlighting several problems with the door. He felt the use of electrical instead of hydraulic actuators was insufficient to ensure the safe operation of the door, and that the floor would be prone to failure without the venting, and that in such a scenario, the aircraft would mostly likely be unflyable. He concluded by pointing out

DC-10-10 • TC-JAV • Turkish Airlines • London Heathrow • May 6 1973
Photo Steve Fitzgerald

this exact failure sequence had taken place in static testing in 1970, and that would most likely take place again in the future.

Sunday, March 3, 1974 was a bright spring day in northern Europe when Turkish Airlines TK981 landed at Paris Orly from Istanbul with 167 passengers on board. Fifty disembarked, leaving 117 onboard for the flight's final destination of London Heathrow. Due to a British Airways strike, 218 stranded London-bound passengers joined the flight, filling every economy class seat and two of the twelve first class seats. Thirty minutes late due to the scrum for seats, TK981 took off at 12:32pm local time, initially heading east, before making a turn to the north towards the English Channel. At 12:40pm, passing 12,000 feet, the bulk cargo door blew open, instantly depressurizing the cargo hold. This time a much greater section of the passenger cabin floor collapsed, probably due to the weight of a full load of passengers. Three pairs of occupied passenger seats were blown out through the hole and the controls for number two engine plus all the controls for the control surfaces on the tail – rudder and elevators – were completely severed, along with all three hydraulic systems which also disabled the remaining flight controls – ailerons and spoilers.

The nose dropped and the ship accelerated into an unrecoverable dive. Seventy-seven seconds after the loss of control, TC-JAV Ankara smashed into the Ermenonville forest at 430 knots. At such force, the aircraft instantly disintegrated into millions of pieces, some of which can still be found at the site. Only forty bodies were recognisable from the 346 onboard. Remains of nine passengers were never found at all. It was the worst air disaster in history.

The investigation unearthed corruption and incompetence in about equal measure. McDonnell Douglas certainly bore much responsibility but the dual role of the FAA – both to regulate aviation but also to underpin the success of the entities engaged in aviation-related commerce, whether building or flying aeroplanes – also came under harsh scrutiny. American 96 hadn't been enough to spur the aviation establishment into action. It took the Turkish 981 accident and resultant gigantic loss of life to get the latching mechanism completely redesigned, and the installation of adequate venting in the cabin floor.

The disaster in France undermined what was up to that point a fantastic sales success and a rugged, reliable machine (in the first five months of service, American and United only cancelled one flight each for technical reasons). In the immediate aftermath of the crash, VIASA, KLM, Western and Varig all took delivery of their first DC-10s, followed by Sabena (the first DC-10-30CF in Europe), Korean Airlines and Philippine Airlines. August 5 saw the third anniversary of DC-10 service, by which time 158 aircraft had been delivered to twenty-eight airlines, with the global airline fleet having racked up 609,000 hours of service.

The DC-10 was proving itself in airline service not only on the trunk routes of the United States it was initially designed for, but on long haul trips around the globe. The slightly smaller size of the craft compared to the Boeing 747 made it ideal in the "long-and-thin" market segment, meaning long haul trips with thinner demand. This manifested itself in two ways; firstly with major carriers who were operators of 747s on the fattest routes but who also operated to secondary long haul destinations, such as Northwest Orient to Tokyo, who might fly 747s out of Los Angeles, but could profitably use their DC-10-40s from a smaller city of origin such as Seattle. The other manifestation was with smaller carriers such as who could fly out of their home base with widebody service, but without the burden of having to sell the extra seats of a 747, such as Air New Zealand out of Auckland all the way to London.

As the 1970s continued, demand for air travel dipped below expectations due to inflation and high energy prices. A few DC-10s were built without buyers as McDonnell Douglas vowed to maintain production as their forecasts showed that the market was cyclical and that orders would appear, and by 1977 that proved to be prophetic as American Airlines bought three more DC-10s, followed by orders from Nigeria Airways, Wardair Canada, Japan Airlines, World Airways and British Caledonian. In 1978 McDonnell Douglas increased production to 2.1 airframes per month as more orders came in from Martinair, VIASA, Laker Skytrain, Swissair subsidiary Balair, and Singapore Airlines.

What looked like a very bright future for the DC-10 ended on May 25, 1979 when American 191 crashed inverted after takeoff into a caravan park just outside Chicago O'Hare airport with the loss of all 271 onboard plus two on the ground. During the takeoff roll, engine number one under the left wing separated and smashed onto the runway. After liftoff, the pilots correctly slowed slightly to the engine-out climb speed; however, the departing engine had wounded their bird. Damage to the leading edge of the wing depressurised the hydraulic system that kept the leading edge slats on the left wing extended. Aerodynamic forces caused the slats on the left side to retract, thereby increasing the stall speed of the wing; the right wing, with slats extended, had a lower stall speed. With the ship's actual airspeed in between the two speeds, the left wing stalled while the right wing kept flying, rolling the aircraft sharply to the left. The other fatal injury suffered by N110AA was electrical, depriving the cockpit crew of certain crucial instrumentation including the stick shaker that warned of an impending stall, so the cause of the roll was a mystery to the pilots, who could take no effective action.

In the wake of the crash, engine pylons and thrust link attachment bolts were inspected on DC-10s worldwide. Surprisingly, severe damage was found in the bolts of DC-10s belonging to United, Continental and American Airlines. With the shadow of inaction after American 96 back in 1972 that had led to the Paris disaster hanging over the FAA, the DC-10's type certificate was revoked for US-flagged aircraft on June 6, grounding the type in the US and banning foreign operators from flying their DC-10s in to the country (Freddie Laker, ever resourceful, began flying from London to Windsor Ontario in Canada and bussing his customers across the border to Detroit).

Because the damaged aircraft appeared to be confined to just three US airlines, attention was soon turned to their methods of removing engines and pylons. Since McDonnell Douglas did not have the authority to mandate maintenance procedures, United American and Continental had devised a method of performing engine an engine change whereby, instead of removing the engine from the cowling before removing the cowling and pylon from the wing, they were removing and replacing the whole assembly with a forklift which saved nearly 150 man-hours per engine change. The procedure had begun on DC-10-30s without incident due to greater design tolerances and a stronger pylon structure built to take the extra weight of the heavier -30 engine.

With the cause of the crash established, the FAA restored the type certificate on July 13 and service resumed. Some US carriers noted lower than usual customer load factors but by October numbers were back to where they had been before the grounding.

Unfortunately for the DC-10, two more fatal accidents with a month harmed the reputation of the aircraft at a time when it needed a clean run. On October 31, Western Airlines 2605, known as El

Tecolate (the Night Owl, in Spanish) from Los Angeles to Mexico City crashed on landing due to pilot error, killing seventy-two passengers and a construction worker on the ground; and on November 28, Air New Zealand's Antarctic sightseeing flight 901 crashed into Mount Erebus with the loss of all 257 onboard after the crew descended below the height of surrounding terrain, with their situation complicated by an error in the navigation database which was later covered up by the airline.

Neither accident was the fault of the aircraft but sales, at that point hovering around 350, dried up. The safety record of the DC-10 wasn't the only reason – Asian airlines, traditionally a strong market for the DC-10 as even their local flights tended to be operated by widebodies, were standardising on the Boeing 747, especially Singapore Airlines, Thai and Malaysia. Meanwhile the Airbus A300 was undermining the DC-10 from below, offering slightly less seating but with only two CF6 engines, offering consequently lowering ownership, maintenance and fuel costs (Eastern Airlines' costs with their A300 operations were less than two-thirds of the cost of their Lockheed L1011s).

VII. DC-10 SWANSONG

At the turn of the decade, to refresh the type, McDonnell Douglas proposed three updates. The DC-10-61 would be a domestic people mover with a 40 ft (12.2m) stretch; the DC-10-62 would have intercontinental range with a lesser, 26½ ft (8m) stretch; and the DC-10-63 incorporated the full stretched fuselage of the -61 with the intercontinental range of the -62. These new versions were aimed at Air New Zealand, Swissair, and United, however a weak global economy and the shadow of 1979's crashes meant these proposals were not taken up.

Airline deliveries in the 1980s were at a low rate, mostly the last of historic orders placed by the likes of Varig, Canadian Pacific, British Caledonian and Japan Airlines. One of the most important orders of the whole programme was placed by the US Air Force on December 19, 1977 when the DC-10 was chosen to be the platform for the Advanced Tanker Cargo Aircraft Programme (ATCAP) and an order was placed for twelve machines, to be known as the KC-10. This order was later expanded to sixty airframes, making the USAF the second-biggest DC-10 customer after American (66) – beating United (59) into third place by a single airframe.

The KC-10 was based on the DC-10-30CF but with the deletion of main deck windows and other airline-related equipment. The first example flew on July 12, 1980 and in October the first air-to-air refueling sortie was performed. The KC-10 was fitted with a centreline refueling boom extending from the rear fuselage as well as a drogue-and-hose system on the starboard side of the fuselage. Additionally, the final twenty deliveries included wing-mounted pods for added refueling locations. As a transport, the KC-10 could carry a payload of 66,225 kg (146,000 lbs) and up to seventy-five personnel. The first deliveries were to the USAF's Strategic Air Command (SAC) based at Barksdale AFB in Louisiana in March 1981, with the next fifty-nine being delivered throughout the decade up to November 29, 1988.

DC-10-63 McDonnell Douglas

Today the fifty-nine strong KC-10 fleet is mostly found at Travis AFB outside San Francisco in northern California, and McGuire AFB in northeast New Jersey (one aircraft was written off on September

KC-10A • 79-0434 • USAF • Paris Le Bourget • June 1981
Photo Jacques Barbé

17, 1987 when an explosion and fire destroyed the aircraft during maintenance at Barksdale AFB). Some questions were asked about the future of the fleet during 2015 budget debates, since the KC-135 fleet is larger, and the KC-46 (derived from the Boeing 767) coming online creates three separate fleets of tanker transports. However the KC-10 is unique due to its freight-carrying capability – it is able to carry fighter jet support personnel and equipment on overseas deployments while simultaneously refueling the fighters en route. (Incidentally, the budget issues made public the hourly cost of a KC-10 in flight: $21,170.)

The KC-10 programme was instrumental in keeping the production line open throughout the 80s, although a few late airline orders came in from Toa Domestic Airlines of Japan (renamed Japan Domestic Airlines by the time of delivery) and Biman Bangladesh, who already operated four secondhand machines acquired from Singapore Airlines back in 1983.

Biman bought one final aircraft from the manufacturer, delivered on December 30, 1988, named New Era and registered S2-ACR; after serving its entire quarter-century career at Biman, New Era was the last DC-10 to fly passengers when it was retired in a blaze of publicity on February 22, 2014 at the end of a weekend of nine packed sightseeing flights-to-nowhere for airline enthusiasts out of Birmingham England and ferried back to Dhaka for scrapping.

The late 80s saw a number of meaningful changes at Long Beach. In 1983 it was decided that the stretched DC-9-80 aka Super 80 would become the MD-80, and an application to the FAA was made to officially amend the type certificate. On March 10, 1986, the FAA allowed the MD- designation on the type certificate and from that point on, MD-81, -82, -83 or -88 was stamped on the aircraft nameplate.

In May of 1988, a highly symbolic torch was passed, when McDonnell Douglas announced that it had sold the rights to manufacture spare parts for all Douglas Commercial aircraft from the DC-3 to the DC-8 to Gulfstream Aerospace. This allowed Gulfstream, at its Oklahoma City factory, to fabricate any part or tooling using technical data supplied by Douglas, which for many years fully occupied a team of over 200 staff.

And perhaps most symbolic of all; the very last DC-10 – the last Douglas Commercial airframe of any kind – rolled off the line the same month and after a six-month delay due to licencing issues, was delivered to Nigeria Airways on June 25, 1989, making way for a widebody successor: the MD-11.

DC-10-30 • S2-ACR • Biman Bangladesh Airlines "New Era" • Birmingham • February 2014 Photo Simon De Rudder

Final assembly work of the first MD-11 aircraft being conducted on the East Ramp of the Long Beach site. Photo McDonnell Douglas via John Wegg

2 The story of the MD-11

I. TEN BECOMES ELEVEN

As early as 1979, McDonnell Douglas were looking at evolving the DC-10. Three Series 60 variants were discussed, using the same evolutionary scale as the final DC-8 variants – the -61 was a forty-foot (12.2m) stretch, but with only transcontinental range; the -62 a mere twenty-six foot (8m) stretch but with a new wing and true intercontinental range; and the -63, which would bring together the people-moving capabilities of the -61 with the wing, performance and range of the -62. The -61 and -63 fuselage would be able to seat over 500 passengers.

To research the potential of a new wing and the burgeoning technology of winglets, in 1981 McDonnell Douglas leased N68048, a 1973-build DC-10-10 from Continental Airlines for winglet testing to reduce wingtip drag, with a flight test programme that began on August 31, 1981 at the company's test base in Yuma, Arizona.

The following year McDonnell Douglas began discussing the DC-10 Super 10 (the naming convention following early MD-80s that were known as the DC-9 Super 80). This became the MD-EEE (Ecology-Economy-Efficiency), then the MD-100, incorporating a

Photos McDonnell Douglas/Kevin Stokes collection

digital two-man cockpit and the fruits of the winglet research data. These developments were encouraged by long range Series 30 DC-10s commanding high prices in the second-hand market.

The launch of a new aircraft was postponed due to a final uptick in orders for DC-10s – ten freighters for FedEx, plus a batch of passenger aircraft – two for Thai, two for Japan Air System and one each for Biman Bangladesh and Nigeria Airways, which allowing time for further consultations with future customers.

Two preliminary designs were unveiled in 1985: the MD-11-X10 which utilized the same fuselage length as a DC-10, and the MD-11-X20, a stretch variant with a fuselage 22.3 ft (6.8m) longer than the existing platform. Two engine options were considered: the Pratt & Whitney PW4460 and the General Electric CF6-80C2.

McDonnell Douglas went to the airlines in July 1985 with the aircraft that was now the MD-11. The frozen design was 18ft 6in (5.66m) longer than the DC-10, with 8ft 4in (2.54m) inserted ahead of the wing and 10ft 2in (3.12m) inserted behind the wing. Range was 6,700 nautical miles (12,000km), with a passenger capacity of up to 405 seats in a high density all-economy layout (approximately forty rows of ten seats per row). The lower deck would have room for thirty-two LD3 containers. The freighter variant would boast a cavernous 14,600 cu-ft (413 cu-m) of cargo space on the main deck and another 6,850 cu-ft (194 cu-m) downstairs.

Although McDonnell Douglas were no longer operating at the same commercial level as Boeing or Airbus, who were both in the position of being able to offer a full family of aircraft (admittedly the

Airbus A330 and A340 only existing on paper), McDonnell Douglas fully understood the need to offer commonality to its airline customers wherever possible, and so the MD-11 was the first to offer what would become known as the Advanced Common Flight Deck (ACFD) which would later be incorporated into the MD-80 update, the MD-90 (and MD-95, which entered service as the Boeing 717-200). The all-new digital cockpit would feature state-of-the-art glass avionics to be operated by a two-person flight crew.

One of the most notable changes to the design of the MD-11 compared to its predecessor was the size of the horizontal stabilizer. A design element that made the DC-10 one of the most stable airliners ever built (DC-10 project pilot Cliff Stout said it flew "like a swan") was the large 1,338ft^2 (120.4m^2) stabilizer. The MD-11's longer fuselage put the tail control surfaces further out from the centre of the moment arm, which allowed the horizontal stabilizer to shrink by nearly thirty percent, to 920ft^2 (82.8m^2). The new stabilizer design was also fitted with a 2,000 gallon (7,570 litre) fuel tank which not only added range but also helped with in flight stability by moving the centre-of-gravity rearwards.

The McDonnell Douglas sales team were able to solicit orders for ninety-two aircraft from Alitalia, British Caledonian, FedEx, Korean Air, Swissair, Thai, Varig, SAS, UTA French Airlines, Air Europe, and Dragonair of Hong Kong, and thus emboldened, McDonnell Douglas were able to announce the official go-ahead for the MD-11 on December 30, 1986.

With the project formally underway, subcontractors were locked in, starting with McDonnell Douglas Canada who would build the wings at its Malton plant adjacent to Toronto airport. General Dynamics down in San Diego were tasked with building the fuselage aft of the cockpit, Alenia (Italy) the vertical stabiliser, and CASA (Spain) the horizontal stabiliser.

As had been the case with the beginning of the DC-10 programme, a pre-production mock-up was built, known as the Development Fixture aircraft. This was a precision base used to test the installation of wiring, routing, clearances and systems throughout the aircraft and although never intended to fly, was built to tolerances similar to that of an airworthy machine.

Assembly of the first true MD-11 began on the existing DC-10 production line at Long Beach on March 9, 1988. In October, as the last DC-10 – Ship 446, destined for Nigerian Airways as N3024W – rolled off the line, the first wing-and-body join for the MD-11 took place.

First MD-11 line 447 at Long Beach in January 1989. Photo McDonnell Douglas

The array of custom options available on the DC-8 had virtually sunk the company, and was a significant factor in the need for the McDonnell merger; yet the lessons had apparently not been learned, and thirty years later history was repeating itself at Long Beach as the MD-11 was undoubtedly hobbled by launching the programme with four variants: the standard passenger model (initially the MD-11-X20), the combi MD-11M (also known as MD-11C or MD-11CB in McDonnell Douglas literature), the freighter MD-11F, and the shorter MD-11-X10 (which had a standard length DC-10 fuselage, a variant that was dropped due to lack of customer interest). Additionally, there were three engine options – P&W, GE and Rolls-Royce.

MD-11 line 449, 448 and 447 at Long Beach in June 1989.
Photo McDonnell Douglas

Rollout of the first MD-11 line 447 at Long Beach in September 1989
Photo McDonnell Douglas

In addition, the "good problem" of extremely high demand for the narrowbody MD-80 (at one point American Airlines alone had more than 300 on order at one time) and development of its successor, the MD-90 meant that resources needed to jump-start the MD-11 were lacking and the first ship wasn't complete until September 1989. The roll out, traditionally a big milestone in the life of a new aircraft, was not marked by a ceremony as it was thought that such an event would only draw attention to the lateness of the programme. It was moved to the East Ramp on the evening of October 11 where the MD-11 team completed pneumatic, hydraulic and electrical final functions and installed the vertical stabilizer and winglets.

The controls and systems were proof-tested and the first MD-11 was released to the Douglas Aircraft Flight Test team without ceremony. So far behind schedule was the programme that the first ship, registered N111MD, was in the paint bay only long enough to be polished and have titles and airline customer logos applied; getting airborne without another week lost was of such importance. As 1989 came to an end, total orders and options stood at 312 aircraft.

For the first flight, the commander was chief project pilot John Miller, a British emigrant to the USA and former Royal Air Force test pilot who flew the Vulcan and Canberra bombers, and as a graduate of the Empire Test Pilots School went on to fly the legendary TSR.2 strike / reconnaissance testbed. During a three-year exchange posting to Edwards AFB he flew the B-52 mothership for the X-15 as well as the B-58 Hustler chase plane for the XB-70. Staying in the US, he gravitated to McDonnell Douglas and was on the first flights of the DC-10-30, the refuelling pod-equipped KC-10, and the MD-87.

In the right seat was McDonnell Douglas chief pilot for advanced technology and special projects Tom Melody, whose USAF career included flying the F-100, F-105, F-106, T-38, C-130 and the WC-135 (a rare specially-modified C-135 deployed to detect nuclear explosions by collecting particulate debris and gaseous effluents in the atmosphere). Melody was closely involved with in the development of the glass cockpit systems for the MD-11 and MD-87 and was a project pilot on the MD-88. Also onboard was flight test co-ordinator Fred Scheiner and specialist flight engineer Jack Bowman.

The four-man crew took the first MD-11 into the air on January 10, 1990 from Long Beach runway 12. Fog kept the first flight from getting underway until 12:30pm when after a short 2,500-foot take-off roll, the MD-11 climbed away at 190 knots heading out over the Pacific west of Catalina Island to a specially designated block of airspace where it underwent a series of basic handling and quality flying tests. Flight controls and landing gear, including the emergency systems, were put through their paces. Also evaluated were functional systems such as avionics, air conditioning and communications.

Because of the weather delay, part of the flight scheduled to take place over Edwards Air Force Base had to be cancelled. Instead, John Miller decided to fly the tri-jet to the company research base of Yuma via Blythe, California.

Prior to boarding of the maiden flight are (from left to right) Tom Melody, co-pilot; Fred Scheiner, flight test coordinator; John Miller, chief project pilot; and Jack Bowman, MD-11 technical specialist. Photo McDonnell Douglas

The prototype N111MD makes its maiden flight on January 10, 1990.

Photo McDonnell Douglas via Nico Braas

A runway-side view of the maiden flight. Photo McDonnell Douglas

Before ending the two hours fifty-six minutes flight, the jet made four runway approaches. The flight was almost completely without incident, with controls and stability checked at 23,000 feet overhead Edwards AFB followed by a climb to 25,000 feet accelerating to 300 knots. The only disappointment was a minor software glitch which prevented the planned autoland but Miller landed the aeroplane manually without incident.

From that point on, N111MD was mostly used for the certification of the General Electric CF6-80C2 engines and was flown on seventeen out of the next twenty-two days including the four days that consecutively followed the successful maiden flight, illustrating the reliability of the machine.

The second MD-11, N211MD, was flown (fully painted!) from Long Beach to Yuma on March 1, 1991 and was mostly used as an advanced avionics test bed. It was the first MD-11 to perform a long-haul flight, operating an eight hour thirty minute sector soon after its first flight.

The third ship to join the test programme was N311MD, the only Pratt & Whitney-powered aircraft in the test programme, getting airborne for the first time on April 26, by which time lead ship N111MD had clocked up 177 hours and N211MD 111 hours aloft.

N411MD took to the skies on June 5. This ship was mostly used to test the navigation systems onboard, and on July 26 performed a sixteen hour, thirty-five minute flight for navigation checks around Alaska and the Arctic, at the time the longest-ever flight performed by a trijet. The challenge for the navigation equipment was that as the aircraft crossed the true (geographic) pole, the cockpit displays had to instantly redraw the ship's orientation as the heading flipped from north to south at the moment the pole was crossed, complicated by the fact that the three computers that comprised the inertial reference system independently calculated the aircraft's position and had to agree the point of transit before signalling the two navigation displays to change simultaneously. Additionally, on two of

Inside the fourth test aircraft N411MD used to test navigation systems.
Photo Brian Bostick

The second aircraft N211MD used as an advanced avionics testbed.

Photo McDonnell Douglas via Johan Visschedijk

The third ship N311MD powered by Pratt & Whitney engines.

Photo McDonnell Douglas

The fourth test aircraft N411MD on a visit to Federal Express in Memphis, TN in August 1990.

Photo Brian Bostick

the four polar transits, Flight Management System computers were deliberately failed to bring back-up systems into operation. It should be noted that even at the best of times, polar navigation presents a unique challenge, especially when leaving the pole, as every direction is south.

The fifth and final machine to join the test programme was N514MD which was mostly used to check for function and reliability (F&R). This was put to the test on October 22 when, after a short hop from Yuma to Dallas-Fort Worth, the aircraft left for Seoul, completing the sector in fourteen hours and fifty minutes. On October 24, the aircraft continued on to London Gatwick, home base for two of the original launch customers, Air Europe and British Caledonian.

The flight from Seoul to London traversed the entirety of the Soviet Union, the first time a US aircraft had operated a test flight in Soviet airspace. Although only thirty-seven people were aboard, the aircraft was weighted with ballast to simulate a load of 281 passengers and crew. The leg home to Yuma took over fifteen hours to complete due to an overhead visit to the North Pole for further navigation accuracy checks en route. The round-the-world flight was crucial for monitoring and calibrating parameters such as crew workload, fuel management, and the reliability and accuracy of autoflight and navigation systems.

To prove function and reliability, N514MD also operated on busy multiple sector days, with routings including Yuma – Minneapolis – Pittsburgh – Boston – Philadelphia – Atlanta – Yuma, a pattern that at one point was repeated three times in three days.

The MD-11 was presented to the regulatory bodies as a new design and not a DC-10 variant, adding complexity to the certification process but representing a break from the past and ensuring the perception in the eyes of customer airlines that this was the most modern, state-of-the-art technology that existed. And so after a test programme that had lasted for ten months and 2,000 flight hours, the MD-11 was certified by the FAA on November 8, 1990 in a ceremony that took place on the tarmac at Washington Dulles airport. The actual certificate was handed to McDonnell Douglas president Robert H. Hood Jr. by FAA administrator Admiral James B. Busey, which also covered the General Electric CF6-80C2 engine. Up to the point of the MD-11 getting certified, McDonnell Douglas had spent $3.3 billion and directly created over 10,000 jobs at Long Beach and 400 at Yuma – plus myriad subcontractors across the USA and around the world.

The Pratt & Whitney PW4460 powered MD-11 was certified the following month, on December 18, 1990, thanks to the work of N311MD which performed 258 flights and logged 373 hours. Certification for autoland in Cat IIIb conditions (100 metres of forward

The fifth test aircraft N514MD MD-11 emerges from the paint hangar in August 1990 finished in Delta livery. Photo McDonnell Douglas

visibility and a decision height for land or go-around of zero feet) was issued on April 23, 1991 for Pratt & Whitney powered MD-11s and on May 17 for those with General Electric powerplants after 911 autopilot-controlled approaches (at least a third of which involved a go-around, so the number of actual landings was less). The autoland certification process took eight weeks and was led by John Miller, and mostly took place at the Mojave Air & Spaceport in central California.

The smoothness of the certification was put down to the excellent co-operation between McDonnell Douglas and the FAA, whose inspectors were invited to ride along on development test flights, a first for the Douglas Aircraft Flight Test team.

The first MD-11 handover at Long Beach. Photo McDonnell Douglas

The European Union's JAA, Joint Airworthiness Authorities, mirrored the thumbs up from the FAA on October 17, 1991, and with the aircraft certified, customer deliveries were able to begin, starting with the handover to launch customer Finnair in a lavish ceremony at Long Beach on November 29, 1990. OH-LGA (nicknamed "Olga" by Finnair crew) was flown out of California to her new home in Finland on December 7 and after a series of crew training sorties, the MD-11 flew her first revenue passengers on December 21 on a holiday flight from Helsinki to Tenerife before taking over from DC-10s on flights to New York and Asia shortly after. Korean Air and Delta Air Lines were next to receive their new trijets. The MD-11 was flying passengers at last.

II. "MR CRANDALL ON LINE ONE"

The sophisticated avionics gave initial operators a hard time. American Airlines parked their first four aircraft for a short period to iron out glitches in the onboard fault reporting software experienced with the first delivery, and Delta Air Lines carried a Honeywell avionics specialist on every flight for months.

But that was within the normal parameters of teething troubles experienced by a new aircraft entry into service. The world began learning of the MD-11's more fundamental shortcomings when American Airlines voiced concerns shortly after getting their aircraft into service. Despite performance guarantees, the engines were burning too much fuel, mostly due to higher-than-expected airframe drag. Other customer airlines, such as Delta, agreed. Fuel burn on

Pratt & Whitney-powered machines was 6.7% over guarantee and the General Electric-powered ships were 5% over. This resulted in reduced range or payload, both of which were critical as the MD-11 was intended for long-range transpacific flights.

McDonnell Douglas were, of course, aware of the problem and had already begun remedial work at the time of delivery. Their Performance Improvement Programme (PIP) came in stages. Phase I began in early 1992 and reduced drag by a couple of percent by drooping the ailerons four degrees in the cruise, and fitting seals to the outboard flaps. These initial improvements added 100 nautical miles (185km) to the MD-11's range. Phase II included structural modifications which saved weight, allowing an increase in fuel carried, thereby extending range by another 250 nautical miles (463km) in November 1992. Phase IIIA added seals to the ailerons and even moved the cockpit windscreen wipers from a horizontal to a vertical position to reduce drag. Phase IIIB added a new larger intake fairing for the tail-mounted centre engine which weighed 400 lbs (180kg) less and reduced drag by 1.5% (however this was one of the only fruits of the PIP that could not be retrofitted to existing aircraft, and was fitted to the 129th MD-11, delivered to KLM and registered PH-KCE, onwards). The final phase, IV, was a package of seals for the wings and undercarriage and a redesigned flap hinge fairing.

The engine manufacturers also went to war to help the MD-11 programme hit the numbers that had been promised; General Electric were able to get fuel burn down by 1.5% with improvements to the high pressure compressor, high pressure turbine and tail pipe. Pratt & Whitney were able to realise a 2.7% fuel burn reduction in similar areas and with a modification to the inlet cowling.

With all these modifications in place, the MD-11 was finally able to meet its original design guarantees. However, by this time

Artist impression of Air Europe MD-11 powered by Rolls-Royce engines.
Photo McDonnell Douglas

the damage to the MD-11's reputation was done. American Airlines cancelled thirty-six of its fifty orders, Singapore Airlines cancelled all of theirs, British Airways disposed of the order they had inherited from British Caledonian, China Southern dumped their six, Air Outre-Mer seven, Minerve two, and SAS their twelve. Dragonair's order went next. Delta Air Lines cancelled twenty-five, leaving fifteen orders in place. Other cancellations were due to bad luck – the war in the Balkans meant JAT had no need for their three and Air Zaïre went bust (two aircraft).

British charter airline Air Europe was the only customer to have taken up the Rolls-Royce Trent engine option, with an order for six aircraft and options for twelve more to be used on new long haul routes to the United States, the Far East and Australia. The airline had been extremely ambitious since its 1979 launch but the downturn in traffic at the beginning of the 90s due to the Gulf War that followed Iraq's invasion of Kuwait at the end of 1990 left the airline wildly overextended and a shut down was inevitable. Alas, without this order, the Rolls-Royce engine option for the MD-11 had no takers and this variant was dropped, much as the RB.211-powered DC-10-50, also known as the DC-10R, had been dropped in the 1970s when British Airways couldn't be convinced to place an order (they bought twenty-nine Lockheed L-1011s instead).

However mixed the appeal of the MD-11 was once its performance shortcomings were revealed, some airlines needed the capacity or were otherwise able to power through and maintain their commitment to the MD-11. Other aircraft in a similar size, although retrospectively considered to belong to the same generation, were not immediately available – the Airbus A340 did not enter service until March 1993 (with Lufthansa) and the Boeing 777-200 (which, in its early non-ER incarnation, only had enough range to fly from northern Europe to the eastern seaboard of the United States – barely intercontinental and not yet a worthy substitute for the MD-11) in June 1995 (with United Airlines).

III. IN SERVICE

American Airlines originally ordered fifty machines but as the shortfall in performance became apparent, deliveries ended with the nineteenth aircraft. After the first delivery the aircraft was grounded and the next four remained at Long Beach until at least the initial improvements were built in. The flagship route to Asia out of their fortress hub at Dallas-Fort Worth to Hong Kong which was supposed to show off the capabilities of the MD-11 was in fact never operated even after all the performance improvements were incorporated. The initial cabin configuration was 16F 66J 163Y, later changed to 18F 52J 163Y. As Boeing 777-223ERs came online, the MD-11s were mostly moved to the Atlantic. As early as January 1996, the first MD-11 was converted to a freighter and sold to FedEx, with the last to leave the fleet going at the beginning of 2002.

Delta Air Lines' experience with the MD-11 was more positive. Firstly, they were able to lease two early-build machines from Mitsui & Co which had originally been intended for Air Europe, before receiving their own machines. The Mitsui lease made it possible for Delta to be second carrier to operate the MD-11 after launch customer Finnair. The Delta machines were configured with 50J and 210 (or 219) Y seats. The fifteen-strong fleet served until 2004 in a wide variety of missions, such as the transpacific routes out of the short-lived Asian-focused hub at Portland PDX to Tokyo, Seoul, Osaka and Nagoya; most European destinations out of Atlanta; and even short domestic trips within the mainland United States (many American avgeeks who wanted to fly on an MD-11 but didn't have the budget to fly intercontinental had many chances to fly one between Atlanta and Orlando, a scheduled route for years). Although it is doubtful that Delta would have bought more MD-11s, it is said that only when Boeing announced the closure of the MD-11 line at Long Beach did Delta's plans of adding to the fleet end. The fleet was retired in 2004 in favour of Boeing 777-232ERs and -232LRs.

US supplemental carrier World Airways operated thirteen airframes, both passenger and freighters. The airline's bread-and-butter was military charters and supplying additional capacity to other airlines. Their MD-11s wore several liveries including Malaysia Airlines, Garuda Indonesia, CityBird, Philippines, Aer Lingus, Saudia, El Al and STAF Cargo.

Some of the World Airways aircraft were configured with 409 economy seats, the highest of any MD-11 operator. On the other end of the comfort spectrum was their service on behalf of oil and gas logistics company Sonair, the Houston Express to Luanda (with a fuel stop in Cape Verde) which offered a comfortable ninety-one business and 138 economy seats. Among MD-11s, only the Saudi Royal Flight's pair of VIP machines (HZ-HM7 and -HM8) had a more generous layout.

Because of Helsinki's northerly location, Helsinki represents little-to-no deviation between most city pairs between Europe and Asia, and, beginning in the 1980s, Finnair had developed a profitable role funnelling travelers from second-tier cities in Europe that lacked nonstop connections to Asia through Helsinki, turning sleepy Vantaa airport into a bustling mini-hub with a flotilla of widebody departures every evening to the likes of Tokyo, Beijing, Hong Kong and Seoul,

D-AERB • LTU Photo McDonnell Douglas

fed by dozens of Douglas DC-9s and MD-80s coming in from all over Europe. The small size of the terminal made fifty minute connection times viable, and their seven long range DC-10-30s were replaced by seven MD-11s which served the polar routes to Asia for twenty years, until they were replaced by Airbus A330s and A340s.

Swissair received the first of sixteen in March 1991 and they became the airline's flagship, flying throughout the network. The airline even bought German charter airline LTU's four aircraft secondhand to make a fleet of twenty ships. As well as incorporating all of the PIP, Swissair did additional structural modifications of their own to create a unique subtype, the MD-11AH, for Advanced Heavy. The aircraft were deployed on the airline's flagship routes to North and South America, as well as Asian ports including multi-leg trips such as Singapore via Karachi and Bangkok.

After being known as a conservative and highly profitable airline, around the turn of the century Swissair went on a buying spree of shares in other airlines, most notably Belgian flag-carrier Sabena which, while a highly respected name in aviation with a global network that included the likes of Mexico City, Tokyo and much of francophone Africa, had not historically been a profitable airline; plus shares in a disparate portfolio including LOT, Turkish Airlines, Air Europe Italy, South African Airways, LTU, and Portugalia. Under what was known as the "Hunter Strategy" the purchase of shares in Aer Lingus, TAM Brazil and Alitalia was also considered. The investment in German leisure carrier LTU also involved Swissair buying LTU's four MD-11s.

However these investments created a cashflow crisis that Swissair, once known as 'the Banker's Airline' could not survive, and the airline was declared bankrupt on October 1, 2001. A new airline, Swiss International Air Lines, was launched in early 2002 using the operators certificate of local carrier Crossair, inheriting fourteen of the twenty Swissair MD-11s as the beginning of the new airline's long haul fleet. Although they were painted in the fresh white colours of the alpine nation's new flag carrier, within eighteen months they had all been replaced by a new fleet of Airbus A330s and A340s.

Alitalia was the operator of five unique combis, the only such aircraft built. In addition, they received three full passenger machines to make a fleet of eight, replacing DC-10-30s and some 747-243Bs on long haul routes to the Americas including long flights from Rome to Rio and Sao Paolo, and to Asia. The passenger fleet was withdrawn from service around 2005, with some aircraft being sold on, and the combis being used as pure freighters by CargoItalia until 2009.

Independent Belgian carrier CityBird bought three MD-11s off the line from McDonnell Douglas, and also leased three from US supplemental carrier World Airways. The airline flew their distinctive dark green trijets on scheduled routes from Brussels to San Francisco, Las Vegas, Los Angeles, Mexico City and Orlando. They were also used on charter flights to beaches in far-flung hotspots in Cuba, the Dominican Republic, Kenya and Guadaloupe, with a 371 seat configuration – 36J and ten-abreast 335Y. Two of the planes, OO-CTC and 'TS were leased to Sabena, a keen DC-10-30 operator, from April 1997. They were reconfigured for Sabena with a more spacious 48J and 249Y layout. One machine was dedicated to the Brussels-Bamako-Conakry-Brussels triangle, while the other served Johannesburg. They also did some transatlantic flying including Newark, Montreal, Sao Paolo and Cincinatti in 1998, and Newark and Montreal in 1999. 2000 saw service to Monrovia-Robertsfield, Banjul, and Ouagadougou.

The two machines were returned to CityBird in March 2001 when Sabena received their own A340s. In a crisis for Belgian aviation, CityBird went bankrupt in October 2001, one month before Sabena, giving rise to a new national carrier, SN Brussels Airlines, who serve Belgium with a fleet of nine A330s, thirty A319s and A320s, and eight Avro RJs.

In Asia, Korean Air was an early recipient, using their five machines throughout the network with a 20F / 30J / 223Y configuration on routes to California, Australia, Europe as well as short hops within Asia. However the small fleet was an oddity and when the airline began to receive A330s and 777s, they were converted to freighters, starting with HL7372 and soon followed by the rest of the fleet, in a pattern that would be followed by many other passenger MD-11 operators.

B-150 • China Airlines • November 1992 Photo McDonnell Douglas

China Eastern Airlines, based in Shanghai, took five passenger and one freight models. Destinations included Seattle, Brussels, Madrid and Chicago. Two passenger liners were converted to freighters in 1999, the rest in 2003.

For Asian carriers such as Garuda (nine machines) and Thai (four), their MD-11s were never more than a subfleet, so they moved around the network with no particular signature route.

China Airlines (of Taiwan)'s four were used to form Mandarin Airlines which served Amsterdam via Bangkok to the west and Vancouver to the east as well as regional destinations such as Hong Kong and Bangkok, and occasional trips to Australia substituting for the airline's Boeing 747SPs. Eva Air, Taiwan's other carrier, flew three passenger liners and nine freighters.

The Garuda nine were sold to Varig who already had three factory-fresh, making up a substantial fleet flying from Sao Paolo to European capitals (including London to Copenhagen and Paris to Amsterdam with local traffic rights). Brazilian competitor VASP grew their own MD-11 fleet to nine, starting with a first delivery in February 1992. On July 27, 1996 they opened an ambitious service to Osaka via Los Angeles with PP-SPK specially named *Kasato Maru* after the ship which carried the first Japanese immigrants to Brazil in 1908. VASP cancelled its long haul services due to financial difficulties in 2000. Brazilian carrier TAM was keen to get into the long haul business in 2006; unable to wait for their first Boeing 777-200ERs, Boeing leased them a pair of ex-Varig passenger MD-11s for an interim eighteen months from early 2007 until late 2008.

Loyal DC-10 operator Japan Airlines flew ten MD-11s, named "J-Birds" with each ship carrying the name and likeness of a different bird. After ten years of service on mostly long-haul routes out of Tokyo Narita as well as long and thin trips such as Osaka Kansai to London Heathrow and to Los Angeles, they were all sold to United Parcel Service (UPS), who became one of the biggest operators of the MD-11 with thirteen delivered new from Long Beach and another twenty-four acquired secondhand.

The descriptive list of MD-11 operators is not complete without KLM, without question the most loyal Douglas Commercial airline customer of all time. The love affair began with the DC-2 which operated the scheduled route from Holland all the way to Australia (in fact a regular flight on the route was entered in the October 1934 MacRobertson Air Race between London and Melbourne and came second only to the de Havilland DH.88 Racer which had been purpose-built for the race). DC-3s and DC-4s served the airline with honour, and KLM was the only airline customer for the DC-5, of which only twelve were built. Needless to add, KLM ordered fleets of DC-6s and DC-7s for the post-war propliner age, and the DC-8 and DC-9 for the jet age that followed. The DC-10-30 served the airline's thinner long haul routes alongside 747-206Bs, and when the MD-11 was launched, KLM were quick to place an order for ten.

Unlike other airlines who replaced their MD-11s with 777s or A330s, KLM retained the fleet for their entire working lives right through the early 2000s until by the middle of the second decade of the twenty-first century, they were the last airline in the world to fly MD-11s in passenger service. In 2014, the last year of service, the diminishing fleet mostly operated to Toronto and Montreal, with some extra flights in summer to San Francisco, Los Angeles and the odd daytime rotation to Dubai.

The final day of MD-11 passenger flight, and since Biman Bangladesh had withdrawn their elderly ex-Singapore Airlines DC-10s in February of the same year, the last day of widebody passenger McDonnell Douglas flight anywhere in the world, took place on October 25, 2014 with KLM 672 from Montreal to Amsterdam with PH-KCE. The trip was mostly booked by aviation historians and enthusiasts, current and retired air crew, and ex McDonnell Douglas employees, some of whom had worked on the development of the type in Long Beach. The flight operated across the Atlantic and into Schiphol airport before dawn, where it was met by a water cannon salute by the airport fire service just shy of its final parking position at the gate. After that, KLM operated three enthusiast charters on (suitably) November 11, 2014 with PH-KCD; with the parking brake set on the last one, never again would airline passengers look up from the gate or ramp to see the distinctive and proud centre engine speared through the tail.

PH-KCI above Maho Beach, St. Maarten in November 2003   Photo Sam Chui

The last delivery customer for the MD-11 was Lufthansa Cargo, who ordered eight aircraft in 1998, and converted the additional six options to firm orders in 1999, all of which came after McDonnell Douglas was merged with Boeing. The choice was an interesting one but was no doubt influenced by a very low price for the final machines to be built, and in any case Lufthansa Cargo has a history of employing different aircraft types to the parent airline, including the DC-8-73s which the MD-11s were largely replacing, another type never operated by Lufthansa itself. Lufthansa Cargo added two ex-VASP machines and three ex-Alitalia to make nineteen. The hub of operations for Lufthansa Cargo is Frankfurt with focus cities Sharjah, Miami, and Nairobi. The last eight MD-11s were all for Lufthansa Cargo, and the last machine weas finished on October 2, 2000. D-ALCN was handed over to the customer airline on January 25, 2001. It was the end of an era.

1990	1991	1992	1993	1994	1995	1996	1997	1998	1999	2000	2001	Total
3	31	42	36	17	18	15	12	12	8	4	2	200

MD-11 deliveries by year

IV. SECONDHAND OPERATORS

Despite a successful military and space division, the MD-11 (and MD-90) was McDonnell Douglas' last throw of the dice, and with the commercial programme a washout, the company was no longer viable as an independent entity. McDonnell Douglas was taken over by Boeing on August 1, 1997.

Along with many of the DC-8s, DC-9s, DC-10s and MD-80s, the 200 MD-11s built continued to fly the world's air routes and receive tech support from the new mothership, Boeing.

In its second life as a freighter, the MD-11 found a niche that served owners of converted airframes well as, with lots of cubic capacity and lots of thrust, the MD-11 turned out to be well-suited for cargo hauling. It will have been of some consolation to their original owners that in the 1990s and early 2000s, MD-11s commanded a handsome secondhand sale price.

MD-11 freighters went into service with a wide range of carriers, such as Ethiopian Airlines who had a pair of cargo haulers operating to Europe and China out of their Addis Ababa base between 2009 and 2015. Aeroflot operated three on lease from Boeing from January 2010 until the end of 2013. Shanghai Airlines Cargo operated four between 2006 and 2013. US operator Gemini Air Cargo flew four ex-Varig machines from 2000 and 2008.

A major second-hand operator is Centurion Skylease, a Miami-based airline group that consists of two sister companies, Sky Lease Cargo, originally founded as a subsidiary of Challenge Air Transport, and Centurion Air Cargo, which was previously known as Tradewinds Airlines. In total, the two airlines have employed thirteen MD-11s – five under the name Centurion, and eight under the name Skylease (six of the latter all came from the China Eastern subsidiary China Cargo Airlines aka Cargo King), although they share the same yellow and red corporate livery and ultimate ownership. Today only four of the fleet is active, mostly on the Centurion side of the business.

The last major acquisition of MD-11s was by Western Global Airlines, a Los Angeles-based operator with around ten on strength, flying on behalf of other airlines including FedEx as well as regular and ad hoc charters for a range of corporate clients. The fleet are all white, with the only ornamentation being their registrations.

V. THE WORLD ON TIME

Today, the biggest MD-11 operator is FedEx, who received twenty-two ships directly from the manufacturer (including the first two off the line, N111MD which became N601FE and N211MD which became N602FE), and added forty-three secondhand for a total of sixty-five, fifty-six of which are active at the time of writing.

Although FedEx had the Airbus A300 already in service, the MD-11 was the first true electric jet with a Flight Management System (FMS) computer and a fully glass cockpit including six large Display Units (DUs). For pilots coming from the DC-10, 727 or 747 Classic, the transition was described by FedEx (and ex Flying Tigers) pilot John Dickson as, "Like going from steam gauges to the space shuttle." The latest addition to the FedEx fleet was initially coined the Lawn Dart after a childrens' toy popular in the seventies because of it's raked good looks. Eventually that term was replaced by the more generic names — Mad Dog or The MD.

Internationally, the longest MD-11 trips at FedEx exceeded twelve hours, such as Memphis to Tokyo (Narita), or Paris to Subic Bay, requiring an augmented crew of four, normally one captain and three first officers.

In later years as the Boeing 777-200ERF took over as the FedEx flagship, MD-11s migrated to domestic trips including some busy local trips as short as forty-five minutes, such as Memphis to Atlanta or to Dallas-Fort Worth. The very shortest flights were positioning legs between San Francisco and Oakland, or Newark to JFK. These were enjoyable but demanding for crew, as the enormous thrust powering an empty aircraft made the MD-11 a bit of a handful, and transitioning from a departure regime to an arrival regime within minutes required the crew to be thinking far ahead of the aircraft's actual progress.

MD-11 crews were initally all based in Memphis, although both Los Angeles and Anchorage became MD-11 domiciles. (Although Los Angeles was a crew base and saw regular MD-11 operations, most LA-based crew deadheaded to and from other cities of the world to join up with existing scheduled MD-11 trips. Crew schedules varied from simply out-and-back trips from Memphis to fourteen day international trips around the globe.

FedEx stations that saw the most amount of MD-11 activity were the airline's global superhub in Memphis, followed by Anchorage, Osaka (Kansai), Tokyo (Narita), Paris (Charles De Gaulle) and Dubai. As passenger liners were sold by their owners and converted to freighters, FedEx added forty-three secondhand aircraft to the twenty-two they bought new from McDonnell Douglas, for a total of sixty-five through the books. Although the MD-11 is being gradually overtaken by the Boeing 777-200ERF for high capacity long haul trips and 767-300ERFs on domestic and mid-haul runs, a whopping fifty-six MD-11s remain active at FedEx at the time of writing, plying a combination of domestic and international routes. This is by far the biggest MD-11 fleet ever seen and with the aircraft paid off, and FedEx's vast amount of experience with the type, the MD-11 will be seen flying the purple colours for many years to come.

VI. IN SUMMARY

On first glance, the MD-11 can be said to have been doomed by its shortfall in performance, and that airlines were too quick to dismiss it, as the implementation of the Performance Improvement Packages did pretty much get the aircraft back to the numbers guaranteed in the sales brochure.

But the forces at work against the MD-11 were far greater. It can be said that the fate of the Douglas Aircraft Company was sealed as early as the mid 1950s; ceding the first race of the Jet Age to Boeing handed the Seattle company a massive first-mover advantage with the 707 and left Douglas playing catch-up for the next three decades. While the DC-8 was a safe and reliable machine and 556 machines sold is by no means a bad outcome, those sales actually break down into a bewildering number of subtypes, and each customer variation cost Douglas money; alas the degree of customization was the high price that had to be paid to pry customers away from Boeing.

In the sizeable niche of short haul jet transport Douglas did meaningfully give Boeing a run for its money with the DC-9, but this brought its own host of problems, most notably resourcing a large production run while the country was engaged in a very costly war in southeast Asia, sucking up young men, cash and raw materials alike, all of which could have been applied to large-scale civilian programmes like building jet airliners. Later, the success of the MD-80 took resources away from developing the MD-11.

The merger with McDonnell Aircraft Corporation was a compromise in some senses but a lifeline in others, and the resulting DC-10 could have put the reorganized company back on top. Despite the engineering triumph of the 747, Boeing did not have a particularly good decade in the 1970s, with their two newest programmes, the jumbo and the 737, struggling to find their niche. (The 737 in particular did badly in the early 70s, with less than twenty sales a year, and took a decade to reach 500 sales, with Ship 500 delivered to Gulf Air in 1977 – only an order from the USAF saved it from cancellation. At the time of writing in October 2016, there have been more than 9,200 737s delivered, with over 4,000 on order, and more than one a day rolling off the line. In stark contrast, 1972's total of twenty-two ships equalled less than two deliveries per month.)

The stage was set for a windfall, however, two things stopped the DC-10. The first factor was Lockheed's decision to build an identical competitor in the form of the L-1011 Tristar, which doomed both types from achieving true break even. McDonnell Douglas estimated the size of the market to be 900, and Lockheed said 1,000. The reality came remarkably close, with 446 DC-10s, 250 L-1011s and 245 Airbus A300B1, B2 and B4 twin jets (the -600R series of the A300 came later and can be excluded) for a grand total of 941 widebody people-movers (within nine sales – one per cent – of the averaged-out market estimate of 950). For McDonnell Douglas to have netted half the total is impressive, but the second factor that put the brakes on the DC-10 was undoubtedly the black halo of notoriety around the aircraft's safety record, especially in the wake of 1979's *annus horribilis* in which American 191, Western 2605 and Air New Zealand 901 killed 603 people in the space of 189 days, even if the latter two accidents were unrelated to the aircraft type.

The lack of profitability at McDonnell Douglas meant a significant handicap going into the MD-11 programme – a lack of funds and resources for research and development. And as it happened, the MD-11 design team were starting with a very low tech platform, as the DC-10 made a virtue out of being a very rudimental design. Lockheed took time to create an L-1011 packed with engineering hacks that made it the most hi-tech airliner in the world in the 70s. It had an all-flying horizontal stabilizer and sophisticated direct-lift spoiler function for vertical speed control on approach. The S-bend intake for the centre engine allowed room on the vertical stabilizer for a gigantic rudder, which in turn allowed the wing mounted engines to be much further out from the fuselage, and that in turn created bending relief for the wing, saving significant structural weight.

The DC-10 design team eschewed all of these in favour of getting their aeroplane into the air first. The slogan at Long Beach was "fly before they roll" – get the DC-10's first flight done before the first L-1011 was even rolled out of the factory. Not only did the low-tech approach make such a victory possible, it made the DC-10 popular with airlines and pilots as it was reliable and rugged where the L-1011 was considered over-complicated and had a slightly greater tendancy to "go tech". Certainly one can look to the success of the competing types in the second-hand market as an interesting barometer of which of their differing design philosophies "got it right" – DC-10s flew for a wide range of second tier carriers around the world in some pretty remote locations for many years after its initial owners sold them on, whereas outside the bubble of the huge engineering operations found at the likes of Eastern Airlines, British Airways and Cathay Pacific, L-1011s rarely flourished or even lasted long.

As the 80s dawned, Boeing was making huge technological strides with the implementation of sophisticated avionics in the course of creating not only the 747-400 but also the 757 and 767, the latter two sharing a pilots' typerating, so aircrew could fly the two types interchangeably. Lockheed may have been bowing out of the civilian airliner business but Airbus, the new kid on the block, was preparing to leapfrog even Boeing to make a mark with its true fly-by-wire family, the A320 narrowbody series and A330/A340 widebody, all of which could be flown on a single pilots' typerating.

One major element in the sales arc of the MD-11 cannot be discounted: the third engine had finally become redundant. The Airbus A300 was the first widebody with only two engines (and starting with the A300B4FF "forward facing" in 1982, the first widebody with only two flight deck crew, another first for Toulouse) and Boeing's 767-200ER went a step further by pioneering long overwater flights on two engines. The 1980s bore no comparison to previous eras when engine reliability had been far more dubious. Until 1976, twins were restricted to flying within sixty minutes of a runway; that year Indian Airlines began flying their A300B4s up to ninety minutes from land on sectors across the Bay Of Bengal and the Arabian Sea, and in 1985 the FAA certified the 767 to fly ninety minutes of single-engine flying time from a runway under certain specific conditions, a code of conduct that became known as ETOPS – Extended Twin Operations – and was soon extended to 120 minutes. This allowed TWA to begin the first transatlantic operation using a twin-engined jetliner, which was from their hub at Saint Louis to Frankfurt in May 1985.

This rewrote the map of where airlines could fly. Big airlines were able to operate directly out of their fortress hubs to more spokes, and smaller airlines could plant a flag on foreign soil for the first time, such as US regional carrier Piedmont Airlines out of Charlotte North Carolina, who bought 767-204ERs and opened up direct flights to London and Frankfurt in the mid 80s. Even on mainline routes like London to Chicago or Toronto to Frankfurt, two engines meant less maintenance, less chance of a technical delay, less fuel burn, and smaller planes allowed more frequency, a crowd-pleaser especially for business travellers. The role for four-engined aircraft remains, but from now on it is only to provide extra thrust needed for very heavy machines, like the Boeing 747 or the Airbus A380. (The A340 was something of an exception in this regard, although its four engines were slimline CFM56s, just like on a Boeing 737, and – at least at the time of the launch of the aircraft – four CFM56s were as efficient as two of the kind of powerplants found on a widebody twin. And – to be fair – the A340 wasn't a massive sales smash either, with a total of 377 built, 247 of the standard -200/-300 and a disappointing 131 of the upgraded -500/-600.)

Cargo operators FedEx, Centurion Sky Lease, Western Global Airlines, Lufthansa Cargo and UPS continue in operation. The type is gone from passenger schedules but will remain a familiar site at airports around the world for some years to come. The Douglas dream of commercial airliners flies on.

Photo Felix Gottwald

CK's chapters were mostly written in San Francisco and dedicated to dear H with love and gratitude — "even the most unpossible dream is real when you're dreaming" — xoxo

soundtrack to writing – Tangerine Dream, Clogs, Philip Glass, Gary Numan, The Cure, Klaus Schulze, Tomita, Miles Davis and Mew with thanks to Amoeba Music in Haight-Ashbury & City Lights Books in North Beach

special thanks to Lori's Diner at 336 Mason Street that closed after thirty years of serving San Franciscans as this book was finished – lots of love and thanks to Marta Delfino, Kathy Maloney, Zaya Nayamzaya, Stephie Hermosillo and Kathi Nolte

The MD-10

The MD-10 is a DC-10 that has been refitted with a digital two-person Advanced Common Flightdeck, as found on the MD-11 as well as the MD-90 and Boeing 717 (MD-95). The genesis of the programme was with Federal Express, who had large fleets of both DC-10s and MD-11s and acquiring a large fleet of more DC-10s from United and American.

The first stage of the conversion was the installation of a main deck cargo door with the same dimensions as that found on an MD-11, and a rigid cargo barrier in place of a nylon cargo net, to protect the flight deck in the event of a high-G deceleration in an accident. Structural changes allowed a higher gross payload – the series -10 payload rose from 124,000 lbs (56,240 kgs) to 143,500 lbs (65,091 kgs) and the series -30 payload rose from 163,000 lbs (73,930 kgs) to 180,000 lbs (81,720 kgs). MD-11 landing gear and brakes were fitted to carry the extra weight.

Since the aircraft were being prepared for another few decades' of flight, other heavy maintenance modifications included the replacement of wiring looms and other items to improve future reliability and also with a view to saving weight where possible.

The most meaningful modification to turn a common-or-garden DC-10 into an MD-10 was to strip out the flightdeck and replace it with the Honeywell VIA2000 EFIS (Electronic Flight Instrument System) cockpit identical to the MD-11 (or MD-90), the Advanced Common Flight Deck (ACFD). The huge advances in avionics tech since the dawn of the DC-10 meant that although the ACFD dispensed with the role of the flight engineer in favour of a two-person cockpit, in the avionics bay, twenty-two computers were replaced by just three. This meant that the MD-10 and the MD-11 could be flown by pilots interchangeably, merging the two pilot groups at FedEx, the MD-10's only customer. Other avionics upgrades included the installation

N386FE • Boeing MD-10 Freighter • Phoenix-Mesa, AZ • April 2000

Photo David J. Hamilton

of satellite communications systems (known as SATCOM), global positioning systems (GPS) and future air navigation system (FANS) compatibility.

Although the MD-11 and the MD-10 shared a common FAA Type Certification, and therefore common checklists for normal operations, there was no fly-by-wire attenuation of differing flight handling characteristics (as on the Airbus family); and abnormal procedures differ between the two models. This requires a dedicated flight training simulator and a dedicated Quick Reference Handbook (QRH) for the MD-10. It also necessitated dedicated differences training sessions, both in ground school and in the simulator.

An operational difference was the air system on the MD-10 which was manually operated at all times, therefore requiring some extra attention on the pre-takeoff checklist. In addition, the throttles sat a little higher, the flap lever operated a little differently and the engine start switches were on the overhead panel. Otherwise, the difference between the MD-10 and the MD-11 upon entering the cockpit were hard to spot.

The first aircraft to be converted was N386FE, a 1973-build DC-10-10 that began life as N1821U with United Airlines, and was bought by FedEx at the start of 1998. After completion of the conversion, it first flew out of Long Beach on April 4 1999 under the command of Boeing test pilot Joe Goodlove, with Gary McCellan in the right seat and flight test engineer Wayne Anselmo in the jumpseat. All of the planned elements of the flight were accomplished in the four hour and twenty-five minute sortie which concluded with a smooth landing at Mesa in Arizona. N316FE was the second test aircraft to join the programme, a dedicated freighter delivered new to FedEx in October

N1821U • Long Beach • July 1998

Photo Pascal Van Cuyck

1988, the third-to-last DC-10 built. Between the two machines, thirty-three airports were visited and over 1,400 approaches, go-arounds and landings were performed.

The FAA and FedEx were involved throughout the test programme and on May 9 2000 the MD-10 was certified, with N386FE and N316FE handed over to FedEx on the same day in a ceremony at Mesa.

Many subcontractors were involved in the conversions, including the Boeing Airplane Service Centers (BASC) in San Antonio and Wichita, SR Technics in the United States and Zurich, and Aeronavali in Venice, Italy.

Eighty-two MD-10s were produced: sixty-four MD-10-10s (with twenty-six active at the time of writing) and eighteen MD-10-30s (fifteen active at the time of writing). Two aircraft have escaped the grip of FedEx. N330AU, a DC-10-30 originally N101TV delivered to Transamerica on April 19, 1973 and sold to FedEx in April 1984 as N301FE and converted to a freighter. At the beginning of 2010 FedEx retired the aircraft and donated it to Project Orbis, the flying eye hospital where it remains in service as a flying teaching hospital, restoring sight to people suffering from treatable eye conditions, registered N330AU. N314FE was sold to TAB (Transportes Aeroes Bolivianos) and reregistered CP-2791 on July 9, 2013, one of the last DC-10s built, originally delivered to FedEx on August 26, 1988.

The consensus around the MD-10/-11 fleet pilots is that flying the MD-10-30 is the most enjoyable due to its combination of excellent performance, lack of automation, and classic DC-10 stability during the landing phase. To the contrary, however, the MD-10-10 is less beloved, due to its derated engines and unrefined wing which gives it a less-than-stellar performance, especially for pilots accustomed to operating the MD-11.

Regardless of the subtype, the MD-10 remains significant as it was the first full-scale and successful modification of an aircraft originally designed for the standard compliment of three crew members to requiring only a captain and a first officer, and extended the life of dozens of early 1970s widebodies far into the twenty-first century, way beyond that of its contemporaries such as the Airbus A300, Lockheed L-1011 and Boeing 747 Classic (-100, -200, -300, SP).

Brand new MD-10 cockpit of N68056 (ex CO DC-10-10CF) during conversion at Aeronavali Venice in March 2006

N560FE • Memphis • June 2005

N302FE • MD-10-30 • Anchorage • July 2006 Photo Kevin Stokes

The MD-12

Although it will have been obvious from the inside that McDonnell Douglas' path back to being a mainstream competitor to Boeing and Airbus was increasingly steep, the company did not give up the fight, and produced two paper successors to the MD-11, both known as the MD-12.

Double-deck wide-body MD-12 Photo McDonnell Douglas

The first started life as a simple stretch of the trijet but quickly evolved into a four engined double decker bearing a striking resemblance to the future Airbus A380, measuring 208 feet (63.4 metres) with a wingspan of 213 feet (64.9 metres). The fuselage was twenty-four feet three inches (7.39 metres) wide and twenty-seven feet eleven inches (8.51 m) high. A memoradum of understanding was signed in November 1991 with the Taiwan Aerospace Corporation, and the design was unveiled in April 1992. First flight was scheduled for late 1995, with deliveries commencing in 1997. With no airline customers coming forward, Taiwan Aerospace got cold feet, and McDonnell Douglas lacked the resources to go it alone on such an ambitious project.

MD-XX Stretch Photo McDonnell Douglas via John Wegg

Retreating but not giving up, McDonnell Douglas launched the MD-XX at the Farnborough Air Show in June 1996, a more traditional upgrade of the existing MD-11 design in two variants. Both had a 213 foot (64.9 metre) wingspan, but the Stretch was lengthened by thirty-two feet (9.8 metres) compared to the MD-11 and offered accomodation for 375 passengers in a typical three-class configuration, or 515 in all-economy, with a range of 7,020 nmi (8,080 mi; 13,000 km). The MD-XX LR was the same length as the MD-11 with seating for 309 in a typical three-class arrangement, and featured a range of 8,320 nmi (9,570 mi; 15,400 km). However, as with the double decker, the company simply did not have the financial resources to launch the project, and in October 1996 the McDonnell Douglas board of directors announced the end of the "second" MD-12, the MD-XX.

3 MD-11 in Detail

This chapter covers a description of the basic versions, weights and performance, dimensions, flight controls, engines, cockpit, passenger cabin configurations, galley and cargo configuration and aircraft systems.

Photo Felix Gottwald

General Description

In comparison to the DC-10, the MD-11 incorporates a longer fuselage, new engines, advanced aerodynamics including winglets, a new horizontal tail design, a low-drag tail cone, interior features that provided more flexibility in interior configurations, digital avionics and a totally new two-crew flight deck that will later used to retrofit DC-10 cockpits for FedEx.

The MD-11 was conceived as a long-range airliner and was first offered in three different versions, the all-passenger version (MD-11P), the Combi with a mixed passenger and cargo interior (MD-11C) and the all-freighter version (MD-11F). Two other versions followed, the Convertible Freighter (MD-11CF) in 1991 and the Extended Range version (MD-11ER) in 1994 for a total of five versions.

MD-11 (131 built): the Passenger variant, sometimes referred to as MD-11P, was produced from 1988 to 1998. It was the first version on offer at launch of the aircraft in 1986, and was delivered to American Airlines (19), Delta Air Lines (17), Swissair (16), Japan Airlines (10); KLM (10), and other airlines with fewer aircraft.

MD-11C (five built): the Combi was the third variant on offer at launch in 1986 and was designed to accommodate both passengers and freight on the main deck, which featured a rear cargo compartment for up to ten pallets, each measuring 88 by 125 inches (2.2 m × 3.2 m) or 96 by 125 inches (2.4 m × 3.2 m). The main deck cargo compartment was accessible by a large rear port side cargo door, which measured 160 by 102 inches (4.1 m × 2.6 m). The main deck cargo volume was 10,904 cubic feet (308.8 m3). Additional freight was also carried in below-deck compartments. The MD-11C could also be configured as an all-passenger aircraft. All five aircraft were manufactured between 1991 and 1992 and delivered to Alitalia, the only customer for that variant. In 2005 and 2006 the airline converted them to full-freighter configurations to be operated by Alitalia's cargo division. Following that division's closure, the five aircraft were returned to their lessor in January 2009.

MD-11CF (six built): the Convertible Freighter variant was launched in 1991 by an order from Martinair for three aircraft plus two options. The MD-11CF featured a large forward port side cargo door (140 by 102 inches (3.6 m × 2.6 m)) located between the first two passenger doors, and could be used in an all-passenger or in an all-cargo configuration. As a freighter, it could transport 26 pallets of the same dimensions (88 by 125 inches (2.2 m × 3.2 m)) or 96 by 125 inches (2.4 m × 3.2 m)) as for the MD-11C and MD-11F for a main deck cargo volume of 14,508 cubic feet (410.8 m3) and offered a maximum payload of 196,928 pounds (89,325 kg). All six MD-11CFs were delivered to Martinair (four) and World Airways (two) during 1995. The two World Airways aircraft were converted to freighter-only in 2002.

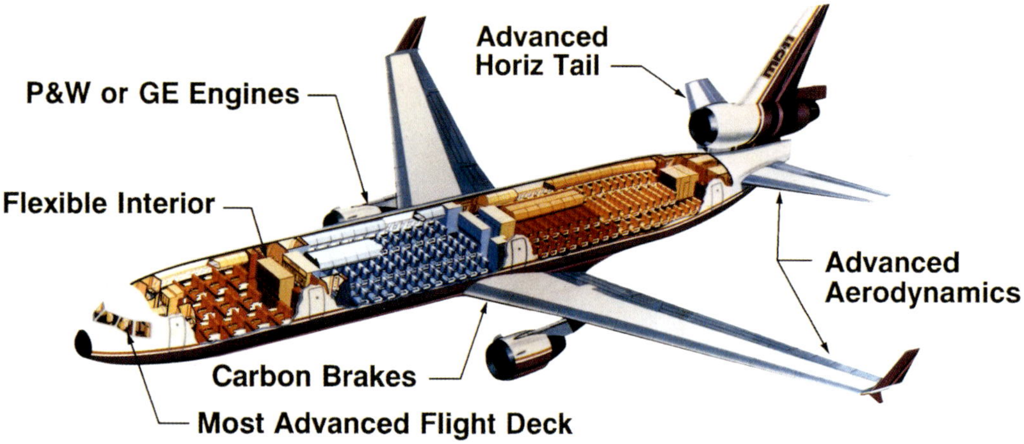

Version	Built
MD-11P	131
MD-11C	5
MD-11CF	6
MD-11F	53
MD-11ERP	5
Total	**200**

Weight Summary (LB)

Aircraft	MTOGW	MLW	MZFW
DC-10-30	572.000	403.000	368.000
MD-11	602.500 (1)	430.000 (2)	400.000 (3)
MD-11 Combi	602.500 (1)	458.000	430.000
MD-11 Freighter	602.500 (1)	471.500	451.300
MD-11 Convertible Freighter	602.500 (1)	471.500	451.300

(1) Optional = 605,500 - 610,000 - 618,000 - 625,500 LB
(2) Optional = 458,000 LB
Optional = 430,000 LB

MD-11F (53 built): the Freight transport aircraft was the second variant on offer at launch in 1986 and was the last and longest (1988–2000) manufactured version. The all-cargo aircraft featured the same forward port side cargo door (140 by 102 inches (3.6 m × 2.6 m)) as the MD-11CF, a main deck volume of 15,530 cubic feet (440 m3), a maximum payload of 200,151 pounds (90,787 kg) and could transport 26 pallets of the same dimensions (88 by 125 inches (2.2 m × 3.2 m) or 96 by 125 inches (2.4 m × 3.2 m)) as for the MD-11C and MD-11CF. The MD-11F was delivered between 1991 and 2001 to FedEx Express (22), Lufthansa Cargo (14), and other airlines with fewer aircraft.

MD-11ERP (five built): the Extended Range version was launched by the manufacturer at the Singapore Air Show in February 1994. The MD-11ER incorporated all the Performance Improvement Program (PIP) options, including a maximum takeoff weight of 630,500 pounds (286,000 kg) and an extra fuel tank of 3,000 US gallons (11,000 l)) in the forward cargo hold[to offer a range of 7,240 nautical miles (13,410 km), an increase of 400 nautical miles (740 km) over the standard passenger variant. MD-11ERs were delivered between 1995 and 1997 to Garuda Indonesia (three) and World Airways (two). As of February 2007, only one Finnair MD-11ER has been converted to MD-11 with the removal of the extra fuel tank.

MD-11 Boeing Converted Freighter (BCF) - Boeing and its group of international affiliates offer a conversion of used passenger airliners into freighters. The MD-11BCF is one of the models offered.
Note: Some or all the features of the MD-11ER, including the higher MTOW of 630,500 lb (286,000 kg), part or all of the PIPs aerodynamic improvements packages and composite panels were fitted to later built MD-11s (except the extra fuel tank), and could be retrofitted to any of the variants, except for the PIP Phase IIIB larger aft engine intake. Some airlines, such as Finnair, Martinair and FedEx, made the structural changes required to allow their aircraft to have the higher MTOW. Swissair's sixteen newly-delivered aircraft were retrofitted with all the features except for the extra fuel tank and were so-designated MD-11AH for Advanced Heavy.

An ex TAM MD-11 under freighter conversion

AIRCRAFT DIMENSIONS

WING	
AREA (NOT INCL WINGLETS)	3,648 FT^2
SWEEP ANGLE	35 DEG
WINGLETS	
UPPER SEGMENT SWEEPBACK	40 DEG LE
LOWER SEGMENT SWEEPBACK	47.3 DEG LE
OVERALL AREA, EACH SIDE	40 FT^2
HORIZONTAL TAIL	
AREA	920 FT^2
SWEEP ANGLE	33.5 DEG

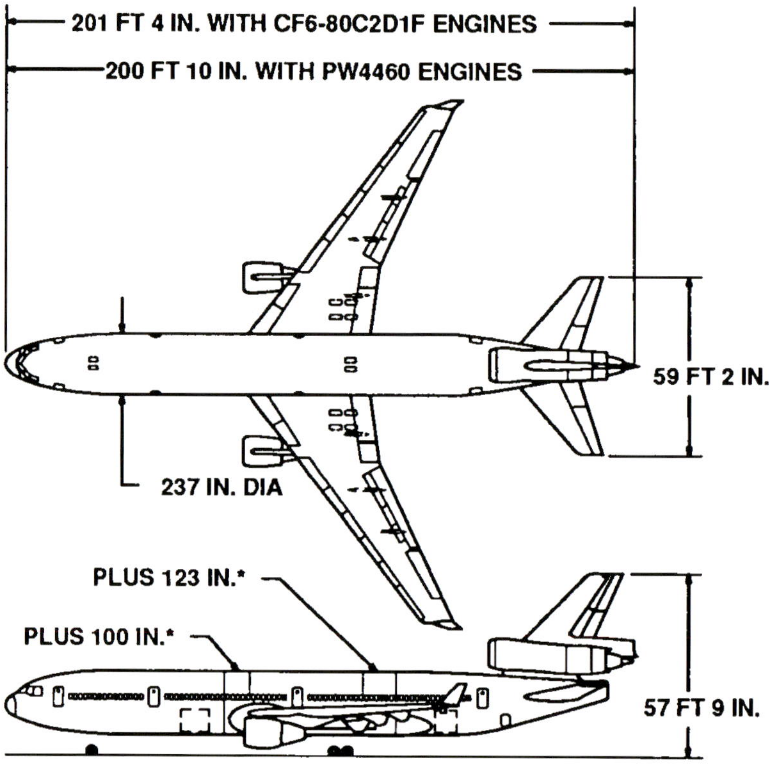

*OVER THE DC-10-30/40

CARGO CAPABILITY LOWER DECK

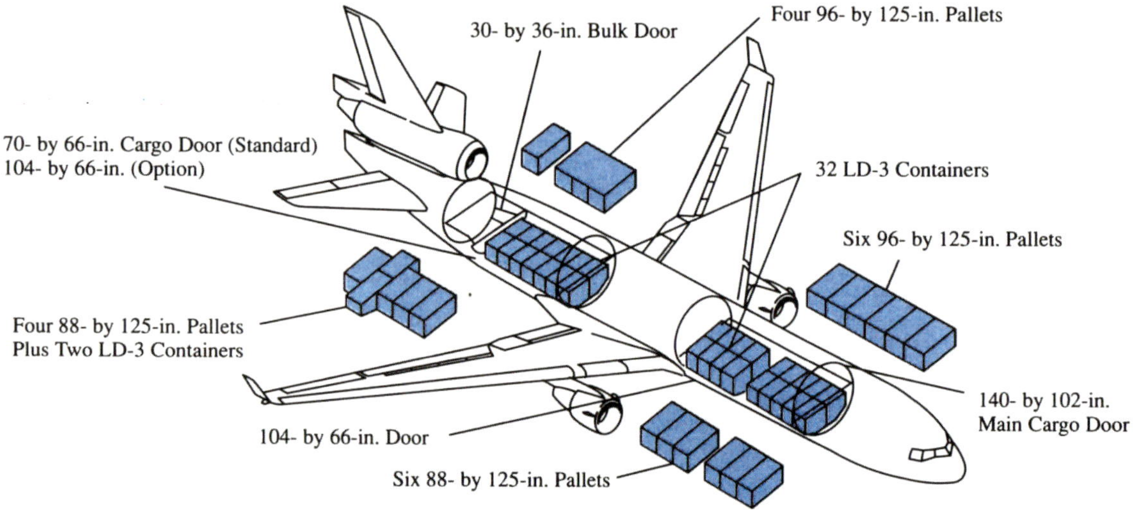

The aft lower cargo door
Photo Benoît Denet

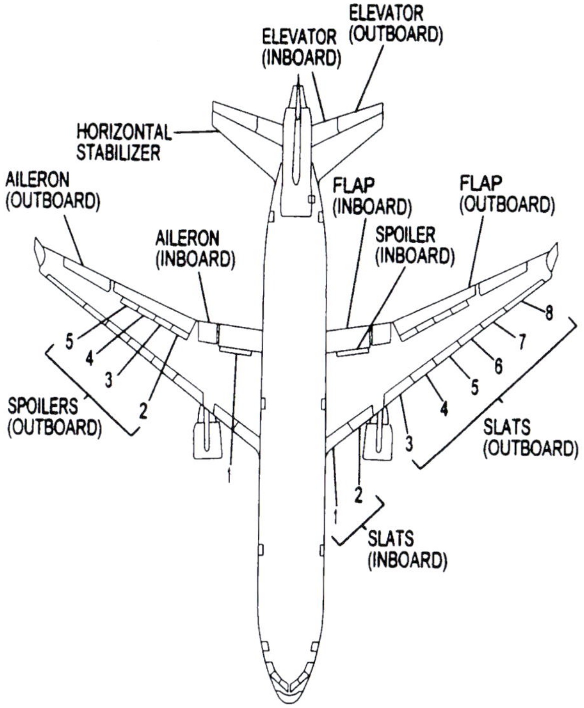

Interesting study of China Eastern B-2173 with slats and flaps deployed - Los Angeles April 2010

Photo Sam Chui

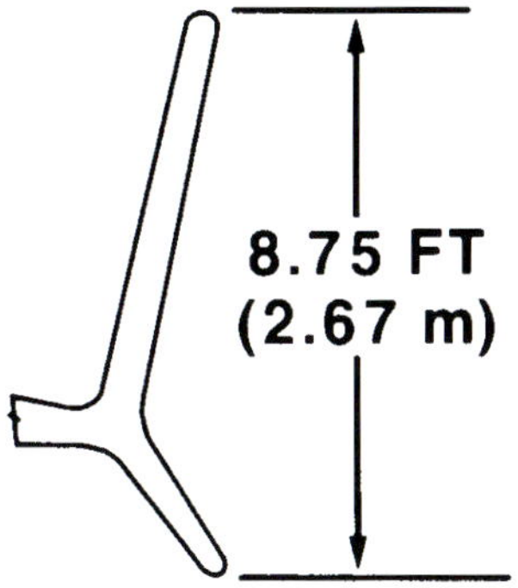

To give maximum operating efficiency for long range flight, at high speed, the MD-11 wing uses an outer-wing air foil and winglets, The combination of the winglet and the trailing edge camber decreases drag

Right photo John Wegg

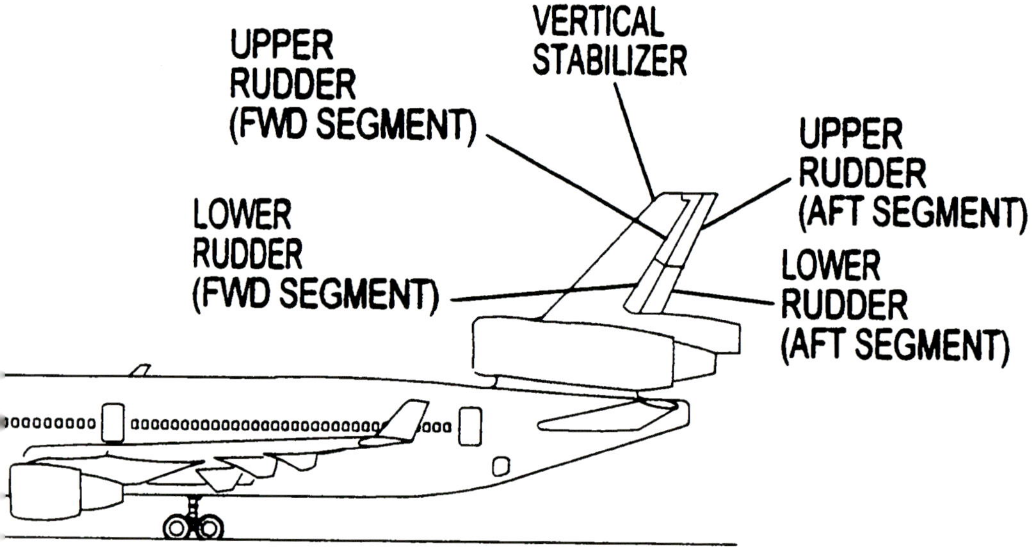

China Eastern MD-11 B-2171 at Long Beach in May 1993 Photo John Wegg

Advanced airfoils on China Eastern MD-11 B-2171 at Long Beach in May 1993 Photo John Wegg

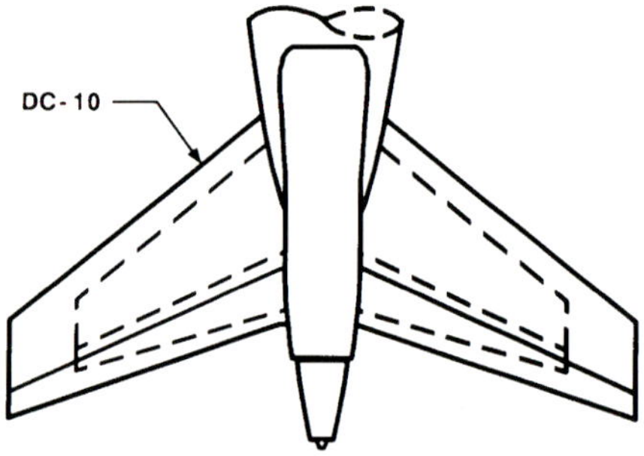

There is a 30% reduction in size of the MD-11 horizontal tail over the DC-10 tail. This reduction along with advanced construction materials reduces overall weight some 1,900 pounds.

N592FE climbing out of Anchorage in August 2007 Photo Michael S.Prophet

Engines

The three world's major engine manufacturers, General Electric, Pratt & Whitney and Rolls-Royce developed engine variants to power the MD-11 aircraft.

The General Electric CF6-80C2 is a direct derivative of the CF6-50 used on the DC-10-30 aircraft and is the result of an international co-operation. SNECMA of France, MTU of Germany, Volvo Flygmotor of Sweden and Fiat Aviazione of Italy contributed in the development of the engine. Testing started in May 1982 and the engine was certified in mid-1985. The GE CF6-80C2 version for the MD-11 is the highest rated CF6, producing 61,500 lb.

The Pratt & Whitney PW4460 and PW4462 engines are members of the PW4000 commercial engine family. The PW4000 was designed with a large engine core allowing thrust growth by increasing the fan diameter and changing the low-pressure spool. The engine was launched in 1982 and was certified in 1986. Besides the MD-11 aircraft, this engine also equipped the Airbus A300 and A310, the Boeing 747-400 and 767.

Both GE and P&W engines are high bypass ratio turbofan engines. The bypass ratio is the proportion of airflow through the fan at the front of the engine and the airflow through the core of the engine. The high bypass engine is fuel efficient and quieter. Both GE and P&W engines and equipped with the FADEC (Full Authority Digital Engine Control) system interfacing with the auto-throttle and FMS (Flight Management System) contributing to the fuel economy and reliability.

General Electric CF6-80C2D1F at Miami in January 2016

The large pylon-hinged nacelle doors expose the entire engine. For simplicity, these remain on the aircraft during an engine change, seen here on Centurion Air Cargo's N986AR at Miami in January 2016

Note the difference in size and shape between the exhaust cone of the GE and the P&W engine.

GE has two different cones: One short standard cone (top left photo by Brian J.Gore via John Wegg), and the long and straight cone (top right photo by Michael S.Prophet).

PW has a much shorter cone as pictured on wing-mounted engine on the left (picture by John Wegg).

Also obvious is the difference between the straight cowling profile of the GE aft engine (bottom left photo by Frank de Koster, bottom centre photo by GVH) and the P&W aft engine (right photo by Guy Viselé). Even though the P&W PW4460/PW4462 has a slightly larger fan diameter than GE CF6-80C2D1F engine, there is no difference in the aft engine air intake cowlings. A difference that was more notable in the aft engine air intake cowlings of the GE and P&W powered DC-10-30s and DC-10-40s.

A self-contained built-in platform for maintenance and inspection is located at the aft engine. This feature was originally designed for the DC-10 aircraft, however on the MD-11 due to a larger engine and relocation of accessory on the engine, it was not really usable. Two sections can be opened forward and aft.

Looking forward (right photo) and aft (left photo) from the tail dock platform

Looking down from the tail dock platform

The tail cone aft compartment access door provides access to the tail dock via a built-in ladder

Photos André Kuiper

Tail cone assembly of Centurion Air Cargo N986AR at Miami in January 2016

Engine removal from PH-KCH at VCV in August 2012 Photo André Kuiper

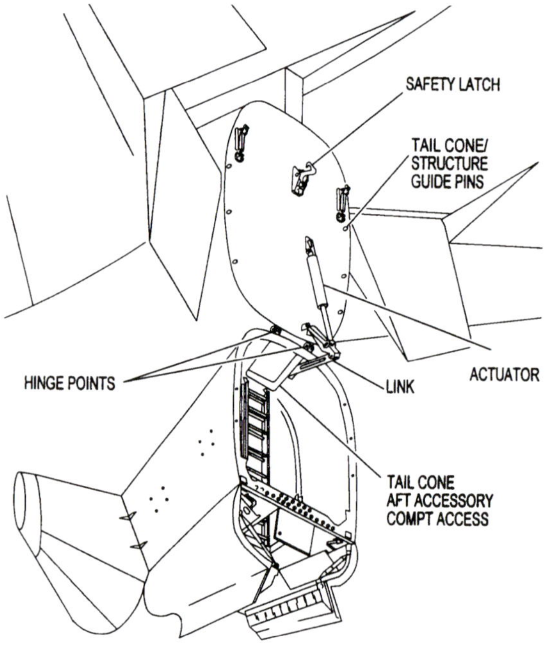

The Rolls-Royce RB211-524L was the third engine type to be offered to the MD-11. With an extra fan radius of 9-inches (2.41m) and improved core components, a higher take-off thrust of 65,000 lb was planned. UK charter operator Air Europe was to be launch customer for the Rolls-Royce engine, however following the bankruptcy of parent International Leisure Group (ILG), the airline was forced to cease operations in 1991. Consequently, the Air Europe MD-11 orders were canceled and as no other airlines was interested in the RB211-524L, the Roll-Royce engine option was dropped.

Of the 200 MD-11s built, 119 aircraft were equipped with GE engines, 67 were delivered with Pratt & Whitney PW4460 engines and 14 were delivered with the higher thrust PW4462 engines. Compared with DC-10 aircraft, Pratt & Whitney managed to place a much higher number of engines as only 42 out of the 446 DC-10 aircraft built were equipped P&W engines (22 for Northwest and 20 for JAL-Japan Airlines) whereas all other 404 DC-10s were powered by GE engines. An interesting design feature is the standard pylon that can carry either a GE or P&W engine without modification.

MD-11 Swissair Pratt & Whitney PW4460 in Zürich on August 30, 1992
Photo John Wegg

		CF6-80C2D1F	PW4460	PW4462
Thrust Ratings				
■ SLS Ideal Takeoff	(lb_f)	61,500	60,000	62,000
■ SL Flat Rate	(ºF)	86	86	86
■ Max Cruise 35,000 ft, Mach 0.82	(lb_f)	11,000	11,400	11,400
■ Cruise SFC	$\frac{lb}{lb/hr}$	1.76	1.69	1.69
■ Max Climb 15,000 ft, 330 KCAS, ISA	(lb_f)	24,900	22,200	22,200
Fan Diameter	(in.)	93.0	93.6	93.6
Length	(in.)	158.9	132.7	132.7
Dry Weight	(lb)	12,920	12,500	12,500

Landing Gear

The MD-11 main and centre landing gear are conventional in design. The right and left main gear are interchangeable with minor changes. The shock struts are strengthened to permit the added weight. The nose gear has a strengthened lower drag brace and external lugs added to the strut piston for weight and balance. To accommodate the Bendix carbon brakes, 24 inch diameter forged aluminum main and centreline wheels are installed. These wheels have better corrosion protection and a 50,000 mile warranty. The tyres on the main and centreline gear provide a double-overload capability.

Nose gear, Center gear and Main gear of N545JN

All Photos Benoît Denet

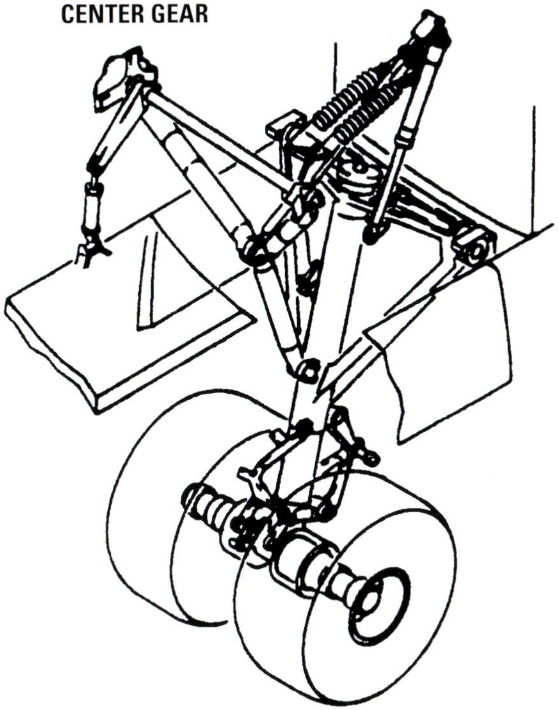

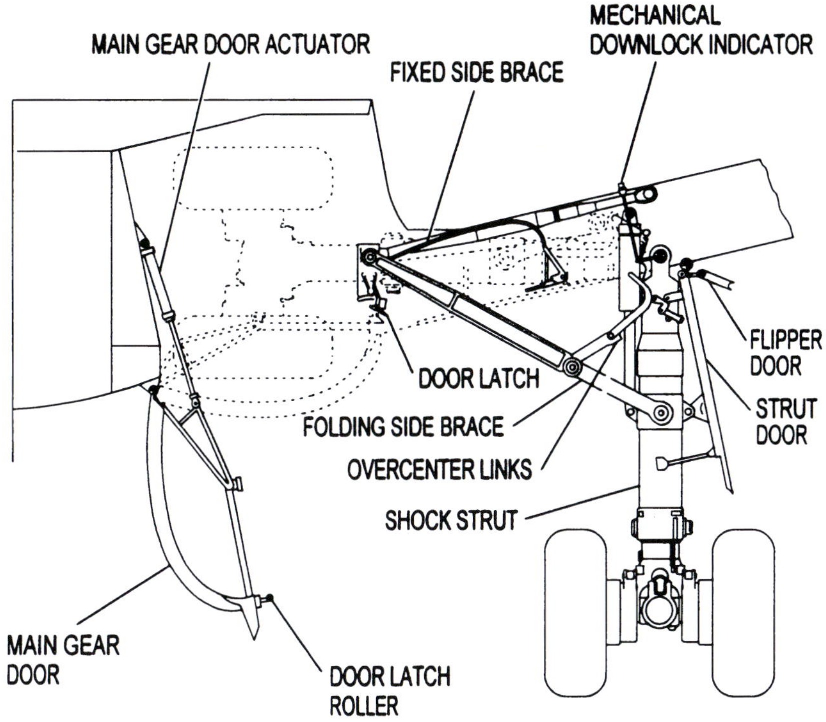

A rare picture of Western Global N412SN without center gear extended at Stansted March 2016 Photo Michel Huart

Flight Deck

Compared to the DC-10 aircraft, one of the MD-11's key features is the two-pilot flight deck. McDonnell Douglas engineers designed hardware and software systems so that functions previously performed by the flight engineer could now be performed by "automatic controllers". Before designing the MD-11's flight deck, McDonnell Douglas asked a committee of pilots from potential MD-11 customers for advice. The committee's goal was to integrate the cockpit's function and layout in such a way as to give the two-pilot crew access to all the information it needs, presented in the most effective way possible. At the pilots' suggestion, the electronic instrument system display units -the heart of the MD-11's automated information system - were located on the instrument panel, six abreast. These 8-inch by 8-inch, color cathode ray tubes (CRTs) dominate the instrument panel and provide the flight crew with instantaneous speed, heading, altitude, navigation, engine/alert, and system data.

1. Flight Control Panel
2. Electronic Instrument System (EIS)
3. Primary Flight Display Unit 1
4. Source Input Select Panel
5. Primary Navigation Display Unit 2
6. Engine & Alert Display Unit 3
7. Gear handle & lights panel
8. Centralized Fault Control Display Unit (CDU)
9. Control pedestal
10. Overhead Systems Control panels
11. Electronic Instrument System (EIS)
12. Alert Lights
13. Light Control panel
14. Primary Flight Display Unit 6
15. Primary Nav. Display Unit 5
16. Oxygen Mask Stowage Box
17. Systems Display Unit 4
18. Multi-Function Control Display Unit (MCDU)
19. Standby Altimeter, Airspeed & Altitude Indicators

Cockpit of KLM PH-KCE at Montreal on October 24, 2014 a few days before its final scheduled flight to Amsterdam

Cockpit of Thai Airways' HS-TMF at Phuket in December 2006 Photo Sam Chui

Nose gear steering wheel provides nosewheel steering up to 70 degrees left or right of the neutral position Photo Benoît Denet

First officer's control wheel on KLM PH-KCE at Montreal on October 24, 2014

Electronic Instrument System (EIS)

The six color CRT Display Units (DUs) are arranged in two horizontal groups of three on each side of the landing gear handle. The outer two DUs are the Primary Flight Displays or PFDs. Inboard of the PFDs are the NDs or Navigation Displays with four pages selectable from the captain and first officer's EIS control panels. Inboard of the left ND is the Engine and Alert Display or EAD. Inboard of the right ND is the Systems Display or SD with ten selectable pages. The flight crew can access multiple screens or pages on system display units (DUs) by means of the Systems Control Panel (SCP) located immediately aft of the throttle quadrant on the pedestal.

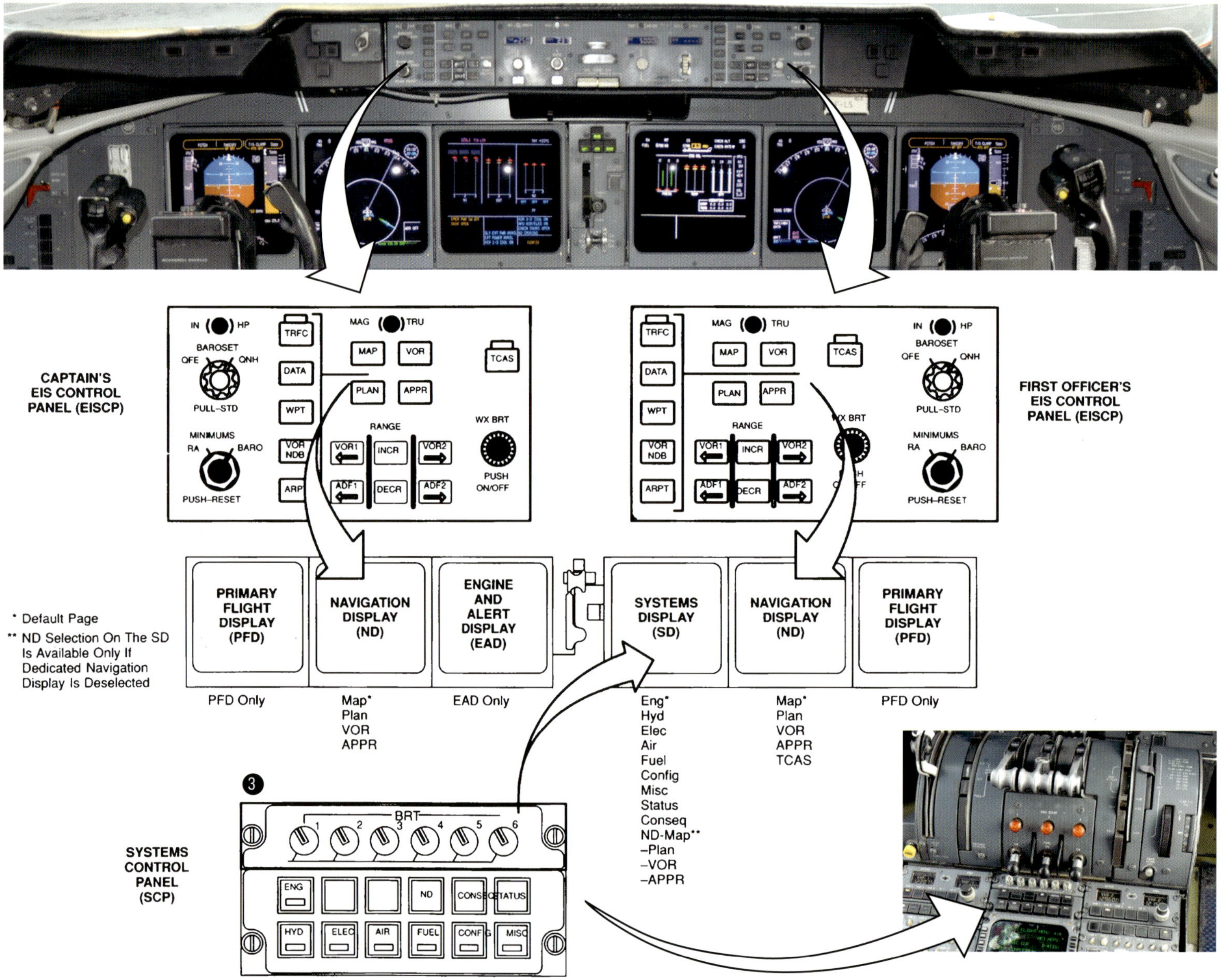

Overhead Systems Control Panels

1. Overhead Circuit Breaker panel
2. Pedestal Floodlights
3. Cockpit speaker
4. Cargo Fire panel
5. Inertial Reference System
6. Cockpit Area Microphone
7. Cargo Temperature
8. Windshield Left Wiper Control
9. Engine Ignition Control
10. Aircraft Lighting
11. Engine Fire shutoff lever
12. APU Control
13. Hydraulic Systems Control
14. Cockpit speaker
15. Cabin Pressure Control
16. Map Lights
17. Anti-ice Control
18. Windshield Right Wiper Control
19. Electrical System Control
20. Environmental Control System - Air System Control. Two configurations: one for CARGO one for PAX
21. Fuel Systems Control

Pedestal

1. Cockpit surveillance camera screen
2. Standby horizon & altitude indicator
3. Spoiler Handle
4. Brake Control panel
5. Thrust Reverser Levers
6. Long Trim Handles
7. Fuel Switch (3)
8. Park Light
9. Radio Panel
10. Digital Audio Control Panel
11. Weather Radar Control Panel
12. TCAS Panel
13. Communication Radio Panel
14. Aileron Trim Knob
15. Rudder Trim Knob
16. Service Interphone Handset
17. Multi-Function Control Display Unit (MCDU) provides automatic lateral & vertical flight guidance and control. Combined with the Flight Management Computer Units (FMCU), it is called cslectively FMS or Flight Management System
18. Flap/Slat Handle
19. Engine Throttle Levers
20. Engine Start Switch (3)
21. Flap take-off selection thumbwheel
22. Systems Display Control Panel
23. Communication Radio Panel
24. Digital Audio Control Panel
25. Cockpit Entry Control Panel
26. Centralised Fault Display System (CFDS) comprised of a Centralised Fault Display Interface Unit and a third Multi-Function Control Display Unit or MCDU
27. Entry Light
28. ADG deploy handle - needs to be pulled aft and lifted to deploy (by cable) the ADG.

PH-KCE at Montreal on October 24, 2014

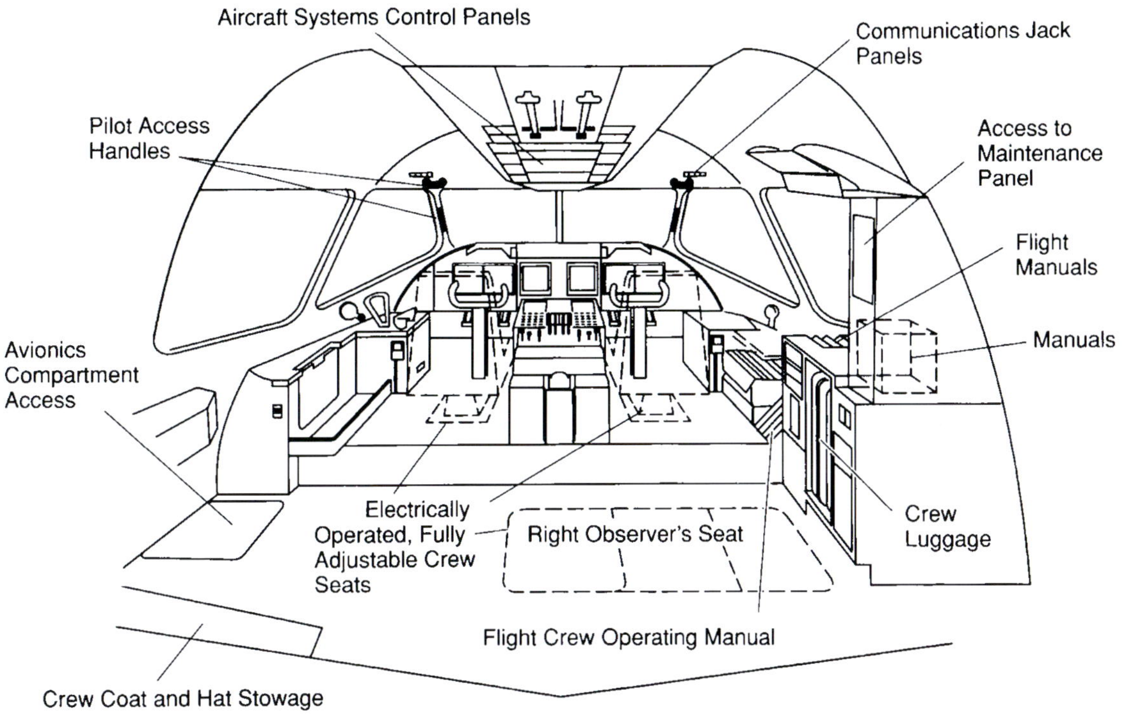

Cockpit of Varig PP-VTJ at Los Angeles in April 2006 – note the absence of a second large observer's seat behind the captain's seat Photo Sam Chui

Aircraft Interiors

McDonnell Douglas designed maximum flexibility into the interior of the MD-11. Track-mounted galleys and lavatories, interchangeable equipment, and other features provided MD-11 operators with a wide range of configuration options and the possibility of rapid conversion from one configuration to another.

Passenger seat possibilities are numerous, from a low-density 22 first, 56 business and 226 economy all the way up to 409 all-economy seats.

Original Swissair first class four abreast seating introduced in 1999 providing extra space, privacy and additional features, and retained by Varig, seen here between flights at Los Angeles in April 2006 on board PP-VTJ, previously HB-IWK Photo Sam Chui

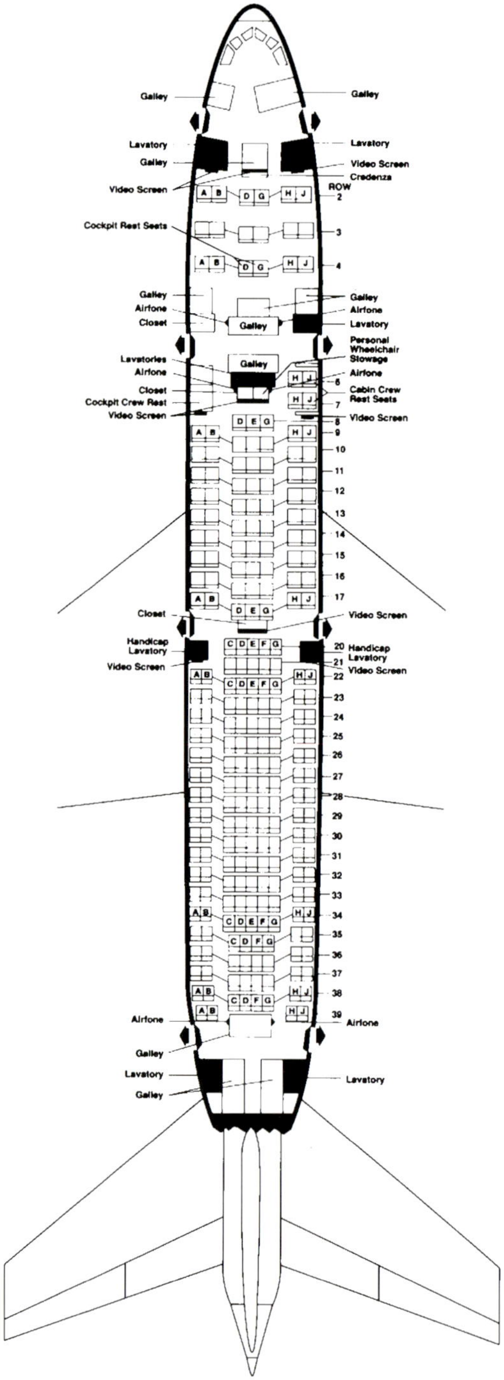

A typical three-class seating arrangement used by American Airlines' MD-11 Luxury Liners; six-abreast first class sleeperettes, seven-abreast business class recliners and nine-abreast economy class seating, carrying 251 passengers in total: 18 first class, 70 business class and 163 in economy.
American Airlines

Finnair's Business Class interior onboard OH-LGA while operating AY091 from Bangkok to Hong Kong in September 2004

KLM World Business Class onboard PH-KCD in March 2013 from Dubai to Amsterdam (KL 430). Only two rows in the section between door 1 and 2 in a six abreast configuration

Thai Business Class of the MD-11 HS-TME in a seven abreast configuration January 2005

Thai Royal First Class of the MD-11 HS-TMF in a six abreast configuration February 2005

Photos Sam Chui

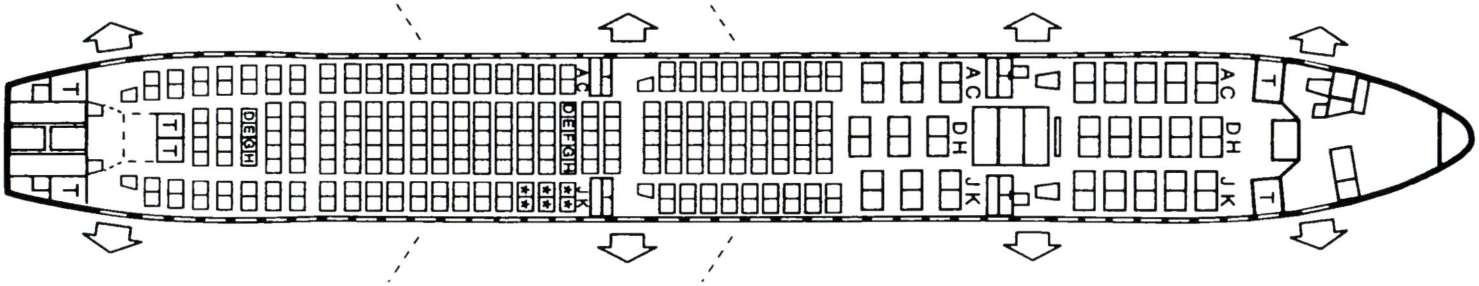

The two-class seating arrangement used by Sabena MD-11s carrying 297 passengers in total (48 Business Class and 249 Coach/Economy)

(Sabena Belgian World Airlines)

Nine-abreast economy class seating in a 2-5-2 configuration aboard Thai Airways' HS-TME in January 2005 Photo Sam Chui

Ten-abreast economy class in a 3-4-3 configuration onboard World N272WA, at Miami in September 2013 Photo Jannik Femerling

Nine-abreast economy class in a 3-3-3 configuration on KLM's PH-KCB at Amsterdam in November 2014 Photo Michael S. Prophet

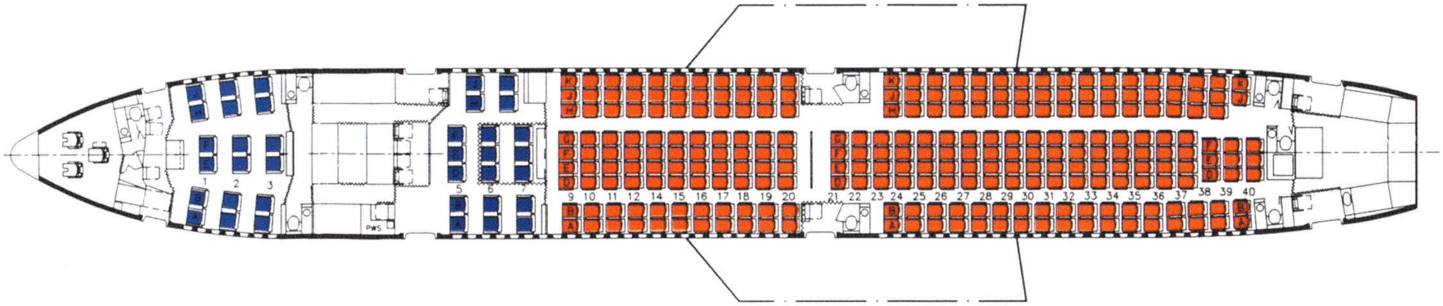

When delivered, KLM's MD-11s had a two-cabin configuration and could carry 297 passengers: 37 World Business Class and 260 Tourist Class. Seats were arranged in rows of two, four and three. (KLM)

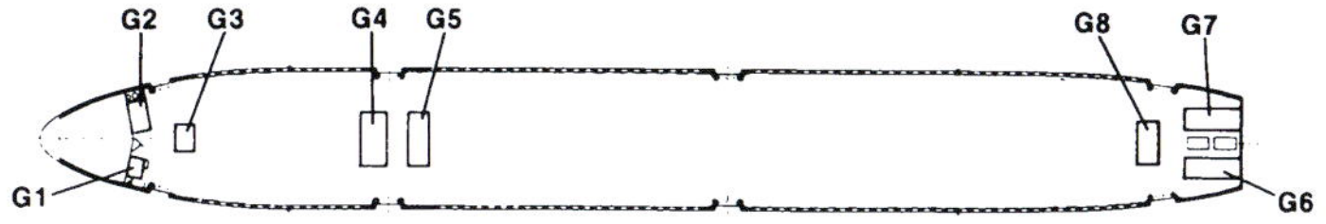

Each airline had the opportunity to procure galleys that fit particular requirements. The all-passenger MD-11P had a baseline configuration of eight galleys providing capacity for two and a half meals per passenger and space for 38 carts.

KLM cabin crew during a break in the rear galley on board PH-KCE during the last passenger revenue service, from Montreal to Amsterdam on October 24, 2014

An unique feature at KLM was the Purser Workstation. From this station with one cabin window, the cabin crew was controlling Inflight Entertainment, Cabin temperature (partial adjustment), and the cabin lights. It was located between Door 2 and the World Business Class section - seen on PH-KCB at Amsterdam in November 2014 Photo Michael S.Prophet

Main Deck Flexible Passenger/Cargo Mix

STANDARD

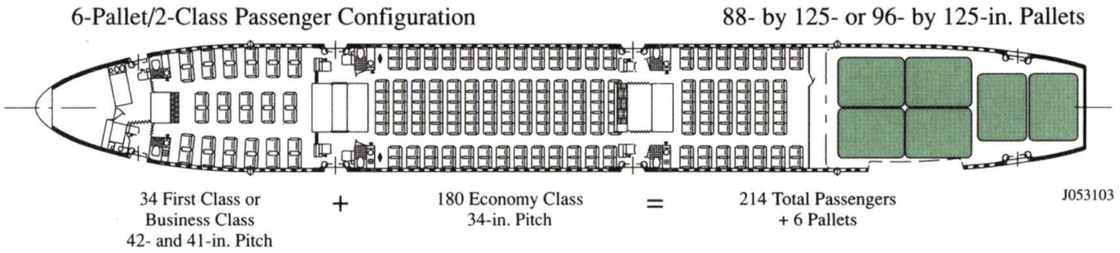

OPTIONS

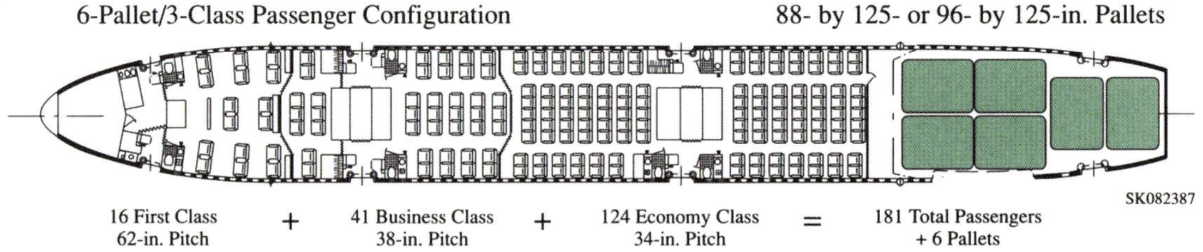

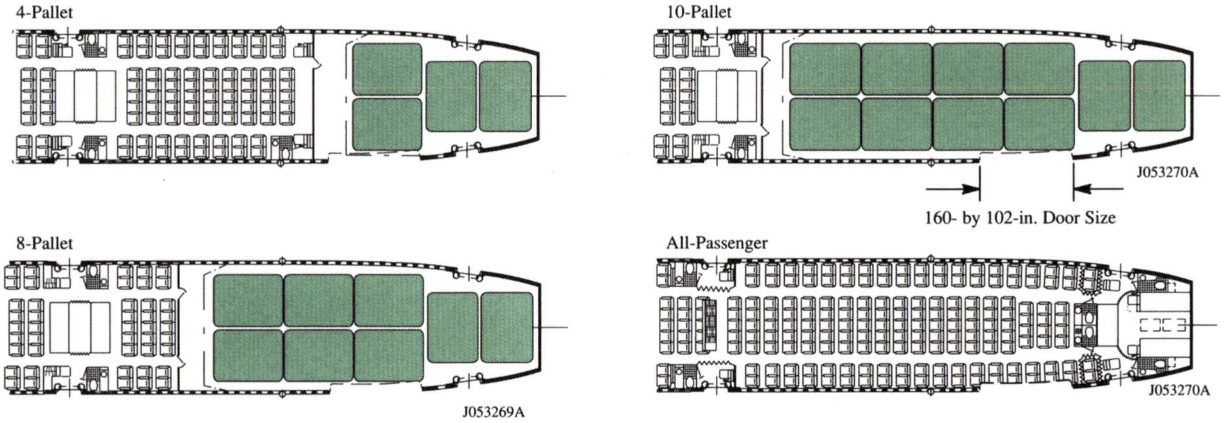

The Combi was normally operated in a six pallets configuration; however main deck flexibility allowed the transport of up to 10 pallets

The MD-11 Combi has a large 160 by 102 inches (4.06 x 2.59 m) cargo door in the rear port side fuselage Photo David Bartoli

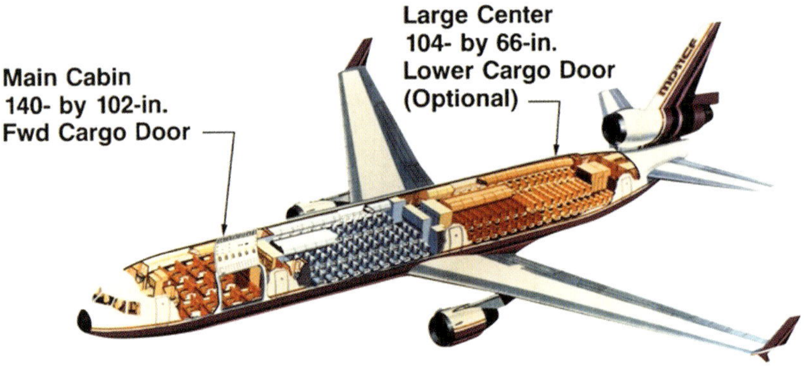

The MD-11CF Convertible Freighter featured a large forward port side cargo door (140 by 102 inches (3.6 m × 2.6 m)) located between the first two passenger doors, and could be used in an all-passenger or in an all-cargo configuration.

All Freighter Configuration 26 Main Deck Cargo Pallets

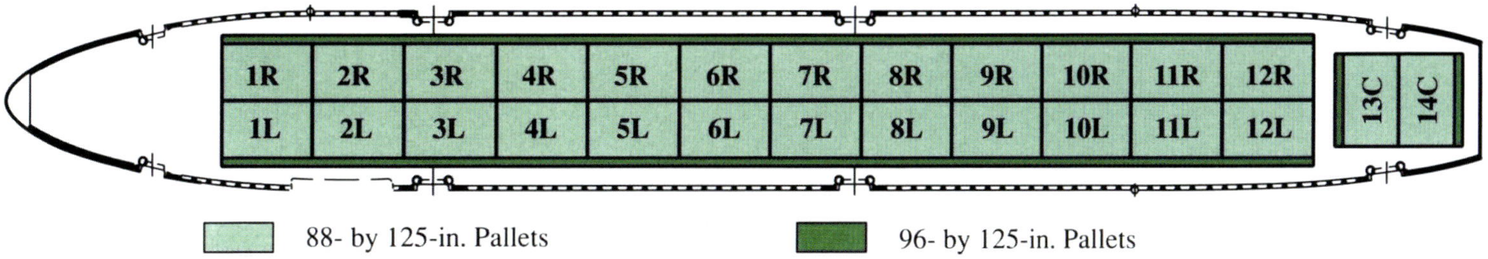

All Passenger Configuration 323 Seats — Two-Class Standard (3-Class Interiors Optiona

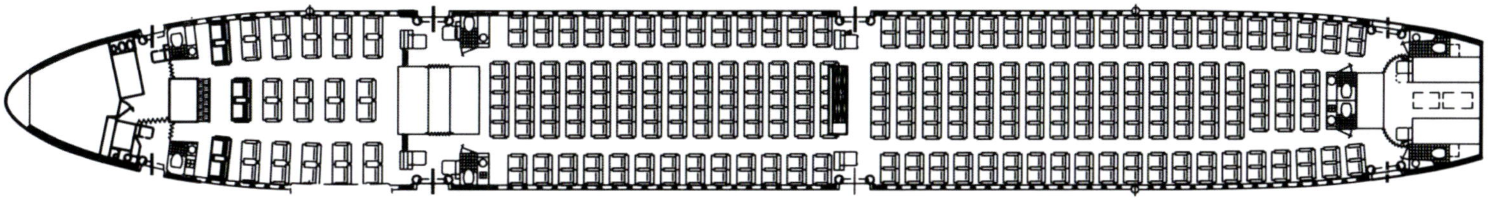

First	34 Seats	42/41-in. Pitch
Economy	289 Seats	34/33-in. Pitch

The MD-11CF could be operated in an all-passenger or all-cargo configuration

PH-MCR is one of the original MD-11CFs delivered to Martinair in 1995, seen here at Miami in May 2014

Photos Benoît Denet

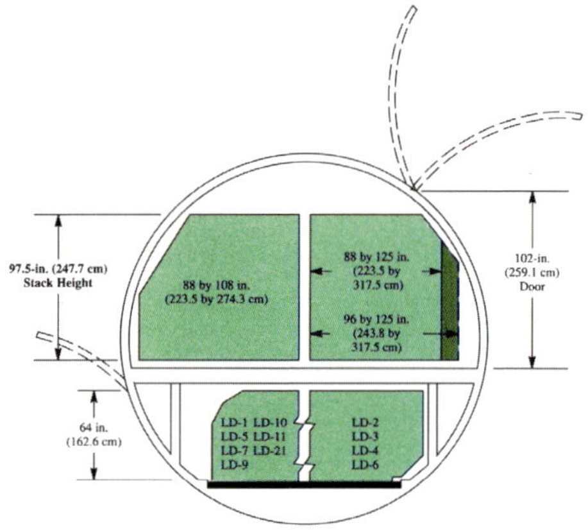

MD-11 Freighter

Design Data

Engine	3	PW4462
Length	(ft/m)	200.9/61.2
Wingspan	(ft/m)	169.8/51.8
Fuel Capacity	(lb/kg)	258,721/117,354
MTOW	(lb/kg)	625,500/283,722
MLW	(lb/kg)	471,500/213,869
MZFW	(lb/kg)	451,300/204,706
OEW	(lb/kg)	251,371/114,020
Cargo Volume	(ft^3/m^3)	21,288/602.8
Gross Weight-Limited Payload	(lb/kg)	194,530/88,237
Net Space-Limited Payload at 8.5 lb/ft^3 (133.6 kg/m^3)	(lb/kg)	180,948/82,077
Range at 180,948 lb (82,077 kg)	(n mi)	3,200
Interior Floor Width	(in./cm)	220/559

Freighter operators have various main cabin configurations between the cockpit and main deck cargo compartment. The main cabin accommodates up to five jumpseats in addition to up to three jumpseats in the cockpit. The configuration depends whether a crew rest compartment is installed and if the galley compartment is separated from the main deck cargo compartment by a cargo barrier net, or a rigid cargo barrier (RCB).

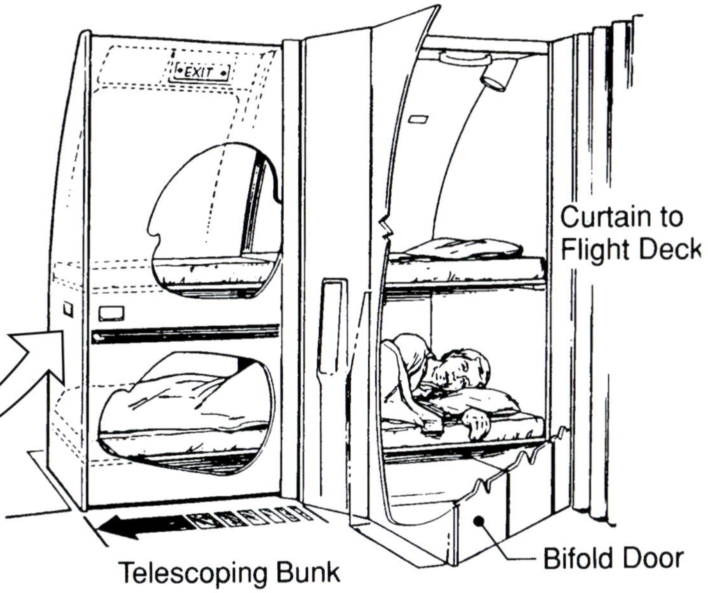

Telescoping bunks can be deployed electrically during cruise flight and therefore blocking door 1L so for in-flight use only! on board Western Global N512JN

Galley area, Note the door emergency control handle - on board N512JN

Photos Benoît Denet

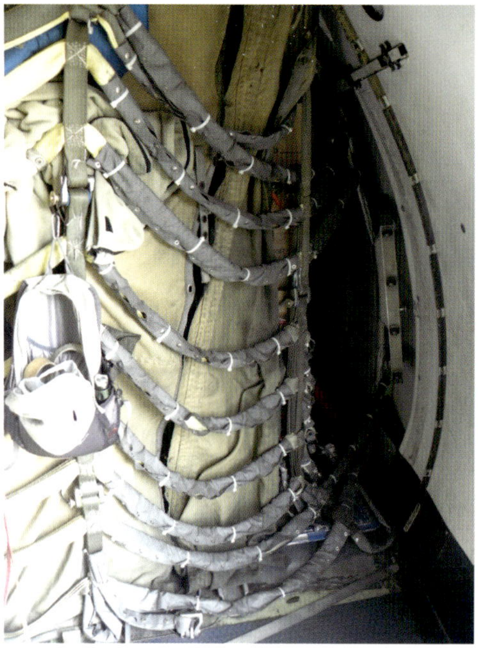

Cargo barrier net, looking from the galley area

Photo Benoît Denet

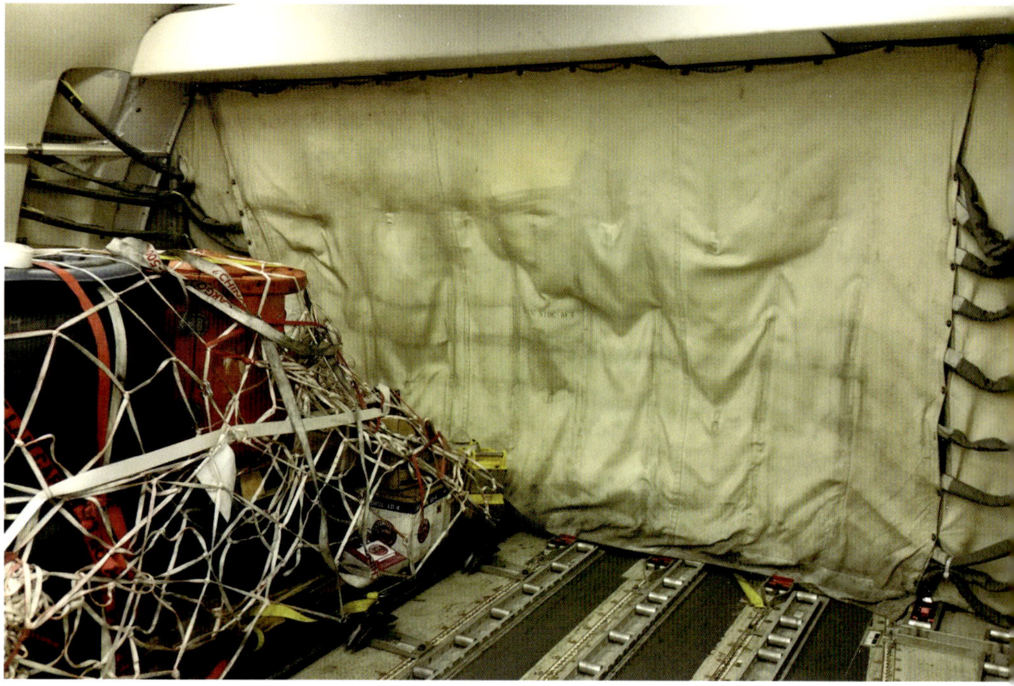

The cargo and smoke barrier net, looking forward

Photo Benoît Denet

During cargo conversion or when replacing the cargo net, the rigid cargo barrier (RCB) frees the space forward of the net that is otherwise kept clear to allow for the net to stretch during an emergency landing.

Operators can then use this space for more baggage stowage or additional business class jumpseats. The RCB incorporates an access door with a viewing window on the left side of the fuselage, a decompression panel on the right side, and a complete smoke barrier.

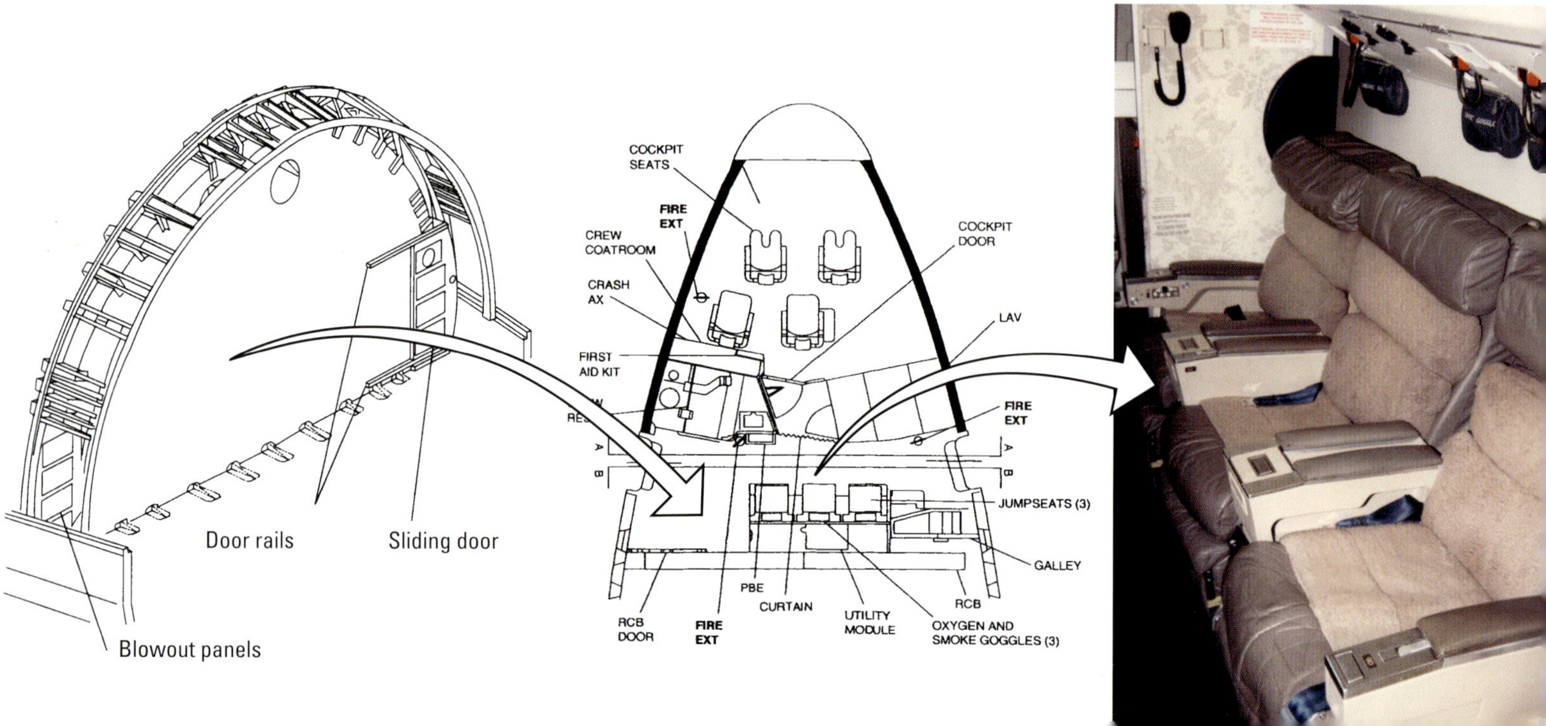

Aircraft Systems

The **air system** supplies pneumatics to the following systems: air conditioning, anti-ice systems, galley ventilation, potable water system, pressurization, the cargo loading system, and cargo heating / ventilation. Conditioned air ventilation of the flight crew and passenger compartments is provided from three air-cycle machines supplied by three independent pneumatic systems. The air conditioning system uses engine compressor bleed air from the main engines during flight; and the engines, auxiliary power unit (APU), or ground source during ground operation. Additionally, the pneumatic systems provide ice protection for wing and horizontal tail leading edges. Engine inlet anti-icing is provided by separate bleed ports from the engine. The PAX LOAD selector, located in the cockpit, controls the flow of fresh air. The flight crew can input the number of passengers on board, and the air conditioning system adjusts circulation accordingly. This capability reduces bleed air requirements and improves fuel consumption. Four internal recirculation fans are used to augment fresh air in order to maintain adequate air movement for passenger comfort. Two fully automatic cabin pressure control systems are installed. In the event that one fails, control is switched automatically to the second system. Manual control of the outflow valve is provided as an additional backup. Forward and aft cargo temperature controls enable these compartments to be used for the transportation of perishables and live animals.

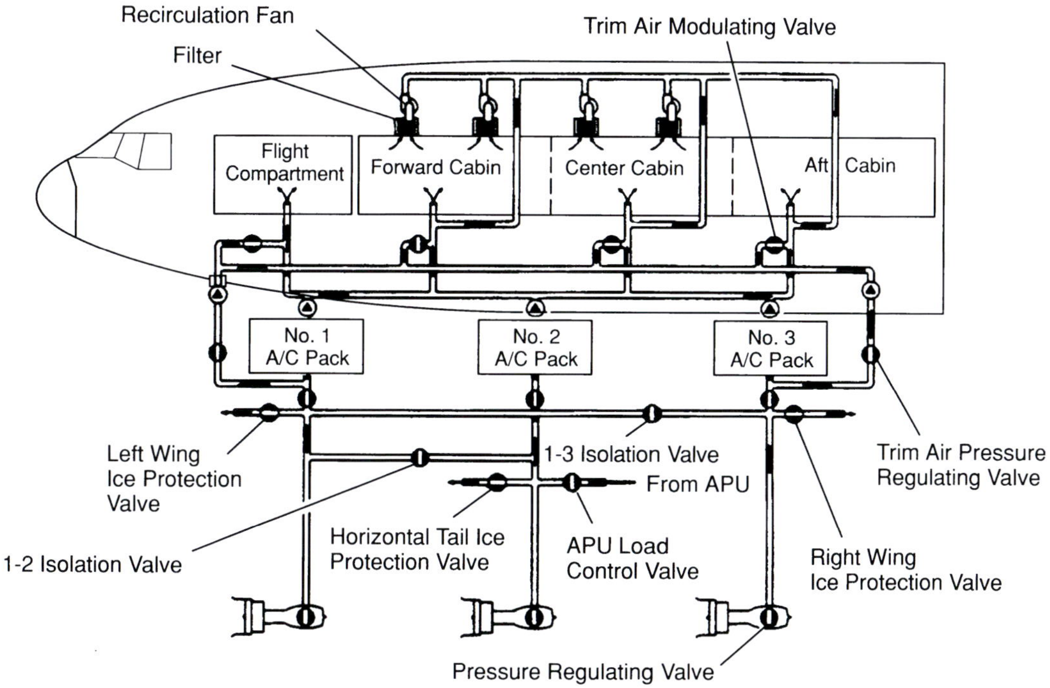

Outflow valve on the left handside in front of the wing Photo André Kuiper

The MD-11 **fuel system** combines advanced equipment with proven McDonnell Douglas components. The fuel quantity gauging system combines direct fuel density measurements and airplane attitude corrections with a digital computer to produce improved system accuracy and greater reliability. The fuel system automatically schedules fuel for centre of gravity control, thus reducing trim drag and increasing fuel economy. In normal operation, each engine is supplied fuel by an independent system from the respective main tank. The center wing auxiliary tank and the tail tank feed the three main tanks. Fuel may be transferred from any tank to any other tank. Fuel is normally supplied to the auxiliary power unit (APU) from the number 2 tank.

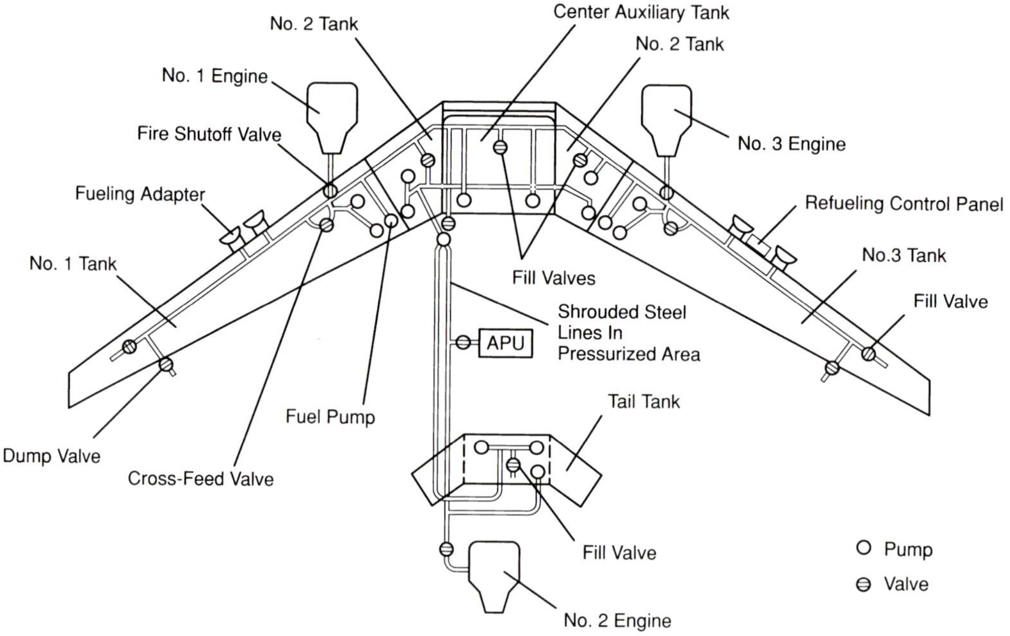

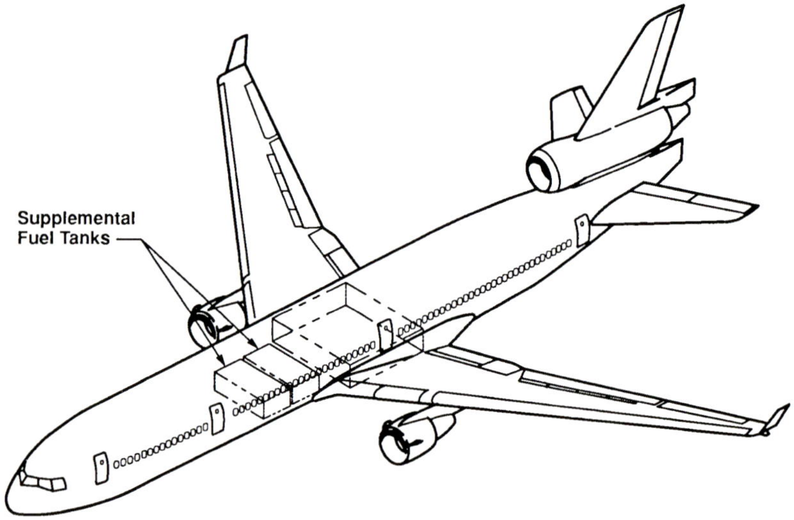

A supplemental and optional fuel system provides for the addition of either one or two tanks located in the lower forward compartment. Fuel tank capacities (assuming density is 6.7 lb/U.S. Gal.) are: for one tank 1,984 U.S. Gal. = 13,293 lb and for two tanks 3,969 U.S. Gal. = 26,592 lb. One tank displaces one pallet, either 88- by 125-inch; 96- by 125-inch, or two LD-3 containers. The two-tank system displaces two pallets, either 88- by 125-inch; 96- by 125-inch; or four LD-3 containers. The supplemental fuel system was designed for "rapid-change," allowing for insertion or removal of the tanks within 12 hours.

Fuel dump during test flight – on board PH-KCI Photo André Kuiper

A three-generator, 115/200-volt, three-phase, 400-Hz alternating current (ac) system supplies power to the primary AC **electrical system**. The three 1 00/1 20 kva integrated drive generators (IDGs), one per engine, are supplemented by a generator on the auxiliary power unit (APU), which is both ground and flight operable. The generator on the APU can provide 120/208-volt, three-phase, 400-Hz electrical power. Three identical generator control units contain the circuitry for voltage regulation, automatic control, and protection, as well as built-in test logic for each generating channel and microprocessor logic to perform automatic functions to control each channel and provide an uninterrupted power transfer from ground to aircraft power.

Finally, a fourth generator control unit is provided for the APU generator. The primary source of DC electrical power is a system of four transformer rectifier units (TRs). The TRs convert 115-volt, 3-phase, 400-Hz AC power into nominal 28-volt DC power and are powered by the AC generator buses. An external power receptacle for ground operation is located on the ground power panel near the nose of the aircraft. It connects external power to the AC generator buses. Additionally, on passenger and combi aircraft, a galley external power receptacle (on ground power panel) connects external power into the galley buses through galley transfer relays (GTR).

Photo André Kuiper

The emergency power system consists of one main 28-volt DC battery, a battery charger, an air driven generator (ADG) and a static inverter.

During an all engines failed situation, or an all generators failed situation, the battery alone (without the ADG) will supply approximately 15 minutes of emergency electrical power to the captain's flight essential equipment.

1. Aft exhaust & APU door
2. APU compt access door
3. APU air inlet door
4. Aft cone and tail dock access

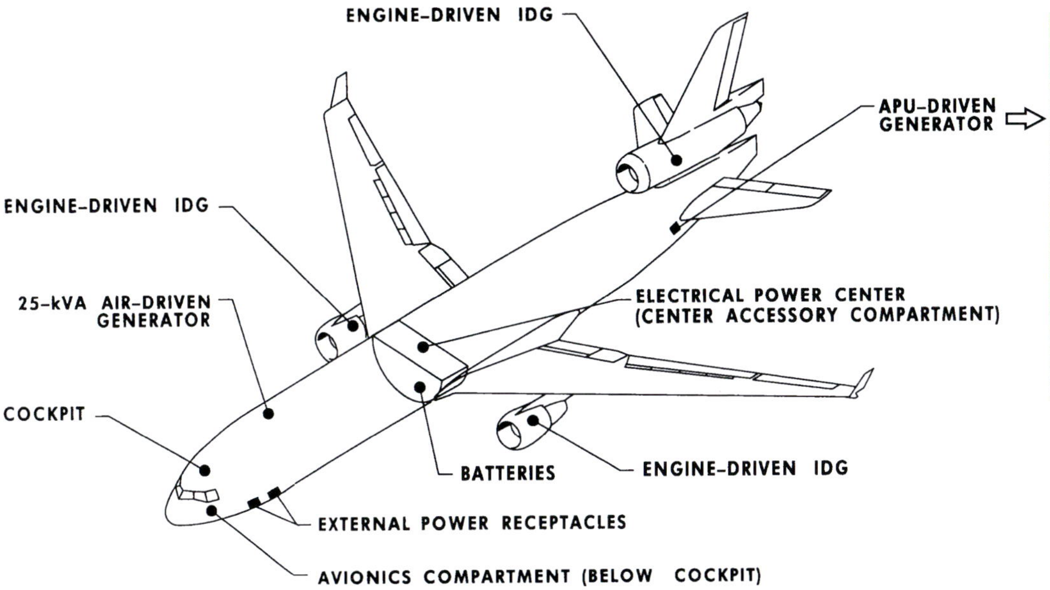

Hydraulic power is supplied by three separate, parallel hydraulic systems. The systems operate continuously at 3,000 psi, and each system is powered by two engine-driven hydraulic pumps. The left pump normally powers its respective system. The right pump is armed to operate if the left pump pressure drops below a predetermined value. Hydraulic system number 3 can also be powered by two electric auxiliary pumps for preflight, ground maintenance, and emergency operations. In an emergency, the air-driven generator (ADG) can supply power to operate the number 1 auxiliary hydraulic pump. Two identical, reversible motor pumps are installed between systems numbers 1 and 3, and between numbers 2 and 3. Pressure can be transferred in either direction. No fluid transfer takes place. The transfer of energy is mechanical. As long as fluid is present on both sides of the reversible motor pump, one system can power the other. Each pump is capable of delivering approximately the same power as one engine-driven pump. Two nonreversible motor pumps provide standby power for upper rudder and horizontal stabilizer operations by powering alternate system number 1 from system number 2, and standby power for lower rudder operation by powering alternate system number 2 from system number 3.

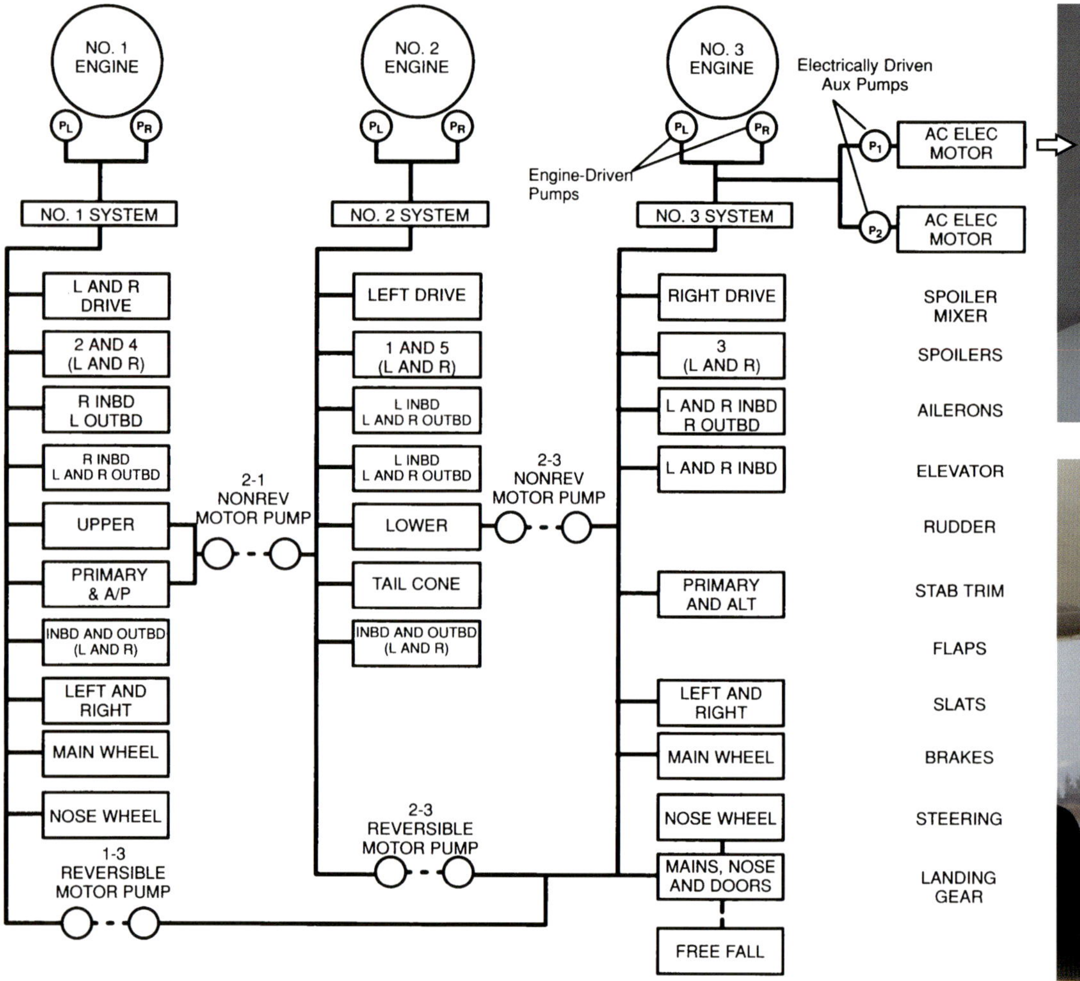

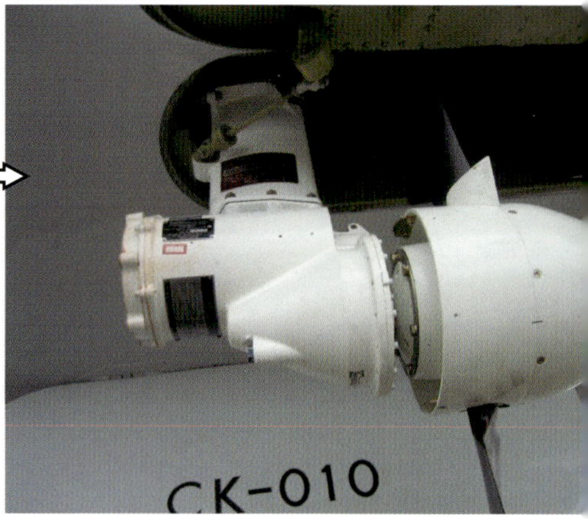

Photos André Kuiper

4 Propulsion Controlled Aircraft

You're flying a large transport plane carrying hundreds of passengers and instantly you are unable to control the airplane – your controls systems have gone out.

This scenario happened on June 12, 1972 on American Airlines flight 96 from Detroit to Buffalo. The DC-10-10, registered N103AA was able to land successfully back at Detroit, aided by the fact that Captain Bryce McCormick had practiced flying the DC-10 after a complete hydraulic failure in the simulator. The same scenario, caused by the failure of the rear cargo door and resulting collapse of the passenger floor, caused the crash of Turkish Airlines flight 981 less than two years later, with the loss of all 346 onboard.

On August 12, 1985, Japan Air Lines flight 123 ended in the world's worst single-aircraft accident with the loss of 520 lives after the rear pressure bulkhead of the Boeing 747 failed, severing all hydraulic lines (and the separation of most of the vertical stabilizer). The pilots' attempt to control the aircraft using engine power was not successful.

After the mid-flight explosion of the centre engine, the damage to UA232 is clearly visible as the aircraft heads for a crash landing into Sioux City

A similar technique was used on another DC-10 on July 19, 1989: United Airlines flight 232 operating from Denver Stapleton to Chicago O'Hare. The DC-10-10, registered N1819U, crash-landed in Sioux City, Iowa after suffering catastrophic failure of its tail-mounted engine, which led to the loss of all flight controls. The crew, led by Captain Al Haynes and assisted by Danny Fitch, an instructor travelling as a passenger, were able to maintain limited control by using the throttles for wing-mounted engines one and three. Asymmetric power achieved a degree of directional control, and simultaneous adjustments was effective for pitch and speed control.

The crew guided the crippled jet to Sioux City's Gateway Airport in rural Iowa and was even able to line up for landing on a runway. Without the use of flaps, slats or spoilers, they were unable to slow down, and the forced landing was at a very high ground speed. The aircraft landed at an extremely high rate of descent due to the inability to flare. As a result, upon touchdown the aircraft broke apart, rolled over and caught fire.

Despite the violent crash, of the 296 people on board, 185 survived. Although 111 passengers lost their lives, the accident is considered a prime example of successful crew resource management due to the large number of survivors and the manner in which the flight crew handled the emergency and landed the airplane without conventional control. The pilots were hailed as heroes and became famous, much like Captain "Sully" Sullenberger in the wake of the Miracle On The Hudson US1549 splashdown in the Hudson.

United 232 definitively demonstrated that the possibility of a total hydraulic failure existed in the event of serious damage, whether caused by unlatched doors, failing structures or exploding engines. Because the DC-10 was affected disproportionately, McDonnell Douglas considered the possibility of creating a formalised and automated control system using just engine thrust to fly and land.

With a system known as Propulsion Controlled Aircraft (PCA) not only is the concept of using throttles only to safely land the airplane a possibility, but was a reality, at least in test flights. This was accomplished by using a specially designed software system a successful flight test program at NASA Dryden Flight Research Center.

The program's humble beginning came from a rough sketch on a TWA napkin that Dryden engineer Bill Burcham drew on a flight to St. Louis for a McDonnell Douglas Aerospace (MDA) meeting. He shared the idea with his traveling companion, Dryden F-15 Project Manager James Stewart. He thought it was a great idea and within five minutes had outlined a test program. They shared it with the people at MDA the next day and they thought it might work too. With

On August 29, 1995, aided by NASA-developed propulsion controlled aircraft (PCA) system, MD-11 N90178 made the first-ever, safe landings of an actual transport aircraft using only engine power for control

the help of Jim Urnes at MDA, they developed and tested the flight software and managed to squeeze PCA into the already existing F-15 research program.

On April 21, 1993, Gordon Fullerton landed the F-15 twice using the PCA system without using any of the flight controls. Over the course of the program, six other pilots flew the PCA equipped airplane and they were all impressed. The plane flew at various altitudes and in unusual attitudes that might be experienced after a major flight control failure. In every test, PCA recovered the airplane successfully.

Ship 560 was registered N90178 and equipped with PCA system. Experimental titles were applied and on August 29, 1995, aided by NASA-developed PCA system, Gordon Fullerton made the first-ever safe landings of a transport aircraft using only engine power for control. Later, on November 30, 1995, improved software enabled a McDonnell Douglas MD-11 to make a final landing at Edwards without the need for the pilot to manipulate the flight controls while using only engine power for control.

The success of the program was the result of a partnership between NASA and McDonnell Douglas Aerospace, St. Louis, with Pratt & Whitney together with Honeywell designing the software used in the aircraft's control computer. NASA Ames Research Center, Mountain View, California, assisted in the program by performing simulations.

For the MD-11, the PCA system used standard autopilot controls already present in the cockpit, together with programming in the aircraft's flight control computers. The aircraft demonstrated software used in the flight control computer that essentially landed the MD-11 without a need for the pilot to manipulate the flight controls and without the use of conventional, hydraulic controls. The PCA concept is simple – for pitch control, the program increases thrust to climb and reduces thrust to descend. To turn right, the autopilot increases the left engine thrust while decreasing the right engine thrust. Since thrust response is slow, and the control forces are relatively small, a pilot would require extensive practice and intense concentration to do this task manually. Using computer-controlled thrust greatly improves flight precision and reduces pilot workload.

Aircraft manufacturers have decided that a PCA system will be valuable for use in the design of future airplanes. When they incorporate this for future design, it will eliminate the need for a less capable hydraulics-dependent backup flight control system. The PCA, also known as the Engines-Only Flight Control System, is patented and currently seeking potential licensees. The PCA has also been featured in NASA Tech Briefs and was the winner of an Exceptional Award in NASA's Space Act Award program. "Now that the technology is proven, I hope to see it incorporated into future aircraft designs," Burcham stated. "I also hope it never has to be used."

The aircraft used in the PCA testing program was later returned to McDonnell Douglas and delivered to Delta Air Lines as N813DE in October 1996 before being converted to a freighter and delivered to FedEx in July 2006. Ironically, the aircraft crashed at Tokyo Narita on March 23rd, 2009.

The technology has not been implanted due to the high hurdle of certification. However the ability to fly and land an airliner after the loss of all flight controls is an invaluable addition to the collective knowledge of the global aviation establishment and is a credit to McDonnell Douglas and the MD-11 development team.

On November 30, 1995, improved software enabled a McDonnell Douglas MD-11 to make a final landing at Edwards without the need for the pilot to manipulate the flight controls while using only engine power for control. With a large NASA sticker above the passenger windows, note the PCA, Pratt & Whitney and Honeywell stickers below

Coming down the steps following the completion of the first and second landings ever performed by a transport aircraft under engine power only on Aug. 29, 1995 are Gordon Fullerton (in front), followed by Bill Burcham, Propulsion Controlled Aircraft (PCA) project engineer at Dryden; NASA Dryden controls engineer John Burken; John Feather of McDonnell Douglas; and Drew Pappas, McDonnell Douglas' project manager for PCA. Note the EXPERIMENTAL title next to door 1R

Bouncy landing for N986AR on runway 18R in Amsterdam, in August 2012 — Photo Simon De Rudder

5 Safety, flying and handling

"It is a pilot's aeroplane. It lands fast and you need to fly it all the way onto the runway. If you are an experienced handling pilot, you will love the MD-11. But for a young cadet who has not flown a jet transport before, it can bite hard."

While the MD-11 has fantastic looks and is an unusual bird for its generation in that it retained three engines when the trend was towards two, the aircraft has a somewhat controversial safety record.

Upgrades to the DC-10 platform that McDonnell Douglas incorporated into their new jetliner were intended to create new efficiencies for its operators. A major change was the placement of the wing on the fuselage relative to that of the DC-10, which results in a more aft center of gravity relative to the center of lift. This reduced the amount of aerodynamic download required on the horizontal stabilizer and elevator during flight, effectively reducing weight the wings must support and thus increasing fuel efficiency. While this does improved control ability it also came with a loss of stability. The other major change was the reduction in the size of the horizontal stabiliser (known colloquially as the tailplane) by forty per cent, reducing induced drag but also comprised the aircraft's natural handling characteristics.

To mitigate the lack of lateral stability, the MD-11 required the use of pitch stability damping in the form of Lateral Stability Augmentation System (LSAS), best understood as a yaw damper that works in the pitch axis. The yaw damper, essential equipment on all jet airliners, reduces the inherent tendency in all swept-wing aircraft to roll and yaw with constant small automated adjustments to the rudder. LSAS is like any fly-by-wire control system – it makes control inputs not commanded from the cockpit with the intention of smoothing out the ride. A flight control computer sums the captain's and first officer's control wheel inputs. When there is no force on the control columns, the LSAS holds the current pitch attitude. When the force exceeds two pounds, LSAS operation is suspended and the elevators are in manual control. When the force on the control column is reduced below two pounds, LSAS holds the newly acquired pitch attitude. The limits on the attitude that LSAS can hold are +30 and -10 degrees. The maximum elevator deflection that LSAS can command is five degrees. If the elevators of an MD-11 at could be observed, they would be seen to be fluttering with a high frequency of pitch inputs under the control of the LSAS.

Additionally, early in the life of the MD-11 it became apparent that the new design had a nasty and unpredictable habit of ballooning excessively nose-up on touchdown, requiring forward elevator input to keep the tail from striking the tarmac, followed by aft elevator to keep the nose from slamming to the ground. In some cases the input required was full forward, and / or full aft. These oscillations usually damped out until the aeroplane was fully stable and established in the roll out. However there were a number of occasions where the tail struck the ground and at least one incident where the nose slammed onto the runway, each causing airframe damage and sometimes being classified by the National Transportation Board (NTSB) as accidents. Some such incidents result in damage to extremities, such as wing tips, wing-mounted engine nacelles, noses or tails. Because a number of these more severe incidents resulted in damage to the tail, they were often simply dismissed as "tail strikes", a somewhat-common event that occurs to most transports from time to time, although use of the term in conjunction with the MD-11 was unhelpful as it hid a more significant malaise, eventually mitigated somewhat by design changes in main gear oleo strut design and reprogramming of spoiler deployment timing upon touchdown.

However, even with the LSAS fitted, it is not controversial to say the MD-11 is a handful to hand-fly – indeed, even among its greatest fans, the challenge of hand-flying the MD-11 is one of its signature characteristics. At best, this makes it a satisfying machine to master, but there can be no escaping the fact that four aircraft crashed in identical accidents, where a high sink rate could not be arrested, resulting in a heavy touchdown followed by a series of divergent bounces, leading to the main spar fracturing, and a crash.

The type's first fatal accident occurred on April 6, 1993 to China Eastern Airlines flight 583 from Shanghai to Los Angeles, operated by B-2171. While not fitting the template of a landing accident that would come to define the MD-11, it could still be considered to be related to the aircraft's slippery handling characteristics in the pitch axis. Over the Pacific at Mach .82 and 33,000 feet, flight crew action inadvertently caused the leading edge slats to deploy, radically changing the profile of the wing and causing B-2171 to go into a

Damage inside of China Eastern B-2171 after an inadvertent deployment of the leading edge wing slats while in cruise flight
Photo NTSB

violent series of pitch oscillations which were so extreme that two passengers were killed and 156 were injured, fifty-three of them seriously.

The investigation revealed five previous incidents of inadvertent deployment of slats in flight, and also several cases of pilot-induced oscillation during recovery from upsets caused by turbulence. With grim prophesy of the landing accidents that would follow, the accident report stated: "The MD-11 is designed to fly with minimal longitudinal stability margin to improve the economic performance of the [aeroplane]. The control column forces needed for manually controlling the aeroplane during normal maneouvres in cruise flight are lighter than those that pilots might have encountered in their past experience in other models of [aeroplane], and they are considerably lighter than the control forces normally used at lower speeds and altitudes." This incident kickstarts the novel Airframe by Michael Crichton which follows the development of the ficticious Northern N-22 widebody airliner which is entirely based on the MD-11.

The first time the difficulty of landing the aeroplane became fully apparent as something that was more than just a quirk was at Newark airport on July 31, 1997, when FedEx flight 14 from Singapore via Penang, Taipei and Anchorage came into land. To illustrate the difficulty pilots faced with the MD-11, N611FE had already suffered underbelly damage landing at Memphis in January 1994 and a serious tailstrike at Anchorage in November of the same year.

The captain had expressed concern about the stopping distance needed for a high weight landing during the descent briefing, as reverse thrust on engine number one (left side) was inoperative, ruling out the use of reverse on number three as well due to the dangers of asymmetrical braking. (In fact the crew had misinterpreted the runway data, and the available stopping distance was greater than they realised). After the captain began to flare to reduce the sink rate, he then let the nose lower to achieve an earlier touchdown, then raised it and increased thrust to slow the plane's descent, then finally pushed the nose down again around the time of the first touchdown. These last control inputs were, the words of the

The morning after the crash of FedEx N611FE at Newark on August 1st 1997

NTSB investigation, "too late and too large" to stabilise the landing. After floating 1,100 feet deep into the runway, the second impact with the ground was on the number three engine and the right landing gear strut which failed, followed by the right wing rear spar. The roll continued and until the MD-11 came to rest off the runway on its back and on fire. The five onboard – two crew and three jump-seaters – escaped via the cockpit windows but the aircraft was totally destroyed.

A Korean Air MD-11, HL7373, was lost just after takeoff from Shanghai's old Hongqiao airport on April 15, 1999. The initiating factor was confusion on the flight deck but the MD-11's handling characteristics certainly played a role. As the flight climbed through 4,500 feet the first officer thought they had busted their clearance which was in fact for a climb to 1,500 metres – 4,900 feet. The captain pushed the control column forward hard enough to put the aircraft

Dynasty 642, B-150 Photo Hong Kong Civil Aviation Department

into an unrecoverable dive; the crash killed all three crew and five people on the ground.

Departing from the chronological narrative, Korean Air sistership HL7372 crashed in Shanghai a decade later. Owned by San Francisco-based aircraft lessor Pegasus Aviation, at the end of its tenure at Korean Air, the ship went on to spend five years at Varig Logistica before being placed with Zimbabwean cargo carrier Avient Aviation and registered Z-BAV on delivery on November 20, 2009. Just nine days later the plane crashed on takeoff at Shanghai's Pudong airport, only thirty miles (fifty kilometres) from the scene of HL7373's loss. The cause was overrotation on takeoff with a tailstrike and overrun, with crew fatigue and complications arising from the use of autothrottles a factor. Of the seven crew onboard, four lost their lives.

On August 22, 1999 there came a carbon-copy repeat of the FedEx crash in Newark when B-150, a passenger aircraft belonging to Mandarin Airlines and operating Dynasty 642 from Bangkok to Taipei via Hong Kong on behalf of China Airlines of Taiwan crashed on landing. 300 passengers and 15 crew were onboard for the transit stop at Hong Kong's Chep Lap Kok airport. With Typhoon Sam twenty-seven nautical miles (fifty kilometres) away, the wind was a challenge, blowing out of 320 degrees at 28 knots gusting to 36 knots, creating a pure crosswind component of 21.4 knots gusting to 27.5 knots (the MD-11 is certified with a crosswind limitation of 35 knots).

It is generally known that an MD-11 will remain only marginally controllable with a fifteen knot tailwind shear at fifty feet or less. As Dynasty 642 flared, power was reduced to idle at twenty feet at the moment the gusty wind changed, conspiring to cause an immediate airspeed loss of twenty crucial knots; the right wing dropped and the number three engine slammed into the tarmac. As with the FedEx crash in Newark, the main wing spars failed, the wing folded up,

FedEx flight 80, N526FE at Narita — Photo Japan Transport Safety Board

Lufthansa D-ALCQ at Riyadh

Photo The General Authority of Civil Aviation of Saudi Arabia

and the aircraft rolled over until it crashed upside down next to the runway. Despite the fire that erupted around the rear of the aircraft, the combination of fast response by the cabin crew, the airport fire service and heavy rain got all but three passengers safely out of the downed bird.

Because the difficulties of handling the MD-11 were now fully recognised, additional training meant that while further incidents of heavy landings continued with regularity, there were no more crashes for a decade, but the MD-11's luck ran out again on March 23, 2009, when N526FE crashed after a series of porpoising oscillations on landing at Tokyo Narita at the conclusion of FedEx flight 80 from Guangzhou. Tragically, the pilots were killed, the first workplace fatalities for FedEx pilots.

Two more MD-11s have been written off due to hard landings since FedEx 80, although in both cases a rollover was averted and the crews were able to survive unscathed – Lufthansa Cargo D-ALCQ was operating LH8460 from Frankfurt to Hong Kong via Riyadh and Sharjah when it crashed on landing at Riyadh on July 27, 2010. Centurion Cargo suffered a similar event at Viracopos, the industrial airport at Sao Paolo in Brazil, on October 13, 2012.

The MD-11's lack of lateral stability may have been exacerbated by some elements of the approach speed calculation, especially on United States-flagged aircraft. A multiplier of about between 1.20 and 1.23 is used to add a controllability margin to V_{S0} (stall speed, or minimum flight speed, in landing configuration) to derive the V_{Ref} (the speed at which one intends to cross the runway threshold before touchdown). Historically, a 1.3 multiplier had been used (including on the DC-10) and indeed the European Joint Aviation Authorities (JAA) still require the 1.3 V_{S0} multiplier to calculate V_{Ref} for European operators. MD-11 Flight Management Systems (FMS)

Centurion Cargo N988AR Photos Carlos M. Rodriguez

operated by European airlines were programed for 1.3 V_{S0} versus 1.2 V_{S0}. For most if not all MD-11s operated by non-European airlines, the 1.2 multiplier was deemed sufficient. This might explain why the European MD-11 operators did not have the type of severe landing accidents that plagued so many other MD-11 operators in the USA and worldwide.

(Another interesting difference between the FAA and the JAA is that the JAA require that V_{S0} be calculated in level flight at one G of vertical acceleration. The FAA allowed this to be done in a steep decent at one G of vertical acceleration. The result of the steep decent method, presumably in a stall recovery maneouvre, reduced V_{S0} by about seven percent, which translates to between nine and eleven knots on the MD-11, depending on landing weight.)

The MD-11 came with another quirk. Like most jet airliners the spoilers on the MD-11 have an asymmetrical function to assist the ailerons in a turn, and a symmetrical speed brake and lift dumping / spoiler function; all of which use the same control surfaces. Speed brakes are deployed manually to reduce lift or speed during flight, and spoilers are deployed manually or automatically to dump lift upon touchdown. The MD-11 has five such panels on the top of each wing. Unlike many jet airliners all five spoiler panels activate when commanded by a turn / aileron control input.

During low level wind shear events the MD-11 wings have actually stalled when on approach and sometimes too low for recovery. When any aeroplane stalls one wing will often stall before the other, especially on a swept wing aircraft. When this happens the wing that stalls first will drop faster than the other wing. During such an event at low level the highest priority is to roll towards wings level to avoid striking a wing tip or wing engine nacelle first. This will require maximum aileron control input away from the low wing. Unfortunately, with such massive spoiler augmentation the amount of lift lost on the high wing due to spoiler deployment can exceed any added lift generated by ailerons on the low wing. Thus, if the aeroplane is dropping due to a low level stall the roll input might actually add to the rate of descent by spoiling lift further.

The MD-11 may be an unusually demanding aircraft but pilots on any complex transport aircraft will find shortfalls and their own work-arounds to compensate and pilots on the MD-11 were no different. A modest speed edit of as little as plus-three knots could significantly reduce the likelihood of a low level wind shear stall or a divergent lateral pitch event. Of course, this required sufficient runway length to safely land with the speed additives, but at the majority of fields where MD-11s operate, even at high landing weights this was rarely a problem.

However, when things did go wrong, the MD-11 may have inherited an ergonomic issue that reduced the pilot's ability to command full up elevator during a maximum effort go around. Control wheel roll travel on the MD-11 is about 117 degrees left or right, as on the DC-6, -7, -8, -9 and -10. This was necessary in order to provide sufficient mechanical advantage during manual reversion in the event of a hydraulic failure. However neither the DC-10 or MD-11 have manual reversion and might therefore function well with much less control wheel travel. In cases where the MD-11 has stalled during low level wind shear events, one wing has invariably dropped faster than the other, necessitating full control wheel roll input away from the dropping wing.

In the case of an event that caused severe damage to an MD-11 landing at Anchorage, the right wing stalled and dropped ahead of the left; the digital flight data recorder showed the elevator deflecting toward full up then reversing to drop slightly and then once again deflecting toward full up. This was a classic example of the ergonomic challenge of a yoke that had so much travel built-in. The flying pilot, in the left seat, had to apply full left control wheel input to attempt to keep the aircraft from landing with an excessive right roll. He was required to bring his left hand – on the yoke – down and across his lap all the way to the right. His wrist also had to rotate 117 degrees counter-clockwise. It was ergonomically impossible for him to apply full up elevator when his right hand was simultaneously applying full ("firewall") throttle. Once throttle was applied and his right hand was available then full up elevator could be commanded. This event has been replicated several times across the operational life of the MD-11; most airliners inherit quirks from their manufacturers' previous designs as not only would it be financially ruinous to start from a completely blank sheet for each new design, but also counter-productive, as the vast majority of elements grandfathered-in are positive, and only rare exceptions prove the rule.

The MD-11 suffered a significantly worse accident rate than other contemporary aircraft type. A widely-used barometer of the safety of any given type is the number of hulls lost (aircraft destroyed) per million departures. Up to the end of 2015, the MD-11 suffered 3.39 hull-losses per million departures; (in other words, one in every 300,000 flights met with disaster). If one restricts the criteria to a fatal crash, the rate is 1.89 per million departures (just slightly better than one fatal crash for every half a million departures). The 747-400 is substantially better at 0.88 hull-losses per million departures, with 1.12 for the Airbus A300-600, and 0.48 for the Boeing 767. Interestingly, the hull loss rate for the DC-10 was 2.92 per million departures (and 1.3 per million departures for a DC-10 crash with fatalities), somewhat better than its successor despite being developed twenty years earlier.

Post-crash reconstruction of the front section of HB-IWF

Photo Transportation Safety Board of Canada

Mention must also be made of the worst accident to befall an MD-11, which was the famous Swissair 111 disaster off the coast of Nova Scotia, while attempting an emergency landing at Halifax. The flight, bound from New York's JFK airport to Geneva, was routine for the first hour but smoke was detected in the cockpit and the crew decided to divert to Boston. Air traffic control suggested Halifax as it was only sixty-six nautical miles away; a descent began. The severity of the situation was not immediately grasped as the pilots discussed dumping fuel and turned away from the airport to allow the flight to descend, however the fire, which was later traced to the power supply of the after-market inflight entertainment system, quickly escalated and caused a cascading loss of flight instruments followed by all electrical power. HB-IWF circled helplessly in the dark once before crashing into the Atlantic Ocean just twenty-one minutes after the first smoke was detected. The accident led to widespread changes in aircraft certification, principally in the field of wiring, fire hardening, and the use of less flammable material especially insulation.

All that said, there is no question that the MD-11 not only fulfilled a unique role in global commerce, especially in its second wind as an in-demand freighter. Captain Dan Dill (retired) flew thousands of hours on the MD-11 as well as the DC-10, 747 Classic and 727, and contributed greatly to this chapter. His words on the positive aspects of flying the MD-11 deserve to be recounted in full.

Situational awareness was perhaps the most spectacular improvement we encountered coming onto the MD-11. Although the MD-11 was not the first "glass cockpit" aeroplane it was certainly by far the most advanced when it went into service. For me, training was extremely challenging, having come from a "steam gauge" background. I was in the first wave of pilots to be trained in the MD-11 and we did not have any cockpit procedural trainers at that time. So all training of the Flight Management System (FMS) had to be done in the simulator, which was premium time and not as suitable for learning the complex menu architectures of the very complex MD-11 FMS.

Additionally, the volume of information made available to the pilot on the six cockpit CRT displays and three Multi-Function Display Units (MCDU) was enormous and initially nearly overwhelming due to the complexity of the multiple pages on each CRT display and the many menu pages on MCDUs. But, as these systems slowly became intuitive there was a new world of situational awareness that I had never seen before on any other airplane.

Added to all these complexities were the frequent software and firmware updates. Sometimes it seemed that just as one started to get used to where everything was there would be a new software update and it would be time again to relearn where everything could be found in the menus. Frankly, we had a significant number of wash outs and most were very experienced captains but with who had little or no previous computer experience.

As the MD-11 matured and as we matured with it things became much more intuitive and eventually the huge pay-offs in improved situational awareness and reduced cockpit workload became very apparent. I say "reduced workload", in reality it wasn't so much reduced as it was reallocated so that most of the workload could be accomplished on the ground or during cruise flight so that workload was reduced during terminal operations. This all amounted to a huge paradigm shift but those who survived the training and check-outs eventually reaped the benefits. The benefits were enormous. Later we got TCAS, GPS, enhanced GPWS, wind shear prediction, ADS-B out and CPDLC, which all added to safety but pilots had to accustom themselves to constant training for the duration of flying the MD-11.

I've heard it said that technology has taken the fun out of flying. I don't agree. For those able to keep up with the technology flying is extremely fulfilling but in different ways than in bygone era. There is little room for "seat of the pants" flying but it's nice to have that ability when all else fails. I found that some of the younger generation adapted more easily to the computerized environment than some of the old timers. But it seemed to me that some of the younger pilots struggled somewhat to make up for lack of seat of the pants experience.

The precision with which the MD-11 flies CAT III approaches to nearly zero-zero conditions and the course and altitude accuracies made possible with GPS and RVSM were never known in earlier aircraft. In fact, it is customary in an MD-11 to provide one or two nautical mile strategic offsets to the right of assigned tracks to avoid the likelihood of a mid-air collision should an aircraft be inadvertently assigned the same track and altitude in the opposite converging direction. While that is an extremely rare occurrence it does happen. In the old days you would probably miss due to the built-in inaccuracies of long range navigation and non-RVSM altimetry. Nowadays, with GPS and RVSM, you will almost certainly hit if such a clearance error occurs. The strategic offset is also used to avoid wake turbulence when following another aircraft on the same track but a higher altitude, sometimes only 1,000 feet higher. While these situations are now commonplace on most modern airliners the MD-11 operators were among the first to learn how to best cope with and benefit from all these new innovations.

When we got the MD-11s there were two environmental improvements. First, the cockpit was very quiet compared with Boeing and Lockheed aircraft I had flown. Second, the MD-11 air conditioning system was apparently equipped with ozone scrubbers. I don't remember reading it in any of our systems manuals but there was an immediate improvement in how our eyes felt after a long international flight. On earlier jet aircraft our eyes would feel like sandpaper near the end of a flight but that went away on the MD-11, which made for a far more comfortable and less fatiguing flight. Sometimes when flying through severe static electrical build-up, the smell of ozone could be almost overwhelming. I was told that was caused by static neutralising the carbon ozone filters.

The cockpit was roomy and comfortable. Visibility was excellent, as it was on the DC-10. The autoflight interface was perhaps the best ever designed, even with minor shortcomings. The aeroplane rode turbulence well, even if stiff compared to Boeing jets. Its Category III (Cat III) landing system was the best I ever experienced by far. I flew about five actual Cat III approaches in a fourteen-year period. At one point we could shoot an approach with ninety metres RVR (300 feet). We might have even gotten to forty-five metres (150 feet) before I retired. I don't remember if it was implemented but it was discussed. On two of the Cat III landings I made, I never saw the runway before touchdown, yet I felt very comfortable flying such approaches. We flew to 100-foot Alert Heights but there was no Decision Height requirement, except at Hong Kong. The MD-11 was very demanding to hand fly, especially without auto-throttles, but it was doable with a lot of concentration.

All in all, it's amazing that just two crew members can take an MD-11 anywhere in the world in just about any type of weather and do it much more efficiently, economically and precisely than possible in earlier airplanes.

Gruppo Alitalia
MD-11
PASSEGGERI
Per la Vostra sicurezza
For your safety
Pour votre sécurité
Für Ihre Sicherheit
Para su seguridad
Para sua segurança
من اجل سلامتك
Γιά τήν ἀσφάλειά σας
あなたの安全のために
Для Вашей безопасности
Kendi emniyetiniz için
Dla bezpieczeństwa pasażerów
Za vašu sigurnost
FOR YOUR SAFETY
MD-11
AmericanAirlines
PLEASE DO NOT REMOVE THIS CARD FROM AIRPLANE
Safety Procedures
MD-11
旅客安全須知
安全のしおり
CHINA AIRLINES
EXIT
OXYGEN
Please do not remove this card from aircraft
CityBird
The Flying Dream
MD11
For your safety
Pour votre sécurité
Voor uw veiligheid
Fur Ihre Sicherheit
Para su seguridad
Please obey the "No Smoking" and "Fasten Seatbelt" signs and all instructions given by your crew members.
For the safety of future passengers please do not remove this card from the aircraft.
MD-11
Passenger
Safety
Information
DELTA AIR LINES
Garuda Indonesia
KARTU PETUNJUK KESELAMATAN
SAFETY INSTRUCTIONS
MD-11
KLM
Safety on board
MD-11
Fasten seatbelt
No smoking
Never smoke in lavatory
Use of electronic devices
Before take-off and landing
Brace for impact
Oxygen
Oxygen
Please do not remove from aircraft
LTU
MD-11
MCDONNELL DOUGLAS
Für Ihre Sicherheit
For your safety
Pour votre sécurité
Para su seguridad
Per la Vostra sicurezza
Kendi emniyetiniz için
VEILIGHEIDS INSTRUKTIES
SAFETY INSTRUCTIONS
MD11
Martinair
TIJDENS START EN LANDING/AT TAKE-OFF AND LANDING
LOSMAKEN/UNFASTEN
TOILETTEN/LAVATORIES
ZUURSTOFMASKER/OXYGEN MASK
NIET GEBRUIKEN/DO NOT USE
For your safety
MD-11
Federal law requires that you review this information.
Follow these instructions, the directions of the crew, and posted signs.
Please do not remove this card from the aircraft.
Monarch Airlines
SAFETY ON BOARD
MD11
SICHERHEIT AN BORD SECURITE A BORD
Please do not remove from aircraft
swissair
Thai
SAFETY ON BOARD
MD-11
MD-11
VARIG
MD-11
Instruções de Segurança
Safety Instructions
VASP
For your safety
Pour votre sécurité
Para su seguridad
Für ihre sicherheit
MD-11
WORLD

DELTA
LTU
AIR MD-11
FINNAIR
DELTA
ARIG
BRASIL

6 Individual Aircraft History

The individual MD-11 aircraft history has been compiled with information extracted from Servaas C. Verbrugge's MD-11 production list available on his airlinerlist.com web site, compiled by José Van Herbruggen, supplemented and collaborated from other sources including from World Airline Fleets News and Aviation Letter.

As the DC-10 and MD-11 aircraft were rolled out from the Long Beach manufactory, they were assigned a "cumulative line number" while the associated manufacturer's serial number or construction number (c/n) do not follow the same sequence and has a much greater significance as it will appear on the actual aircraft data plate and/or its paperwork.

446 DC-10 aircraft were built and therefore 447 became the first MD-11 line number.

The heading for each aircraft history denotes the line number, the manufacturer's serial number (c/n) which coincides with the factory line number, the aircraft type (model), the date of manufacture (mfd) and the engine type being either the General Electric (GE) model CF6-80C2 or the Pratt and Whitney (PW) PW 4462.

The Douglas Aircraft Company data plate of the first MD-11F fuselage 447, serial number 48401, in service with FedEx since June 1991.

Standard abbreviations are incorporated to conserve space. The following most common are:

AL	Airlines	ny	not yet
arr	arrived	oc	old colours
AW	Airways	opf	operated for
bt	bought	own	owned by
canc	cancelled	pkd	parked
conv	converted	r	retired
cs	colour scheme	rgd/r	registered
cvtd	converted	re-rgd	re-registered
dam	damaged	rr, rrgd	re-registered
del	delivered	rt, ret	returned
depa	departed	s	seen
fc	full colours	SCR	scrapped
ff, f/f	first flight	sis	seen in service
frd	ferried	str	stored
ho	handed over	svc	service
Int	International	szd	seized
is	in service	tfd	transferred
L	total landings	tls, tit	titles
lsd	leased	TT	total time (flying hours)
MDD	McDonnell Douglas	unk	unknown
nc	new colours	wfu	withdrawn from use
nn	new name/renamed	W/O	written off by accident
NTU	not taken up	*	new (sub)type after conversion

IATA location identifier three-letter code are used to designate airports.

Most used abbreviations of Financial owners and Leasing Companies

B&BAM	Babcock & Brown Aircraft Management
FSBU	First Security Bank of Utah
GATX (CC)	GATX Capital Corporation
GPA	Guinness Peat Aviation/GPA Group
ILFC	International Lease Finance Corporation
MDDFC	McDonnell-Douglas Finance Corporation
SSB&TC	State Street Bank & Trust Company
WFBN	Wells Fargo Bank Northwest
WTC/Wilm	Wilmington Trust Company

Line	C/N	mfd	model	Engines	
447	**48401**	**02.89**	**MD-11F**	**GE**	**N111MD** 1st prototype, McDonnell Douglas r01.90; f/f 10.01.90; **N601FE** Federal Express "Jim Riedmeyer" del 27.06.91; rgd WTC 06.91, first MD-11 in new FedEx cs s27.06.94 NRT, FedEx r22.06.16

N111MD • the first prototype

Photo McDonnell Douglas

N601FE • Federal Express "Jim Riedmeyer" • January 1993

via R.Verschuur

Line	C/N	mfd	model	Engines	
448	**48402**	**04.89**	**MD-11F**	**GE**	**N211MD** 2nd prototype; McDonnell Douglas r02.90; f/f 01.03.90; **N602FE** Federal Express "Malcolm Baldrige 1990" s28.04.91 MHV, del 29.05.91; own WTC, Federal Express r22.11.16

N602FE • Federal Express "Malcolm Baldrige 1990" • December 1992 via Eddy J.Gual

N602FE • FedEx "Malcolm Baldrige 1990" • July 2003 via A.Hofmann

Line	C/N	mfd	model	Engines
449	**48458**	**05.89**	**MD-11F**	**PW**

N311MD McDonnell Douglas; f/f 26.04.90; **N489GX** GATX/MDD 29.03.91; GATX/China AL 24.09.92; ret GATX 05.02.93, sLong Beach 06.92 full cs/is 03.10; **N280WA** GATX/World/Garuda 23.04.93; own FSBU, arr AMS 23.06.94 after short-term lse; GATX/World AW ret 28.06.94; dep from JFK, white; Ghana AW slsd, s14.10.94; sJFK 11.11.94 with tit; Garuda s05.95; sZRH full World cs; GATX/World AW ret s03.01.97; sPHX grey no tit; City Bird slsd 30.05.97; arr BRU basic World cs ex Taipei, City Bird tit/logo, is 02.06.97 to EWR; GATX/World AW ret 22.07.97; ho at EWR, ret GATX 7.09.97; **N489GX** GATX/CAL/Mandarin AL 23.10.97; sCambridge fc 27.09.97, del to AMS 23.10.97; China AL tfd s11.03.00; sTokyo fc, ret WTC 4.04.01; **N578FE** Federal Express 05.04.01; rr 13.06.01, sVenice 13.07.01 for F-conv, ff 01.11.01, to Memphis 07.11.01, named “Stephen”

N280WA • City Bird • Los Angeles LAX

Photo Frank de Koster

N489GX • China Airlines • Mars 2001

Photo Thomas Kim

Line	C/N	mfd	model	Engines
450	**48419**	**08.89**	**MD-11F**	**GE**

N1750B McDonnell Douglas; f/f 05.06.90, Br Cal NTU; **N411MD** McDonnell Douglas rr 07.90; test aircraft, used for avionics testing, named "The Phoenix"; **N1750B** American AL 28.05.91; **N581FE** Federal Express 28.02.97; Sabretech s28.02.97 ex-AA basic, ro 16.05.97 and rr, reg and tit applied 30.05.97, rgd WTC 16.06.97, lsd till 01.19, named "Joshua". W/O 17.10.99 Subic Bay, Ph. 0(2), overran runway on landing at midnight, "pancaked" water surface, later broke in two parts and became submerged. TT 30278, 5817 L.

N1750B • American • Miami MIA • March 1993 via Eddy J.Gual

N581FE • FedEx / Federal Express • Anchorage ANC • May 1998, a few months before being lost at Subic Bay Photo Ruben Husberg Collection Jacques Guillem

Line	C/N	mfd	model	Engines
451	**48420**	**10.89**	**MD-11F**	**GE**

N511MD McDonnell Douglas r04.90; **N1751A** American AL '1AB' del 01.02.91; Br Cal NTU arr UK 16.07.90 outfitting; s24.04.91 NRT i/s, last service 06.01.96 St Domingo-JFK, ferried to Tulsa, damaged after tipping on tail 01.96 (not confirmed); ferried Tulsa-Phoenix 18.01.96 for freighter conversion by Sabretech, TT 18138, 3344 L; **N582FE** Federal Express bt 22.01.96; ho 17.04.96, is 22.04.96; rr due old reg s02.97, but on ACARS-computer syst already N582FE, rFSBU 04.96, named "Jamie", FedEx r29.07.16

N511MD • American • for outfitting by Marshalls • July 1990 Photo M.Brouyère

N1751A • FedEx "Jamie" still wearing previous American AL reg N1751A • Frankfurt am Main FRA • July 1996 via Eddy J.Gual

Line	C/N	mfd	model	Engines
452	**48421**	**03.90**	**MD-11F**	**GE**

N510MD McDonnell Douglas; arr Cambridge 08.08.90, r08.90; **N1752K** American AL 22.04.91; Br Cal NTU; is 01.05.91; **N583FE** Federal Express 11.06.97; ho Tulsa, TT 23104, 3746 L then sGoodyear AZ 07-08.97, being F-cvtd, s30.09.97 fc, F-conv compl, rr s15.10.97 GAZ, FedEx to SSB&TC, lsd till 01.20; op special charter Louisville-Chitose-Chengdu-Washington 03-06.12.00 as "Panda One"; sNRT 06.04.03 in special (face) panda cs; USB r15.08.05. Named "Nancy" 06.97 to 2008, then "Aquinnah" 2008

N1752K • American • London Heathrow LHR

Photo Frank de Koster

N583FE • FedEx "Aquinnah" on a Charter flight • Liège LGG • November 2011

Photo Jean-Marie Hanon

Line	C/N	mfd	model	Engines
453	**48411**	**04.90**	**MD-11**	**GE**

N514MD McDonnell Douglas; Mit/Air Europe NTU G-MDII rgd MDD 07.90; s22.10.90 DFW prior to dep. for Seoul and London and finally back to Yuma as part of a three day, round-the-world tour; **N891DL** Mit/Delta AL 21.12.90; manuf 09.12.90; **PP-SPD** WTC/VASP 21.01.94; sis 30.01/rToA 28.12.93, Mitsui & Co szd 18.06.99 Toronto, s05.07.99, sMarana 05.09.99 str, s30.12.99 pkd Sao Paulo, s14.03.00 engines and many parts missing; **N703GC** Gemini Air Cargo 20.04.01; rToA 26.10.00, FSB 12.02.01, sis 12.05.01, overhaul Mojave by 27.08.01, ret is, sis 02.09.02 named "Penny", s02.04 named "Dennis Garcia" due ret lessor 04.13, AL ceased 12.08.08, frd Riyadh--GYR 14.08.08; **N382WA** World AW 24.12.08; sTPE 19.10.08, rr res 23.10.08, rr 03.11.08, sis OST 29.12.08 nc, sis OST 03.12, s05.12, frd BWI-MZJ 03.02.14 for storage, WFBN to M48411 LLC (Miami FL) 12.09.14, r25.09.14; **N411SN** Western Global AL r25.09.14; still pkd MZJ, s28.03.15, rr res 22.07.15, old reg s02.09.15 many parts missing, rr 21.12.15, frd MZJ-Mojave 01.04.16, frd Mojave-Ft Myers 31.07.16.

N514MD • Delta • October 1990 via N. Raith

N382WA • World • Nouakchott-Oumtounsy NKC • April 2012 Photo Benoît Denet

Line	C/N	mfd	model	Engines
454	**48412**	**05.90**	**MD-11F**	**GE**

N892DL Mit/Delta AL 21.12.90; Air Europe NTU G-OALM; **PP-SPE** WTC/VASP 30.12.93; rToA 29.12.93, sGRU 7.10.99 wfu, no engines, s30.12.99, s14.03.00 engs and many parts missing; **N705GC** ToA ret 30.06.00; rr 30.06.00, ToA r03.07.00, FSB 30.10.00 now cvtd; Gemini Air Cargo 08.12.00; due ret 12.2012 to FSB, frd Wichita-DFW 09.12.00 after F-cvtd, wlsd to Cielos del Peru in Cielos full cs. by 6.01; Cielos del Peru 07.06.01; ro MIA fc, titles; Gemini Air Cargo ret s09.12.01; s Mojave MHV A-check, Cielos titles painted out, presum retd to Gemini, sBRU 02.02 is, 'Cielos' overtaped, s20.04.02 MHV A-check, now hybrid Cielos csours with Gemini titles again, sKIX 07.04.05 Cielos cs, small FedEx sticker, opf FedEx, WFBN to AFS Inv 50 LLC 11.04.07, opb Gemini, AL ceased 12.08.08, frd Ostend-GYR 14-15.08.08; **N383WA** World AW 10.11.08; rr res 23.10.08, rr 10.11.08, frd OST-VCV 30.11.11 for D-check and repaint fncs, test flight 12.06.12, frd VCV-Baltimore 28.06.12, last svc 04.11.13, frd JFK-MZJ 03.11.13, AFS Investments 50 LLC, M48412 LLC (Miami FL) 22.08.14, r27.08.14; **N412SN** Western Global AL lsd 25.09.14; frd MZJ-San Bernardino 25.09.14, rr res 05.01.15, rr 16.06.15, slsd to FedEx, fis 04.12.15, wfu 25.02.16 ret to WGA, frd MEM-MIA 25.02.16, MIA-LGG 29.02.16

N892DL • Delta • Los Angeles LAX • January 1991- via Brian J.Gore

PP-SPE • VASP • Brussels BRU • September 1994 via P.Lammens

N705GC • Cielos Cargo • Miami MIA • November 2001

Line	C/N	mfd	model	Engines
455	**48449**	**06.90**	**MD-11P**	**GE**

OH-LGA Finnair 07.12.90; first del 29.11.90 and first MD-11 service 21.12.90 HEL-Tenerife; Garuda lsd 01.04.95; on lse, Gar tit + logo; Finnair ret 11.06.95; is fc 15.6, sHKG 10.12.07 Santa Claus cs, last svc 20.04.09, sHEL 13.05.09 white, s11.07.09 N-reg painted, ret BBAM 20.07.09; **N270WA** World AW 20.07.09; own BBAM, N-rgd 21.07.09, frd HEL-ANC-TPE 21.07.09 white, frd to ATL 11-12.08.09 pax ops, frd GRK-GYR 08.02.12 for str, canc 15.08.12 wfu to be brup, sGYR 16.11.12, s20.05.13 many parts missing

OH-LGA was the first MD-11 handed over to a customer

OH-LGA – Finnair – Beijing Capital PEK – March 2001

Cslection Jacques Guillem

Line	C/N	mfd	model	Engines
456	**48407**	**06.90**	**MD-11F**	**PW**

HL7371 Korean Air 24.01.91; F-conv, ff Wichita 18.12.99, del 19.12.99, ret GECAS 01.04.05; **N380WA** World AW 01.04.05; Pasiphae to AFS Inv 68 LLC 01.04.05, sICN 28.03.05 fc, long term parked ATL late 07.09, sMarana 11.11.09 str, s01.05.10, frd MZJ-TPE 29-30.07.10, to ret in svc, sis OST 03.12, 05.12, arr Ostend 04.05.13 for scrapping, minus two engines by 20.05.13, s wfu OST 26.03.14 some parts missing, s10.11.14 being dismantled, scrapped by 24.11.14, Unical Aviation Inc 17.12.14 (although already brup), canc 24.02.15

HL7371 • Korean Air at the manufacturer's Long Beach plan • October 1990

HL7371 • Korean Air • Vancouver YVR • January 1999 - via Chris Melanidis

N380WA • World • Liège LGG • November 2011 Photo Jean-Marie Hanon

Line	C/N	mfd	model	Engines
457	**48408**	**07.90**	**MD-11F**	**PW**

HL7372 Korean Air 25.01.91; arr PHX 04.03.95 for F-conv, compl 21.06.95, depa 27.06.95, Cargo tit, ret Peg. 11.04; **N988PG** Pegasus r29.12.04; arr GIG 24.12.04 HL-rgd basic Varig cs, N-rgd 29.12.04 PegAv II, s19.01.05 still HL-rgd basic Varig-L. cs, s24.01.05 presum N988PG reg painted over; **PR-LGD** Varig Log 18.03.05; sGIG 09.04.05 being painted, rrgd, is 06.05.05, s pkd MIA 06.08, s09.08.08 not in svc; **N408SH** Pegasus Avtn II ret r07.01.09; s str MIA 18.01.09; **Z-BAV** Avient Aviation sMIA fc 25.10.09 N-rgd prior to del, canc 16.11.09, del MIA-LGG 20.11.09; W/O 28.11.09 Shanghai PVG 3(7) after take off roll veered off runway and burnt

HL7372 • Korean Air Cargo -Los Angeles LAX

Photo Frank de Koster

PR-LGD • Varig Log • Sao Paulo GRU • December 2006

Photo Christian Volpati

Line	C/N	mfd	model	Engines
458	**48443**	**08.90**	**MD-11F**	**PW**

HB-IWA Swissair 06.03.91; **N624FE** Federal Express ntu 2002/05; Swiss AL nn 31.03.02; CIT FSC/Crossair r31.03.02, sis 19.09.03 hybrid cs, sZRH 24.03.04 str, sis 24.04.04 hybrid cs, pkd sZRH 06.10.04 fc, s20.12.04 depa to NAP for F-conv; **N624FE** Federal Express r23.12.04; frd to NAP-BGR-LAX 17.08.05, op first revenue svc LAX-MEM 27.08.05 still basic SR cs, sSTN 17.09.05 still basic SR cs, sis CDG 29.04.06 fc, named "Corinne"

HB-IWA • Swissair • Long Beach LGB • March 1991

HB-IWA • Swissair • Los Angeles LAX Photo Frank de Koster

N624FE • FedEx "Corinne" • Dubai DXB • December 2013

Line	C/N	mfd	model	Engines
459	**48444**	**02.91**	**MD-11F**	**PW**

HB-IWB Swissair 30.03.91; Swiss AL nn 31.03.02; Bandung/Crossair r31.03.02, **N625FE** Federal Express ntu 02.05, s14.09.03 basic ocs ZRH, ret lessor 11.03; **PP-VTF** Varig 12.03; sLHR 16.12.03, suffered tail strike MEX 26.01.04, wfu 03.08.04, retd to Central Air Leasing, sGIG 26.08.04 maintenace area basic Varig cs, one eng. missing; **N625FE** Central Air Leasing r28.09.04; WFBN Trustee, F-cvtd at Naples by 01.05, redelivery at ZRH 12.02.05, s17.02.05, s24.04.05 Kuala Lumpur Subang N-rgd ex Varig cs for Transmile, canc 26.04.05; **9M-TGP** Transmile Air Svcs 26.04.05; sSubang fc ar 31.05.05 "ready to enter service", pkd 01.08 after lost USA traffic rights, sSBG 10.08, still pkd s16.09.10; **N644FE** Federal Express 18.01.11; sis fcs 17.11.11, named "Adriana"; frd SLC-VCV 08.11.14 str, s wfu 17.11.15, s10.10.16

HB-IWB • Swissair • Sao Paulo GRU touching down on Rwy 27L • July 2003 Photo Sam Chui

9M-TGP • Transmile • Anchorage ANC • July 2006 Photo Kevin Stokes

Line	C/N	mfd	model	Engines
460	**48445**	**02.91**	**MD-11F**	**PW**

HB-IWC Swissair 22.04.91; Swissair Asia, Swissair tfd s17.08.98, str Zürich 02.10.01, s str 03.12.01 fc, sis 09.01.02 ZRH-LHR, **N626FE** Federal Express ntu 02/05; Swiss AL nn 31.03.02; ro ZRH 09.03.02 fc, Samedan Leasing/Crossair r01.04.02, due wfu late 03.04, due Naples mid 04.04 for F-conv; **N626FE** WFBN 15.04.04; testflt 30.07.04, frd Naples-ZRH 31.07.04 after F-cvtd, sZRH 01.08.04 ex Swiss cs, cargo door installed, N-rgd, N-reg canc 02.09.04; **PH-MCY** Martinair Holland r03.09.04; arr AMS fc 06.09.04, last svc 21.01.12 MIA-AMS, pkd AMS for return to lessor, ret in svc 03.01.13 AMS-MIA-EZE, wfu 19.12.15; frd AMS-MIA-MHV 19-20.12.15 and wfu, reg canc 07.01.16, s30.03.16 no engines, open doors, fcs, s12.10.16

HB-IWC • Swissair, operated only one flight between Cape Town and Zürich in the Swiss International Airlines colors. Swissair name was later removed at ZRH to unveil the new Swiss logo • Cape Town CPT • April 2002 via Br. Emmenegen

PH-MCY • Martinair Cargo • Amsterdam Schiphol AMS • January 2005 Photo Frank de Koster

Line	C/N	mfd	model	Engines
461	**48495**	**03.91**	**MD-11F**	**PW**

B-2171 China Eastern AL 24.05.91; s 26.02.91 Palm Beach in fc; s20.02.04 now converted to freighter; China Cargo AL lsd 03.05; basic ChE cs; **N951AR** Sky Lease Cargo r25.08.10; WFBN 30.07.10 N-rgd, frd PVG-Greensboro 26.08.10, s11.09.10 MIA white, in svc, s10.11.11 fcs, frd MIA-MZJ 08.02.13, frd MZJ-MIA 15.07.13, WFBN, Trustee, sold AFS Investments XV LLC 18.06.14, r18.06.14, lsd to Sky Lease 1 Inc, s pkd MIA 15.01.15 no engines, s30.12.15 wfu, s15.11.16 stripped no engines, doors etc. but standing on u/c

B-2171 • China Eastern • Brussels BRU • October 1992

N951AR • Sky Lease Cargo • Miami MIA • February 2013

Photo Jannik Femerling

Line	C/N	mfd	model	Engines
462	**48505**	**03.91**	**MD-11F**	**GE**

N1757A American AL 02.08.91; N1753 NTU? rg 07.90/WFU 31.03.94, dfw 16.04.94 TT 10796,1518 L; USAfrica AW lsd 19.04.94; frd to Dothan 19.04.94 for work, named "Edward M. Bolton" 04.94, repo 3.02.95 TT 13150,2053 L; American AL repo 03.02.95; Tulsa 3.2, is 22.03.95; **N590FE** Federal Express 23.01.98; TT 23529, 3706 L at ho Goodyear AZ for F-conv, ro and depa 25.05.98, cvtd/rr27.05.98, named "Stan", to SSB&TC, lsd back, USB r15.08.05

N1757A • USAfrica • May 1994 via Bill Hough

N590FE • FedEx • Paris Charles de Gaulle CDG • August 1998

Line	C/N	mfd	model	Engines
463	**48446**	**04.91**	**MD-11F**	**PW**

HB-IWD Swissair 30.05.91; Asia tit s01.02.97, 15.02.97 standard SW; Swiss AL nn 31.03.02; sZRH 03.03.02 basic SR cs, Swiss tit, Bandung/Crossair r31.03.02, sZRH no titles/logo's, **N627FE** Federal Express 02-05 ntu, ret lessor 11.03, s str ZRH 09.10.03; **PP-VTG** Varig 10.03; first svc 26.11.03, sLHR 19.12.03 fc, sGIG 02.07.04 basic cs; N627FE Central Air Leasing 16.07.04; frd to Naples 10.07.04 for F-conv, Bandung to WFBN 16.07.04 N-rgd, to be F-cvtd in Italy, lsd to FedEx as they own the kit and hangar slot for period of cargo conversion, rgd 19.07.04, cvtd, arr ZRH 18.11.04 ret lessor, s28.11.04 in CATRAN interim csours, HB-IWD painted, delivery due 15.12.04 but ntu, remains in ZRH for sale, s08.01.05 still Catran cs, N-reg canc 03.05.05; **9M-TGQ** Transmile Air Svcs 12.04.05; pkd 01.08 after lost USA traffic rights, sSBG 10.08, s 11.04.09 in hangar, being worked on, s16.09.10 str; **N645FE** Federal Express 21.01.11; frd SIN-ANC 09-10.08.11, named "Carmen", WFU 29.05.15, frd LAX-VCV 30.05.15 wfu, s17.11.16

N627FE • CATRAN with "Flowerwings" on engine #2 nacelle and "Sher Flowers" on fin • Zürich Kloten ZRH • January 2005 via Nicholas Scherrer

9M-TGQ • Transmile • Amsterdam Schiphol AMS

Line	C/N	mfd	model	Engines
464	**48447**	**04.91**	**MD-11F**	**PW**

HB-IWE Swissair 14.06.91; arr. own ObF/Asia tit s23.03.97, N628FE Federal Express ntu 2002/05; Swiss AL nn 31.03.02; Outer Banks Fin/Crossair r31.03.02, sis 29.05.04, performed final sightseeing flights 31.10.04, wfu, depa 20.12.04, high cycle/time MD-11; TT 68657, 11314 L end 09.04; **N628FE** Federal Express 04.01.05; F-cvtd as of 01.07.05, frd LAX-PDX 30.07.05 for painting, frd PDX-MEM 10.08.05, first revenue svc MEM-ORD 27.08.05, named "Noah"

HB-IWE • Swissair • July 1991 via Eddy J.Gual

HB-IWE • Swiss • London Heathrow LHR Photo Frank de Koster

Line	C/N	mfd	model	Engines
465	**48448**	**04.91**	**MD-11F**	**PW**

HB-IWF Swissair 05.08.91; crashed en route following inflight fire caused by faulty electricity systems (own BRF) 02.09.98 nr Peggy's Cove, Nova Scotia 229(i); TT 36042, 6560 L

HB-IWF • Swissair • Zürich Kloten ZRH • October 1995 Photo Marco Dotti

HB-IWF Swissair • Genève Cointrin GVA • January 1998 Photo Pierre Rohr

Line	C/N	mfd	model	Engines
466	**48416**	**05.91**	**MD-11F**	**GE**

HS-TMD Thai AW Int 27.06.91; named "Phra Nakhon", op first BRU-BKK svc 08.11.92, s str BKK 30.03.06 nc;
N258UP UPS 06.06.06; sBKK 23.05.06 basic Thai cs rrgd str, F-cvtd as of 06.04.07, sis WAW 08.08.07 fc

HS-TMD • Thai "Phra Nakhon" • Zürich Kloten ZRH • July 2004 Photo Sam Chui

N258UP • UPS • Warsaw Chopin WAW • October 2012 Photo Robert Szymczak

Line	C/N	mfd	model	Engines
467	**48417**	**05.91**	**MD-11F**	**GE**

HS-TME Thai AW Int 15.07.91, named "Pathum Wan"; s29.08.05 ZRH nc, s str BKK 30.03.06 nc; **N259UP** UPS 29.06.06; sBKK 09.07.06 rrgd, basic Thai nc, F-cvtd as of 30.04.07, sis HKG 24.05.07 white, sWAW 03.08.07 fc

HS-TME • Thai "Pathum Wan" via R.Verschuur

HS-TME • Thai • Bangkok BKK • February 2006 Photo Sam Chui

Line	C/N	mfd	model	Engines
468	**48426**	**06.91**	**MD-11SF**	**GE**

N9020Z McDonnell Douglas; sLGB 02.92 metal; **I-DUPA** Alitalia 27.03.92; sLAX still primer 27.03.92, str Rome FCO 07 or 08.03 fc, s25.01.04, s02.10.04, frd MXP-DUB 17.11.04 (for title change), to VCE 17.11.04, full freighter conv, sis 18.05.05 PVG; **EI-UPA** Alitalia rr 10.07.05; Pegasus Avtn MD11-1 r11.07.05, sKIX 27.07.05, ret lessor MIA 10.01.09, sDothan 03.02.09, EI-reg canc 18.09.09; **N986AR** Tradewinds 16.09.09; Pafco 48426 Inc, MSN 48426 LLC 16.09.09 N-rgd, frd DHN-GSO ex Alitalia cs 18.09.09, frd to Miami 20.09.09, Sky Lease I r03.10.09 ("added to operating certificate"), AWAS 48426 Trust r15.12.09, sis SCL 21.03.10 no tit opf Centurion; Sky Lease Cargo nn by 10; sMIA 08.04.10 still basic AZ cs, small Skylease One titles; Centurion Cargo 29.03.11; sMIA 07.02.11 Centurion tit, orange/red fc, wfu 05.09.14 MIA-BOG pkd, AL resumed late 12.14, AWAS 48426 Trust to Centurion 14.04.16, WFBN 14.04.16, lsd to Centurion, slsd to Sky Lease 1 19.04.16

EI-UPA • Alitalia Cargo • Pisa Galileo Galilei PSA • April 2008

Photo Andrea Graziadio

N986AR – Sky Lease I ex Alitalia Cargo – Santiago SCL – April 2010

Photo Benoît Denet

N986AR • Centurion Cargo • Amsterdam Schiphol AMS • June 2011

Photo Frank de Koster

Line	C/N	mfd	model	Engines
469	**48487**	**06.91**	**MD-11F**	**GE**

N1753 American AL 29.08.91; N1754 NTU? rgd 07.90/wfu 24.05.96 Santo D-JFK, Phoenix 30.05.96; **N586FE** Federal Express 31.05.96; cvtd 30.08.96, rr 10.09.96/rFSBU 09.96, named "Dylan"

N1753 • American • Miami MIA • February 1994 via Eddy J. Gual

N586FE • FedEx Express "Dylan" • Las Vegas McCarran LAS • September 2006 Photo Marco Dotti

Line	C/N	mfd	model	Engines
470	**48459**	**06.91**	**MD-11F**	**GE**

N603FE Federal Express 11.09.91, Pacific Harbor Capital Inc bt 11.09.91 and lsd back, named "Elizabeth"; damaged 28.09.94 in Anchorage, right inboard flap vane detached on approach; own WTC, wfu 23.08.14, frd to Victorville 29.08.14, s17.11.15, FedEx r07.09.16, frd VCV-SIN 29.10-01.11.16, ret to svc, s20.01.17 JFK

N603FE • Federal Express • December 1992 via Nicholas Scherrer

N603FE • FedEx Express • Hong Kong Chep Lap Kok HKG • August 2010 Photo Chi Lam Wong

Line	C/N	mfd	model	Engines
471	**48427**	**07.91**	**MD-11SF**	**GE**

I-DUPE Alitalia 27.11.91; named "Arena di Verona", later re-named "Giuseppe Verdi", sLGB 05.07.94 (for repairs?), s20.06.98 LAX is, Team Alitalia tit, wfu 07 or 08.03 Rome FCO fc, s25.01.04, sis IAD 07.06.05 (pax); **EI-UPE** Alitalia rr r27.10.05; Pegasus Avtn MD11-3 Ltd r27.10.05, s13.06.06 Alitalia Cargo titles, no pax windows, full freighter, ret lessor 08.01.09 FCO-JFK-DHN, sDothan 03.02.09; CargoItalia 05.09.09; del SAT-MXP, AL ceased 21.12.11, in maintenance at Singapore-SASCO for maint. since fall 2011, presum impounded there, frd SIN-ANC-VCV 06-07.03.12 for str; **N987AR** Centurion Cargo 07.12.12; WTC rgd 14.11.12, frd MZJ-TUS 29.11.12, MZJ-MIA 09.02.13 fcs, wfu LAX-MIA 20.04.14, pkd, AL resumed late 12.14, sLouisville SDF 19.12.14 optnl, BOG 23.08.15, WTC to Centurion 14.04.16, WFBN 14.04.16, r29.04.16 lsd to Centurion

EI-UPE • Alitalia Cargo • July 2008

Martin Fenner Collection

N987AR • Centurion Cargo • Amsterdam Schiphol AMS • July 2013

Photo Alf van Beem

Line	C/N	mfd	model	Engines
472	**48452**	**07.91**	**MD-11F**	**PW**

HB-IWG Swissair 19.09.91; arr 21.09; Swissair Asia tfd s23.12.95; sZRH 01.02.97 nc; Swiss AL nn 31.03.02; **N629FE** Federal Express ntu 2002/05, s pkd ZRH 6.04.02 Swissair Asia titles, not seen 20.04.02, arr Mojave 14.05.02 for str, s07.06.02, s20.02.03, s19.09.04, own by Central Air Leasing Ltd by 01.05, for F-conversion in Singapore in 2005; **N74WF** WFBN 14.01.05; still str Mojave 23.01.05 as **HB-IWG**, N-reg repainted 20.07.05; **N282UP** UPS 20.07.05; bt ex Central Air Leasing, depa 28.07.05 to ROW for F-conv, N-rrgd res 25.08.05, rr 24.10.05, sHKG 30.03.06 white/grey, s24.04.06 full UPS cs

HB-IWG • Swissair • Zürich Kloten ZRH • October 1991

HB-IWG • Swissair Asia • Zürich Kloten ZRH • January 2001

Photo Richard Vandervord

Line	C/N	mfd	model	Engines
473	**48453**	**07.91**	**MD-11F**	**PW**

HB-IWH Swissair 02.10.91; arr 03.10; Swiss AL nn 31.03.02; sZRH 17.03.02 basic SR cs, Swiss tit, Bandung/ Crossair r31.03.02, frd ZRH-Mojave 02.12.02 for str, basic cs, FedEx **N630FE** due 2002/2005 ntu; **N37WF** WFBN 20.12.02; rr request by WFBN 12.11.02, str MHV, s02.04.03 still old reg, id s05.10.03, s30.06.04 still with HB-reg, depa 14.09.04 repo lsd to Varig, but other aircraft lease was extended instead, sRio-Galeao 19.01.05 being repainted white, repo to be cvtd to freighter at SASCO Singapore by 08.05 for lse to Varig Log as **PP-VTV** but ntu, repo 01.05 to remain pax configured, sGIG 28.02.05 white, N-reg canc 03.05.05; **V5-NMD** Air Namibia lsd 03.05.05; wfu 15.08.06 sZRH 06.09.06 basic cs, for Singapore for F-conv; **N286UP** UPS 05.09.06; sZRH 01.09.06 rrgd, Air Nam cs, s Singapore QPG 15.10.06 full SW cs, for F-conv, F-cvtd as of 05.02.07, sis SYD 07.04.07 white, sis CGN 23.09.07 fc

HB-IWH • Swissair • Genève Cointrin GVA • August 1996 Photo Marco Dotti

V5-NMD • Air Namibia • June 2005

Line	C/N	mfd	model	Engines
474	**48428**	**08.91**	**MD-11SF**	**GE**

N9020U McDonnell Douglas s27.11.91 together with I-DUPE; **I-DUPI** Alitalia 12.12.91; s21.06.98 LAX is Team Alitalia tit, str Rome FCO 07 or 08.03 fc, s25.01.04, s02.10.04, ret in svc frd MXP-DEL 01.11.04, cvtd to full freighter s31.05.05 Venice; **EI-UPI** Alitalia rr r31.08.05; Pegasus Avtn MD11-2 r31.08.05, sKIX 10.09.05, ret lessor 10.01.09 Miami, sDothan 03.02.09; Cargo Italia 06.05.09; del DHN-JFK-MXP, sMXP 07.05.09 olymal delivery salute, Cargo Italia titl, basic AZ cs, frd MXP-ZRH 03.08.09 pkd, AL ceased 21.12.11, arr FRA 21.12.11 pkd, frd to BGR 17.02.12, s str Marana 20.03.12; **N216AW** Wilmington Trust Comp r03.12.12; EirTrade Aviation Ireland 06.12.12, s wfu MZJ 18.11.12, canc 19.12.12 wfu, s25.10.13 AZ bcs no engines

EI-UPI • Alitalia Cargo • Milan Malpensa MXP • March 2008 • Martin Fenner Collection

EI-UPI • Cargoitalia • Liège LGG • March 2010 Photo Jean-Marie Hanon

Line	C/N	mfd	model	Engines
475	**48461**	**08.91**	**MD-11F**	**PW**

B-2170 China Eastern AL 31.10.91; China Cargo AL lsd 09.04; basic ChE cs, ret lessor Celectial Avtn Trading 62 by 11.05.10; **N950AR** WFBN 11.05.10; r12.05.10; Sky Lease Cargo 16.07.10; aka Sky Lease 1/new name of Tradewinds AL, operating certificate, sis SCL 12.08.10 white, often operating for Centurion, sMIA 02.11.10 white, s13.08.11 full Sky Lease cs, WFBN, Trustee, sold AFS Investments XV LLC 13.06.14, r17.06.14, lsd to Sky Lease 1 Inc, wfu 13.09.14 BOG-MIA, pkd, s09.02.17 MIA no tail cone, otherwise complete

B-2170 • China Eastern Cargo • Kansai KIX • December 1999

N950AR • Sky Lease Cargo • Liège LGG • August 2012

Photo Jean-Marie Hanon

Line	C/N	mfd	model	Engines
476	**48434**	**08.91**	**MD-11F**	**GE**

PP-VOP GPA/VARIG 12.11.91; still old cs 08.99, ret AerFi Leasing 13.01.00; **N701GC** Gemini Air Cargo 13.01.00; to be F-cvtd, WTC r13.01.00, F-cvtd and s Sappore is 04.06.00, named "Michael Disalvo", later "Michael D"; AL ceased 12.08.08, frd MIA-GYR 13.08.08, ret lessor; **N988AR** Centurion Air Cargo 03.10.08; own lessor, frd GYR-MIA 13.12.08, s09.01.09 nice yellow/red/white cs, damaged 19.10.09 Montevideo 0(5) hard landing, right main landing gear bent, wing damaged, sis SCL 13.12.09 after repairs, sMIA 20.12.09, rr res 01.12.09, rr 25.05.10, WTC to WFBN 19.12.11 still lsd to Centurion, ext damaged 13.10.12 Sao Paulo Campinas, left main u/c collapsed on landing, engine, gear, wing and runway damaged, s20.12.12, WFBN to Centurion 26.02.13, repo 01.15, not repaired, and now used as instructional airframe for the fire service

PP-VOP • Varig • Frankfurt am Main FRA Photo Frank de Koster

N701GC • Gemini Air Cargo "Michael Disalvo" • June 2006 • Amsterdam Schiphol AMS Photo Simon De Rudder

N988AR • Centurion Cargo • Miami MIA • May 2012 Photo Jannik Femerling

Line	C/N	mfd	model	Engines
477	**48454**	**09.91**	**MD-11F**	**PW**

HB-IWI Swissair 15.11.91; own CIT/Sw Asia s25.04.95 Osaka, normal cs 5.95; Swiss AL nn 31.03.02; **N631FE** Federal Express 2002/05 ntu, CIT FSC/Crossair r31.03.02, sis 20.05.04, s str Zürich 23.10.04, s20.12.04; **N631FE** Federal Express 23.12.04; being F-cvtd at Naples by 01.05, cvtd as of 01.08.05, sOsaka KIX 05.08.05 in svc fc, named "Terra"

HB-IWI • ex Swiss, stored • Zürich ZRH • 2004 via St. Fuchs

N631FE • FedEx Express "Terra" • Paris Charles de Gaulle CDG • August 2010 Photo Sébastien Charousset

Line	C/N	mfd	model	Engines
478	**48435**	**09.91**	**MD-11F**	**GE**

PP-VOQ GPA/VARIG 02.12.91; still old csours 09.99, ret AerFi Leasing 15.12.99; **N702GC** Gemini Air Cargo; frd Rio GIG-Wichita 10.12.99 fc, to be F-conv, N-reg reserved, WTC r07.01.00, F-cvtd., ff 26.04.00, del 29.04.00 IAD, sJFK 14.05.00, arr MHV 14.02.02 for short term storage, sis BRU 08.06.08 add Cargoitalia sticker, Tampa ar 07.08 in PEMCO hangar for maintenance, AL ceased 12.08.08, frd Tampa-ANC-TPE 19.09.08; **N384WA** World AW lsd 24.09.08; sTPE 12.10.08 basic Gemini cs, rr 22.10.08, frd TPE-BWI 31.12.08-01.01.09 hybrid Gem/ World cs, ACMI lease to Arrow Air by 05.09, frd TPE-GYR 05-06.04.12 for str, ret WTC, CIT Leasing bt 30.07.12, r08.08.12, M48435 LLC bt 19.12.12, r08.01.13, frd GYR-MHV 11.01.13, frd MHV-Paya Lebar 24-29.07.13; **N435KD** Western Global AL 07.01.14; frd Paya Lebar-ANC-MHV 07-10.01.14, own M48435 LLC, N-rr res 28.02.14, rr 10.04.14, sMHV 24.05.14 rrgd, is over MCO 22.07.14 and UK 25.07.14, flew EMA-Akrotiri 10.08.14, sis NIM 21.08.14 white, MLA s18.06.15, wetlsd to Allied Air (Nigeria) by 11.07.15, LGG 09.08.15 white, sMIA 12.02.16 presum back from Allied

PP-VOQ • Varig • Frankfurt am Main FRA Photo Frank de Koster

N384WA • World Cargo • Miami MIA • August 2009 Photo Jannik Femerling

Line	C/N	mfd	model	Engines
479	**48450**	**09.91**	**MD-11P**	**GE**

OH-LGB Finnair 07.12.91; BBAM AH 92 LLC r12.02, opb Finnair, sis NRT 28.05.06 Moomin cs, sKIX 16.11.07 Santa Claus cs, relief flight 24.01.10 to Haiti, s pkd HEL 13.03.10 white; **N269WA** World AW 30.09.10; sHEL 06.09.10 white, rrgd, galley overhaul done, due to TPE for overhaul, BBAM Aircraft Holdings 92 LLC, BBAM 92 Statutory Turst 30.09.10, N-rgd 01.10.10, del/in svc 01.12.10 HEL-ATL white, frd KHOP-VCV 07.02.12 for str, presum ret lessor, BBAM Aircraft Holdings 91 LLC ret, sold to Unical Aviation Inc 26.04.12, r10.05.12, sVCV 09.10.12 many parts missing, s24.10.13, canc 26.08.15 wfu, s10.10.16

OH-LGB • Finnair in special Santa Claus livery • Bangkok BKK • January 2006 — Photo Mark Tang

OH-LGB • Finnair in special "Moomins" livery • Kansai International KIX • June 2006 — Photo Steve Hampton

Line	C/N	mfd	model	Engines
480	**48472**	**09.91**	**MD-11F**	**PW**

N30051 McDonnell Douglas sLBG 12.91 and 01.92, Delta tail csours, presum N801DE (or N802DE), not confirmed; **N801DE** Delta AL 13.03.92; r01.92 MDD, 03.92 WTC, still in svc 12.02, wfu by 01.01.03, s str Montreal YMX 03.04 basic onc, frd to Goodyear 02.11.04; World AW 08.12.04; presum the ac frd to ATL 08.12.04, sATL basic DL noc, World titles, sis Gdansk 13.01.05, Delta ret lessor 09.05, now directly lsd to World, sis 31.10.05, WTC to BoNY 29.12.05, UPS 02.05.06 still opb World; Ethiopian AL slsd s03.07.06; basic DL cs, Eth tit, lse for 2 months; World AW ret late 08.06; sis 08.12.07 IAH-Luanda, wfu 23.12.07, due to Singapore QPG for F-conv and lse to UPS; **N294UP** UPS r30.04.08; rr res 12.02.08, sis WAW 26.08.08 white, s06.12.16 new Worldwide Services titles

N801DE • Delta • Los Angeles LAX • April 1992

N801DE • Delta Air Lines • Amsterdam Schiphol AMS

Photo Frank de Koster

Line	C/N	mfd	model	Engines
481	**48473**	**10.91**	**MD-11F**	**PW**

N802DE Delta AL 13.04.92; r01.92 MDD, own 04.92 WTC, dam 12.12.03 Atlanta engine and wing fire during maintenance, s22.04.04 Atlanta minus one engine, other 2 taped up, repaired, frd to Montreal YMX 20.07.05, s30.12.05, WTC to BoNYTC 28.12.05; **N293UP** UPS 28.12.05; frd YMX-ROW 16.05.06 for str till F-cvtd, rr res 26.07.06, rr 06.10.06, F-cvtd as of 10.04.08, sis ANC 30.04.08, HKG 01.07.08 white

N802DE • Delta Air Lines • Amsterdam Schiphol AMS

N293UP • UPS • Sydney SYD • November 2014

Photo Simon De Rudder

Line	C/N	mfd	model	Engines
482	**48481**	**01.92**	**MD-11F**	**GE**

N1759 American AL 19.04.92; F-GKMR Minerve NTU, wfu 22.05.98, to Tulsa 23.05.98; **N585FE** Federal Express 17.06.98; F-conv, SSB&TC 21.09.98, named "Katherine"; USB r15.08.05, sDEL and Chengdu-YVR-YYZ 25.03.13 special Panda Express cs transporting two panda's for Toronto Zoo display for 5 years

N1759 • American • Miami MIA • March 1995

via Eddy J. Gual

N585FE • FedEx Express • Toronto Lester Pearson YYZ • March 13, 2013 delivering of two giant pandas to the Toronto Zoo

Photo Andrea Zaratin

Line	C/N	mfd	model	Engines
483	**48436**	**01.92**	**MD-11F**	**GE**

N1768D American AL 17.04.92; YU-AME JAT NTU; **N584FE** Federal Express 17.10.97; TT 20817, 3344 L at ho, to Goodyear for F-conv, SSB&TC 26.02.98 rrgd, sis STN 26.02.98 named "Jeffery Wellington"; sKIX 08.12.00 with special "Panda One" markings to transport two giant pandas from China to the Smithsonian Institution's National Zoological Park in Washington; USB r15.08.05

N1768D • American • October 1997 via Eddy J.Gual

N584FE • FedEx "Jeffery Wellington" on a charter flight • Liège LGG • March 2011 Photo Jean-Marie Hanon

Line	C/N	mfd	model	Engines
484	**48484**	**10.91**	**MD-11F**	**PW**

D-AERB LTU 19.12.91; ff 09.12.91, wfu 26.10.98; **HB-IWR** Swissair 27.10.98; acceptance flight as D-AERB 27.10.98, TT 28327, 6609 L, frd to ZRH 30.10.98 as HB-, impounded Johannesburg 02.10.01; Swiss AL nn 31.03.02; N633FE Federal Express ntu 2002/05, still str sJohannesburg 31.07.02, s02.02.03 fc, D-checked, ff 03.05.03, frd to ZRH 05.05.03, arr Mojave 08.05.03, s10.01.04, depa 14.08.04 to ZRH; **V5-NMC** Air Namibia lsd 01.09.04; sZRH 30.08.04 newly painted, s31.08.04 ZRH rrgd, wfu 30.11.05, frd to Zürich; **N283UP** UPS 28.12.05; bt ex Central Air Leasing, frd ZRH-Singapore QPG 29.12.05 for F-conv, cvtd as of 25.04.06, sANC 23.05.06 white, s29.06.06 HKG still white/grey

HB-IWR • LTU • Düsseldorf DUS • October 1998 via Eddy J.Gual

V5-NMC • Air Namibia • Frankfurt am Main FRA • 2004

Line	C/N	mfd	model	Engines
485	**48474**	**11.91**	**MD-11F**	**PW**

N30075 McDonnell Douglas; sLGB 12.91; **N803DE** Delta AL 01.05.92; r01.92 MDD/own 04.92 WTC; World AW slsd 26.03.03; due ret 03.04, pkd Houston 05.03, re-enter svc 07.03 IAD-GVA-Kabul, sis 08.08.03 BWI sports charter, full World cs, arr Goodyear by 23.11.04, sis FRA 16.01.05 fc, s05.05 special retro 1970s cs to to fly a group of former Vietnamese orphans back to Vietnam to commemorate the company's dramatic "Operation Babylift" of 1975, Delta ret lessor 09.05, now directly lsd to World, WTC to BoNY 27.12.05, UPS 27.12.05 remains on lease to World, sATL 29.01.08 basic cs no tit; **N296UP** UPS ret 22.07.08; UPS rgd 31.03.06, World retd to UPS and rrgd 22.07.08, F-cvtd 08.08, #38 and last MD-11 for UPS

N803DE • Delta Air Lines • London Gatwick LGW • May 2001 Photo Richard Vandervord

N803DE • World Airways • Frankfurt am Main FRA • September 2005

Line	C/N	mfd	model	Engines
486	**48499**	**11.91**	**MD-11F**	**GE**

EI-CDI GPA/Garuda 31.12.91; own AiF r13.06.96/canc 23.12.96; **PP-VPN** GPA/VARIG 21.12.96; sGoodyear 13.12.03 fc; **N499HE** WFBN r22.06.04; bt ex Airplanes Finance Ltd, sGYR 15.08.04 still Varig cs, moved to the field s21.08.04; **N574FE** Federal Express 29.09.04; still sGYR 14.10.04 RG cs, s02.04.05 at TIMCO ramp, airtest 18.07.05, depa to HNL 19.07.05 for F-conv, rr res 01.07.05, rr 12.08.05, sKIX 23.11.05 now F-cvtd, named "Bryce"

EI-CDI • Garuda Indonesia • April 1992 Photo Schneider Herwart

PP-VPN • Varig • London Heathrow LHR Photo Frank de Koster

Line	C/N	mfd	model	Engines
487	**48455**	**12.91**	**MD-11F**	**PW**

HB-IWK Swissair 03.02.92; Swissair Asia tfd, s18.08.96; s12.04.98 Asia applied with stickers GVA; Swiss AL nn 31.03.02; N632FE Federal Express ntu 2002/05, Bandung/Crossair r31.03.02, s str Zürich 02.04 logos/titles painted over, s01.03.04; **PP-VTJ** Varig 08.03.04; sis LHR 08.06.04, tfd to VRG Linhas Aéreas ar 07.06, continues to be op as Varig, first svc 04.01.07; **N289UP** UPS 12.06.07; frd GIG-Singapore QPG 13-14.06.07 for F-conv, F-cvtd as of 04.01.08

PP-VTJ • Varig • Amsterdam Schiphol AMS

Photo Frank de Koster

N289UP • UPS • Warsaw Chopin WAW • August 2015

Photo Robert Szymczak

Line	C/N	mfd	model	Engines
488	**48413**	**01.92**	**MD-11F**	**GE**

PP-SOW Mit/VASP 14.02.92; PP-SOS NTU, r06.02.92, sis 31.01.00 ZRH; **PP-VQL** Varig lsd r12.05.00; sis LHR 20.07.00, sGIG 26.08.04 no titles, overhaul, ret Mitsui & Comp ar 08.04, frd JNB-Singapore XSP 09.09.04 for F-conv; **N413LT** WFBN 01.10.04; delayed due to taxi damage ar. 04.05 when conversion was almost done, WFBN canc 12.07.05; **D-ALCO** Lufthansa Cargo 12.07.05; green WOW sticker, dam 13.09.09 Mexico City on hard landing, still pkd 10.09, frd MEX-VCV 14.11.09 with nose gear extended, for further repairs, re-certified 18.11.09, frd VCV-XMN 29.09.10, frd and ret in svc 20.11.10, last svc due 23.12.13, frd FRA-TUL 23.01.14 for part-out, TT 82269, 12059 L, canc 28.02.14 wfu

PP-SOW • VASP • Brussels BRU • March 1994 Photo P. Lammens

D-ALCO • Lufthansa Cargo • Frankfurt am Main FRA • August 2011 Photo Frank de Koster

Line	C/N	mfd	model	Engines
489	**48475**	**01.92**	**MD-11F**	**PW**

N804DE Delta AL 06.05.92; own WTC; World AW slsd s14.11.03; sATL, sFRA 04.12.03, white, tit&logo, Delta ret lessor 09.05, now directly lsd to World, sis 28.10.05, WTC to BoNY 27.12.05, UPS 27.12.05, r31.03.06, remains on lse to World, sis 17.07.06, wfu 09.02.08 Krakow, frd to Atlanta 09.02.08, frd to ATL-QPG 16-18.02.08 being F-cvtd; **N295UP** UPS r30.04.08; rr res 12.03.08, frd QPG-HKG-DXB 17-18.07.08 white/silver cs, sis HKG 06.12.08 fc

N804DE • Delta

N295UP • UPS • Anchorage ANC • May 2013

Photo Frank Schuchardt

Line	C/N	mfd	model	Engines
490	**48409**	**01.92**	**MD-11F**	**PW**

HL7373 Korean Air 24.03.92; arr Ph 01.12.95 for F-conv, s01.03.96 convtd, LAX dam 25.05.96, s hangared 06.96 no reg, crashed 15.04.99 nr Shanghai PVG 3(i)+6, on industrial zone minutes after T/O; TT 28337, 4463 L

HL7373 • Korean Air

Martin Fenner Collection

HL7373 • Korean Air Cargo • Los Angeles LAX • July 1996

Martin Fenner Collection

Line	C/N	mfd	model	Engines	
491	**48414**	**02.92**	**MD-11F**	**GE**	**PP-SOZ** Mit/VASP 27.03.92; r13.03.92; **PP-VQM** Varig lsd r12.05.00; sis LHR 04.07.00, s pkd Rio de Janeiro GIG 26.08.04 no titles, ret Mistui & Co 08.04, to be F-cvtd at Singapore XSP; **N414LT** WFBN 01.10.04; canc 07.02.05; **D-ALCP** Lufthansa Cargo 07.02.05; in svc 11.02.05, last svc 17.08.09 frd to VCV for storage, frd VCV-Xiamen 03.09.10, in svc 20.10.10, last svc 27.04.14, frd FRA-Tulsa 12.05.14 wfu, canc 20.05.14

PP-SOZ • VASP • April 1994 via Nicholas Scherrer

D-ALCP • Lufthansa Cargo • Frankfurt am Main FRA • August 2011 Photo Frank de Koster

Line	C/N	mfd	model	Engines
492	**48489**	**02.92**	**MD-11F**	**GE**

N1754 American AL 12.03.92; is 14.03 DFW-San Jose; **N587FE** Federal Express 19.09.96; sSabretech PHX 20.09.96 ex AA basic/s30.11.96, F convtd, rr/s14.12.96 old reg taped/rWTC 01.97, sis N587FE reg 05.97, named "Jeana"

N1754 • American • Miami MIA • March 1993

N1754 • FedEx "Jeana" with previous AA registration and Federal Express sub-titles

Line	C/N	mfd	model	Engines
493	**48500**	**02.92**	**MD-11F**	**GE**

EI-CDJ GPA/Garuda 04.04.92; **PK-GIH** GPA/Garuda rr, s21.09.92; **EI-CDJ** GPA/Garuda rr 10.10.92; **PK-GIH** GPA/Garuda rr, s29.05.95; **EI-CDJ** GPA/Garuda rr, s11.10.95; own AiF r13.06.96, canc 10.04.97; **PP-VPO** GPA/VARIG 09.04.97; sfnc 21.05.97, frd to Goodyear 01.10.03 fc, ret to GECAS, s28.03.04; **N485LS** WFBN r22.06.04; bt ex Airplanes Finance Ltd, sGYR 15.08.04 still Varig cs, s26.02.05, frd to Singapore 10.06.05 for F-cvtd 06.05; **N575FE** Federal Express 29.09.04; rr res 01.07.05, rr 04.08.05, frd NAP-SNN-BGR-LAX 17-18.02.06 F-cvtd, ex Varig cs, sSTN 21.04.06 fc is, named "Sonni"

EI-CDJ • Garuda Indonesia • Frankfurt am Main FRA

N575FE • FedEx Express "Sonni" during a water canon salute for captain retirement

Line	C/N	mfd	model	Engines
494	**48456**	**02.92**	**MD-11F**	**PW**

HB-IWL MDD sLGB 25.02.92, del Swissair 13.04.92; Swiss Asia cs 05.95, s02.06.98 GVA 'Argentina' tit, football logo; Swiss AL nn 31.03.02; N634FE Federal Express 2002/05 ntu, Bandung/Crossair r31.03.02, s hybrid cs 11.02, nc 02.03, s str ZRH 24.01.04 ex Swiss cs, depa ZRH 30.01.04 for GIG, ret lessor 02.04; **PP-VTI** Varig 30.01.04; sis MEX 09.04.04, sPOA 26.02.06, sLHR 26.05.06 add Soccer Team titles/csors, tfd to VRG Linhas Aéreas ar 07.06, continues to be op as Varig, sis FRA 04.03.07, wfu GIG 11.06.07, frd to GRU 12.06.07 ret lessor; **N290UP** UPS 20.07.07; F-cvtd as of 30.10.07, sis 30.12.07 DXB white

HB-IWL • Swissair Asia • February 1996

PP-VTI • Varig with additional "Official Carrier of the Brazilian National Soccer Team" titles and colors • Munich MUC • July 2006 Photo Christian Volpati

Line	C/N	mfd	model	Engines
495	**48410**	**03.92**	**MD-11F**	**PW**

HL7374 Korean Air 20.05.92; sPHX 15.04.97 for F-conv, dep 21.08.97 *F, sLAX 21.01.05 white/dark blue tail HK-rgd; **N989PG** Pegasus Avtn IV ret 11.02.05; arr Rio 23.01.05 pkd basic Varig cs N-reg painted over, s14.04.05 pkd HL-rgd; **PR-LGE** Varig Log s18.06.05; sGRU 18.06.05 fc, in svc, sMEX 12.04.06 tipped on its back during loading, s str VCV 15.06.06 Varig LOG cs, retd to Pegasus, s str 17.08.06, sis REC-FRA 25.11.06,s pkd GRU 23.05.08 minus one engine, still str s 10.08; **N575SH** Pegasus Avtn IV ret r25.06.09; frd GRU-MIA 02.07.09, s str 17.10.09, N-reg canc 25.01.10; **Z-BVT** Avient Aviation 27.01.10; sMIA 12.09 Avient markings, s15.01.10 rrgd, frd MIA-LGG 27.01.10, repo pkd ZRH by 07.13; AV Cargo tfd 29.04.14; frd ZRH-CGK 29-30.04.14; **Z-GAA** Global Africa Aviation slsd s27.06.15; fis 27.06.15 CGK-SIN fcs, wlsd to Emirates AL for flights to Vietnam ar 01.11.15

Z-BVT • Avient • Ouagadougou OUA • April 2012 Photo Benoît Denet

Z-GAA • Global Africa Cargo • Liège LGG • February 2016 Photo Jean-Marie Hanon

Line	C/N	mfd	model	Engines
496	**48496**	**03.92**	**MD-11F**	**PW**

B-2172 China Eastern AL 22.05.92; cvtd to freighter sKIX 02.12.03; China Cargo AL lsd 12.04; basic ChE cs, to Celestial Avtn Trading 62, to WFBN 28.02.11 N-rgd, frd PVG-MIA 14-16.03.11; **N955AR** Sky Lease Cargo 11.03.11; arr GSO, sMIA 19.03.11 full yellow/red cs, WFBN, Trustee, sold AFS Investments XV LLC 19.06.14, s wfu MIA 30.12.15 and 27.11.96 no engines but cowlings still attached, s09.02.17 no engines, no slats & flaps

B-2172 • China Eastern • Beijing Capital PEK • January 2003 Photo Sam Chui

N955AR • Sky Lease Cargo • Miami MIA • January 2013 Photo Jannik Femerling

Line	C/N	mfd	model	Engines
497	**48460**	**03.92**	**MD-11F**	**GE**

N604FE Federal Express 22.05.92; own WTC; named "Hollis", Federal Express r17.11.16

N604FE • Federal Express • Hong Kong Kai Tak HKG • November 1993 via Alfred Lerch

N604FE • FedEx / Federal Express sub-titles • Anchorage ANC • June 2002

Line	C/N	mfd	model	Engines
498	**48457**	**04.92**	**MD-11F**	**PW**

HB-IWM Swissair 01.06.92; Swiss AL nn 31.03.02; Bandung/Crossair r31.03.02, sis NRT 21.03.03 fc, **N635FE** Federal Express 02-05 ntu, s white ZRH 30.09.03, ret lessor s str ZRH 09.10.03, s15.11.03, ret lessor 11.03; **PP-VTH** Varig 12.03; Star Alliance cs sLHR 18.12.03; **N285UP** UPS r10.07.06; cvtd as of 08.11.06, sis PVG 14.02.07 white, CGN 23.09.07 fc

HB-IWM • Swissair • Zürich Kloten ZRH • April 1995 Photo P. Frei

PP-VTH • Varig in Star Alliance livery • Los Angeles LAX • October 2005 Photo Sam Chui

Line	C/N	mfd	model	Engines
499	**48490**	**04.92**	**MD-11F**	**GE**

N1755 American AL 28.05.92; is 29.05 DFW-Tokyo, wfu 22.05.00, Tulsa 24.05.00 TT 30164, 4473 L; **N588FE** Federal Express 31.05.00; rr and to Venice 15.06.00 for F-conv, FSB 30.10.00 now F-cvtd, named "Kendra"

N1755 • American • Manchester MAN • January 1993

George Ditchfield via Martin Fenner Collection

N588FE • FedEx / Federal Express sub-titles • Anchorage ANC • July 2010

Photo Pierre Rohr

Line	C/N	mfd	model	Engines
500	**48429**	**04.92**	**MD-11SF**	**GE**

I-DUPO Alitalia 17.07.92; repairs PHX 01.10.94-11.02.95, str Rome FCO 07 or 08.03 fc, s25.01.04, s02.10.04, sFCO 17.02.05 no longer str, frd Dublin 19.06.05 for sale to PAFC and lse back, ret Rome 19.06.05, sis pax 09.05; **EI-UPO** Alitalia rr r28.09.05; Pegasus Avtn MD-11-4 r28.09.05, sis 08.06 with Alitalia Cargo titles, no pax windows, conv. to full freighter, ret lessor 11.01.09 Miami, sDothan 03.02.09; **N429AN** Centurion Air Cargo r29.05.09; Pafco 48429 Statutory Trust r29.05.09, frd Dothan-Miami 03.06.09, s Centurion fnc; **N984AR** Centurion Air Cargo rr 24.06.09; wfu 06.09.14 BOG-MIA, pkd, AL resumed late 12.14, PAFCO 48429 Statutory Trust sold to Centurion 24.03.15, r08.04.15 ex lse, wfu MIA, s09.02.17 no tail cone, no center gear, no engines but cowlings still attached

I-DUPO • Alitalia TEAM • Milan Malpensa MXP • November 1998 Photo C. Aldo

N984AR • Centurion Cargo • Amsterdam Schiphol AMS • September 2011 Photo Michael S.Prophet

Line	C/N	mfd	model	Engines
501	**48418**	**05.92**	**MD-11F**	**GE**

HS-TMF Thai AW Int 02.07.92; sMojave 22.06.92 hangared, named "Phichit", s str BKK 30.03.06 old cs;
N260UP UPS 31.07.06; sBKK 09.07.06 rrgd, basic Thai oc, HNL s27.04.07 on ferry to Singapore for F-conv, F-cvtd as of 27.08.07

HS-TMF • Thai "Phichit" • Paris Charles de Gaulle CDG • August 1997

N260UP • UPS • Cologne Bonn CGN • May 2016

Photo Rainer Bexten

Line	C/N	mfd	model	Engines
502	**48485**	**05.92**	**MD-11F**	**PW**

D-AERW LTU 10.07.92; ff 16.06.92, manuf 26 or 28.05.92, offic dd 30.06.92, wfu 01.11.98, TT 25916, 6158 L; **HB-IWS** Swissair 05.11.98; frd to HAM as HB- 05.11.98, Bandung (Bermuda) 04.11.98, ro fc 27.11.98, to Zürich 01.02.99, is 08.05.99, str sZürich 03.12.01 fc, to Mojave and taped up 17.09.02, s15.01.03 ex SR cs, s MHV 15.10.04, **N642FE** Federal Express 2002/05 ntu, due for F-conv. in Singapore in 2005; **N71WF** Central Air Leasing 09.11.04; own Central Air Leasing, WFBN Trustee, s white arr ZRH ex F-cvtd Singapore 30.04.05; **9M-TGR** Transmile Air Svcs 10.06.05; pkd 01.08 after lost USA traffic rights, sSBG 10.08, still str s16.09.10; **N642FE** Federal Express 23.03.11; frd Paya Lebar-MEM 16-17.09.11, named "Elise"

D-AERW • LTU • Düsseldorf DUS

Photo Frank de Koster

N642FE • FedEx Express "Elise" • Seoul-Incheon ICN • January 2016

Photo Martin Fenner

Line	C/N	mfd	model	Engines
503	**48491**	**04 .92**	**MD-11F**	**GE**

N1756 American AL 11.06.92; wfu 27.02.01 Tulsa, TT 31657, 4805 L; **N589FE** Federal Express 26.03.01; frd TUL-VCE 27.03.01 for F-conv, rrgd 08.05.01, s05.08.01 after F-cvtd, frd VCE-MEM 14.08.01, first revenue svc MEM-FLL 16.08.01, named "Shaun"

N1756 • American • Miami MIA via Eddy J. Gual

N589FE • FedEx / Federal Express "Shaun" • Dubai DXB • December 2010 Photo Guy Viselé

Line	C/N	mfd	model	Engines
504	**48527**	**05.92**	**MD-11F**	**GE**

N1758B American AL 08.07.92; wfu 16.04.94 DFW, 29.04.94 TT 7455,1099 L; USAfrica AW lsd 02.05.94; frd to Dothan for work, repo 03.02.95 TT 9872,1494 L; American AL repo 03.02.95; Wash-Tulsa 03.02.95, is 01.04.95, wfu 25.11.90 Tulsa, TT 30134, 4465 L; **N591FE** Federal Express 03.01.01; frd Tulsa-Venice 04.01.01 for F-conv, f/f VCE 08.05.01 after F-conv, frd VCE-MEM 11.05.01, FUNB 14.05.01, first revenue svc MEM-ATL 25.05.01, Wachovia r30.05.02, Regions Bank r21.09.06, named "Giovanni"

N1758B – USAfrica "Edward R. Bolton" – Washington Dulles IAD – May 1994 Photo George W. Hamlin

N591FE • FedEx Express • Cologne Bonn CGN • July 2015 Photo Julian Klein

Line	C/N	mfd	model	Engines
505	**48451**	**06.92**	**MD-11F**	**GE**

HS-TMG Thai AW Int 31.07.92; named "Nakhon Sawan", s28.11.98 Long Beach no engs for overhaul, s str BKK 30.03.06 old cs; **N257UP** UPS 04.05.06; sBKK 05.05.06 rrgd, basic cs, depa to ANC 06.05.06, to ROW 07.05.06 basic cs, sHNL 01.11.06 basic TG cs N-reg to QPG for F-conv, F-cvtd as of 13.03.07 at SASCO, sis DXB 11.05.07 white

HS-TMG • Thai "Nakhon Sawan" • Zürich Kloten ZRH • July 2003 — Photo Pierre Gillard

N257UP • UPS in basic Thai colors • Anchorage ANC • 2007

Line	C/N	mfd	model	Engines
506	**48437**	**06.92**	**MD-11P**	**PW**

McDonnell Douglas Fin Corp; wfu sLong Beach 26.06.92 primer (JAT YU-AMF 392 NTU); **N272WA** ILFC/World/Garuda 16.04.93; sZRH 23.4 white,Garuda logo/tit; World AW ret s31.07.93; sCDG full cs; Malaysian AS lsd 22.11.94; dep ZRH, tit, white; Garuda lsd s05.95; sZRH,white,tit; Malaysian AS lsd s24.11.96; fc; Aer Lingus lsd 13.05.98; del TPE-ANC-DUB 13-14.05 full World cs, to SNN 24.05 full Aer Lingus cs, is 27.05.98, wfu 14.12.98; World AW ret 17.12.98; frd to BWI basic Aer Lingus cs, World tit, sMAN 08.03.99 basic Aer Lingus cs, old Saudia tit/tail, DXB-SNN 22.05.99 basic Aer Lingus cs no tit, slsd Aer Lingus 25.05.99, is 28.05.99 fc, due ret mid 12.99; World AW ret 31.10.99; frd SNN-BWI 31.10.99, s11.03.00 Cambridge (basic Aer Lingus cs, Garuda tit/tail) Aer Lingus slsd 21.05.00 SNN, full cs 24.05.00, is 28.05.00, sFRA 3.11.00 basic Aer Lingus cs, retd, sATL 19.10.00 World tit, Aer Lingus basic cs, id s03.02.01; Aer Lingus lsd 26.05.01; sATL 25.05.01 fc, is 28.05.01; World AW ret 09.01; sNUE 01.08.02 basic Aer Linguc cs, World AW titles/logo, sNUE 07.02.04 now fc, sATL 05.08.07 new World cs, WTC r23.09.10, ILFC to WTC 23.09.10, still in svc 01.14 pax config, World ceased ops 26.03.14, frd BWI-GYR 28.03.14, Bank of Utah 02.09.14 (filed 11.09.14) r26.09.14, sGYR str 18.04.15

N272WA • Aer Lingus "Cilian" • Zürich Kloten ZRH • August 1998

N272WA • Garuda Indonesia basic Aer Lingus colors • Shannon SNN • March 2000

via Nicholas Scherrer

Line	C/N	mfd	model	Engines
507	**48528**	**06.92**	**MD-11F**	**GE**

N1759 American NTU; MDD manuf 21.06.92, r07.92, conv to *F 10.92 after TT 25, rWTC 11.92, **N614FE** Federal Express 12.11.92, named "Christy Allison"

N614FE • Federal Express • Hong Kong Kai Tak HKG • December 1995

N614FE • FedEx Express • Viracopos/Campinas VCP • September 2013

Photo Benoît Denet

Line	C/N	mfd	model	Engines
508	**48430**	**06.92**	**MD-11SF**	**GE**

I-DUPU Alitalia 17.08.92; paint 22.08.92-08.09.92 LAX, str Naples, Italy 06.03 fc, s01.02.04, sRome FCO 02.10.04, scheduled LIMC-OMDB 24.11.04 pax svc, sFCO 17.02.05; named "Antonio Vivaldi "; EI-UPU Alitalia rr r25.07.06; own Pegasus Avtn MD11-5 rgd, sis 18.08.06 Alitalia Cargo titles, no pax windows, full freighter, ret lessor, str Rome FCO 01.09, frd to Bangor 13.02.09; **N985AR** Centurion Air Cargo 23.10.09; Pafco 48430 Statutory Trust 23.10.09 N-rgd, frd Dothan-New Iberia ARA 23.11.09, frd AMA-MIA after repaint 07.11.09, named "Frank Fine", wfu 06.09.14 MIA-BOG, pkd, AL resumed late 12.14, reg canc 14.04.15

Alitalia took an early delivery of I-DUPU "Antonio Vivaldi " with a bare metal fuselage but with a fully painted tail section and winglets, and an "Alitalia" title on the cabin roof • Los Angeles LAX • 1992 Photo Jukka Kauppinen via John Wegg

N985AR • Centurion Cargo "Frank Fine" • Amsterdam Schiphol AMS • February 2012 Photo Michael S.Prophet

Line	C/N	mfd	model	Engines
509	**48486**	**07.92**	**MD-11F**	**PW**

D-AERX LTU 22.08.92; ff 25.07.92, wfu 01.11.98; **HB-IWT** Swissair 02.11.98; acc flight as D- 02.11.98 TT 25820, 6095 L, Bandung (Bermuda) r04.11.98, Zürich 05.11.98, is 9.02.99, s str ZRH 03.12.01 fc; **N15WF** WFBN 05.06.02; FedEx **N643FE** ntu (dd 02/05), ret lessor, arr MHV 15.04.02 due for be based at VCV as experimental AC by Boeing, own Central Air Leasing (Focus Aviation mentioned as Management company), to Boeing 20.05.02, still seen MHV 07.06.02, rr 22.06.02, now "experimental" titles, still Swissair csours, to be based at VCV, frd 28.06.02, Boeing FCS Flight testing lsd 18.06.02-9.02, arr MHV 18.09.02 after tests, retd. to Central Air Leasing, s15.01.03 ex SR cs, s10.01.04 SR cs, dep MHV 29.10.04 via Salina KS, arr ZRH 30.10.04, s20.12.04, depa 05.01.05 for Singapore for F-conv, frd LCLK-WSAP 06.01.05, F-cvtd at SASCO, arr ZRH 17.05.05 F-cvtd; **9M-TGS** Transmile Air Svcs 21.07.05; repo LSZH-WMSA 11.07.05, but still at ZRH s13 and 20.07.05, presum depa 20.07.05, canc 21.07.05 to 9M, sis HKG 13.10.05, pkd 01.08 after lost USA traffic rights, sSBG 10.08, still str s16.09.10; **N643FE** Federal Express 22.02.11; frd QPG-MEM 01-02.11.11, named "Haley"

D-AERX LTU • Düsseldorf DUS

Photo Frank de Koster

9M-TGS • Transmile • Anchorage ANC • February 2007

Udo Schaefer via Martin Fenner Collection

Line	C/N	mfd	model	Engines
510	**48476**	**07.92**	**MD-11F**	**PW**

N805DE Delta AL 16.11.92; frd ATL-Goodyear 03.02.03 str, s12.04.03 fc no engines, s23.05.03, s28.03.04 fc, s30.01.05 basic cs, s30.04.06; **N522FE** Federal Express 15.10.04; frd GYR-LAX-HNL 27-28.06.06, rr 28.08.06, F-conv as of 26.10.06, frd QPG-SIN 30.10.06 after F-conv, in svc 04.11.06 SIN-HKG, named "Katelyn"

N805DE • Delta • Los Angeles LAX • April 1999

N522FE • FedEx Express "Katelyn" • landing at Los Angeles LAX after a flight from Honolulu HNL • November 11, 2016 Photo Rudi Kohlbacher

Line	C/N	mfd	model	Engines
511	**48477**	**07.92**	**MD-11F**	**PW**

N806DE Delta AL 20.11.92; own WTC 1.93, wfu by 12.03, s str Montreal YMX 03.04 basic DL cs, World 03.04 ntu/delayed, s13.05.05, Delta ret lessor 09.05, still at YMX 09.05, s30.12.05, WTC to BoNYTC 28.12.05; **N291UP** UPS 28.02.06; frd Montreal-Roswell 02.03.06, rr res 26.07.06, rr 05.10.06, F-cvtd as of 13.02.08, sis CGN 11.05.08 fc

N806DE • Delta • Paris Charles de Gaulle CDG • December 2001

N291UP • UPS • Cologne Bonn CGN • October 2011 Photo Julian Klein

Line	C/N	mfd	model	Engines
512	**48497**	**07.92**	**MD-11F**	**PW**

B-2173 China Eastern AL 10.92; arr TLV mid 8.99 for F-conv, sis 17.12.99; China Cargo AL lsd earl06.04; still China Eastern cs, China Cargo titles, ret China Eastern, sold 15.10.10 by Celestian Avtn Trading; **N952AR** Sky Lease Cargo 27.10.10; WFBN bt/rgd 15.10.10, del PVG-MIA 28.10-02.11.10 Centurion style yellow/red cs, Sky Lease titles, WFBN, Trustee, sold AFS Investments XV LLC 13.06.14, r16.06.14, lsd to Sky Lease 1 Inc, wfu MIA, s09.02.17 no slats, no engines but cowlings still attached

B-2173 • China Eastern Cargo • Los Angeles LAX on runway 25L • April 2010 Photo Sam Chui

N952AR • Sky Lease Cargo • Miami MIA • July 2012 Photo Jannik Femerling

Line	C/N	mfd	model	Engines
513	**48501**	**08.92**	**MD-11F**	**GE**

EI-CDK GPA/Garuda 30.09.92; own AiF 12.06.96, ret GECAS 21.09.97, EI-reg canc 23.09.97; **PP-VPP** GECAS/ Varig 21.09.97; frd MIA-Goodyear GYR 28.06.03 str, s28.07.03 full cs, s04.10.03; **N501FR** WFBN 07.10.03; sGoodyear 13.12.03 fc old reg PP-VPP, s28.03.04; **N576FE** Federal Express 29.09.04; still sGYR 14.10.04 RG cs, s26.02.05, frd GYR--Singapore 04-07.03.05 for F-cvtd by SASCO, FedEx rr res. 04.04.05, s23.05.05 Singapore basic RG cs, frd to Naples 23-24.05.05 for F-conv, F-cvtd as of 12.01.06, named "Keeley"

EI-CDK • Garuda Indonesia • Las Vegas McCarran LAS • September 1992

PP-VPP • Varig in World Cup colour scheme • London Heathrow • November 1998

Photo Richard Vandervord

Line	C/N	mfd	model	Engines
514	**48478**	**08.92**	**MD-11F**	**PW**

N807DE Delta AL 21.12.92; own WTC, final Delta MD-11 flt NRT-ATL arr 02.01.04, s str Montreal YMX 03.04 basic old cs, Delta r28.12.04 ex lse, World AW due 03.04 ntu, frd to GYR 12.05.05, s30.04.06 str; **N521FE** Federal Express 01.06.05; frd GYR-LAX-HNL-GUM-QPG 27-31.05.06 for F-conversion, rr res 23.06.06, rr 22.08.06, F-conv at QPG as of 28.09.06, named "Janie"

N807DE • Delta with 1996 Olympic Games sticker • Frankfurt am Main FRA

N521FE • FedEx Express • Narita NRT • December 2008

Photo Michel Saint-Félix

Line	C/N	mfd	model	Engines
515	**48514**	**08.92**	**MD-11F**	**GE**

N605FE Federal Express 29.09.92; own WTC 07.93, named "April Star", FedEx 27.01.16 ex lse

N605FE • Federal Express • Anchorage ANC • September 1994 via Nicholas Scherrer

N605FE • FedEx / Federal Express sub-titles • Hong Kong Kai Tak HKG • March 1997 Photo Wil Teunissen

Line	C/N	mfd	model	Engines
516	**48523**	**08.92**	**MD-11F**	**PW**

HL7375 Korean Air 10.92; s14.10.99 Kelly AFB, TX, being F-conv, conv. and del 14.11.99, own Sinope Ltd by 2005; **N381WA** World AW Cargo 06.05.05; own LIFT Arizona LLC, sShanghai 02.06.05 fc, add "operated for/ exploite pour Air Canada" titles/logo on fuselage, sis OST 05.12, frd TPA-MZJ 24.01.14 ret lessor, frd MZJ-MHV 03.09.14, Mobility Air LLC 18.09.14, r02.10.14, sMHV str 01.10.15, s12.10.16

N381WA • World with "operated for Air Canada" titles • Brussels BRU • June 2007 Photo Guy Viselé

N381WA • World • Amsterdam Schiphol AMS • June 2011 Photo Frank de Koster

Line	C/N	mfd	model	Engines
517	**48547**	**09.92**	**MD-11F**	**GE**

N607FE Federal Express r10.92; del 13.10.92, r22.04.93 WTC and lsd back, named "Louis III", later "Christina"

N607FE • Federal Express • Anchorage ANC • January 1994

N607FE • FedEx / Federal Express

via Eddy J. Gual

Line	C/N	mfd	model	Engines
518	**48468**	**09.92**	**MD-11P**	**PW**

B-150 China AL s07.11.92; in svc 07.11.92 full old cs; Mandarin AL tfd s17.07.93; China AL tfd s03.03.99; crashed 21.08.99 Hong Kong 2(315) wingtip hit ground on landing in adverse weather, last pieces cut up s09.09.00, only cockpit remains, flightdeck sDodson scrapyard, Rantoul KS 10.04; TT 30727, 5827 L

B-150 • China Airlines • Amsterdam Schiphol AMS

Photo Frank de Koster

B-150 • Mandarin Airlines • Amsterdam Schiphol AMS

Photo Frank de Koster

Line	C/N	mfd	model	Engines
519	**48469**	**09.92**	**MD-11F**	**PW**

B-151 China AL 13.11.92; s20.10.95; Mandarin AL tfd s14.11.95; **B-18172** China AL ret s07.01.00; still full Mandarin cs, s Abu Dhabi 17.08.00, last i.s., s13.06.02 Hong Kong fc i.s., wfu 29.07.02, arr Mojave 8.10.02, s15.01.03 Mandarin cs, s07.03.03 left engine out for overhaul, s05.10.03 str, s10.01.04; **N577FE** Federal Express r29.10.04; frd MHV-Singapore 13-15.11.04 presum for F-conv, sNaples 29.10.05 cargo door installed, basic Mandarin cs, sLAX 12.11.05 tests, for service by 12.05, sKIX 27.12.05 fc, named "Tobias ", wfu 13.04.14, frd to VCV 14.04.14 for str, s wfu 16.09.15

B-151 • China Airlines • Amsterdam Schiphol AMS

Photo Frank de Koster

N577FE • FedEx Express "Tobias" • Anchorage ANC • August 2007

Photo Michael S.Prophet

Line	C/N	mfd	model	Engines
520	**48502**	**09.92**	**MD-11F**	**GE**

N9076Y McDonnell Douglas; EI-CDL ntu, wfu sMojave 31.03.93 due to financial problems GPA not del earlier; **PK-GIG** Garuda Indonesia 30.09.93; Kuta-One AC 3.94, BCC tfd 12.08.97; **N540MD** Kuta Ac Corp 23.09.98; canc 26.01.99; **PP-VQF** Varig 26.01.99; s13.11.98, 12.12.98 Hong Kong fc, no eng, test flight 26.01.99, N-rgd, PP-reg under sticker, Kuta PP-rgd 19.02.99, presum wfu ar 07.06, frd GRU-Naples 31.01.07; **N774BC** Kuta-One Ac Corp r16.02.07; at Venice for F-cvtd, N-reg canc 03.12.07; **VP-BDP** Aeroflot Cargo 03.12.07; sHEL 27.12.07 fc, F-cvtd, outside hangar awaits finalization before svc, del 19.07.08 HEL-SVO, HHN 26.07.08; Aeroflot nn s14.03.10; sNRT Aeroflot titl, ret lessor, frd HHN-VCV 25.07.13, s23.10.14; **N380BC** Kuta-One Ac Corp r06.02.15; Kuta-One Aircraft Corp (Seattle WA) r06.02.15, marketed by Boeing for sale 03.15, still wfu VCV s24.10.15 VP-reg, N-reg canc 21.09.16 wfu VCV, s10.10.16

PK-GIG • Garuda Indonesia • Munich MUC • April 1994 — Photo Schneider Herwart

PP-VQF • Varig • Los Angeles LAX • December 2005 — Photo Sam Chui

Line	C/N	mfd	model	Engines
521	**48548**	**10.92**	**MD-11F**	**GE**

N608FE Federal Express 24.11.92; own WTC, named "Dani Elena", later "Cston", s17.11.16

N608FE - Federal Express "Dani Elena"

via Alfred Lerch

N608FE – FedEx / Federal Express sub-titles – Paris Charles de Gaulle CDG – August 1998

Line	C/N	mfd	model	Engines
522	**48498**	**10.92**	**MD-11F**	**PW**

B-2174 China Eastern AL 16.12.92; F-cvtd s17.08.00; China Cargo AL lsd 09.05; basic China Eastern cs, to Celestial Avtn Trading 43, to WFBN 31.05.11 N-rgd; **N954AR** Sky Lease Cargo r31.05.11; WFBN N-rgd 31.05.11, arr GSO 12.07.11, Miami 17.07.11, sis 06.03.12 fcs, WFBN, Trustee, sold AFS Investments XV LLC 13.06.14 lsd to Sky Lease 1 Inc, s stored MIA 15.01.15 no engines, broken up 2016

B-2174 • China Eastern • Hong Kong Kai Tak HKG • December 1996 Photo Marco Dotti

N954AR • Sky Lease Cargo • stored at Miami MIA • May 2014

Line	C/N	mfd	model	Engines
523	**48404**	**10.92**	**MD-11F**	**GE**

PP-VPJ Varig 30.12.92; sGIG 28.04.03 maint, due repaint nc, arr Marana 21.04.05; **N255UP** UPS 10.05.05; BAHC r02.05.05, rrgd and frd 11-13.05.05 MZJ-HNL-Singapore QPG for F-conv in basic RG cs, cvtd as of 13.09.05, sis 26.11.05 white Osaka, sis CGN 11.06.06 nc

PP-VPJ • Varig Brasil • Amsterdam Schiphol AMS

Photo Frank de Koster

N255UP • UPS • Anchorage ANC • August 2007

Photo Michael S.Prophet

Line	C/N	mfd	model	Engines
524	**48405**	**10.92**	**MD-11F**	**GE**

PP-VPK Varig 30.12.92; **N256UP** UPS 03.06.05; arr Marana 16.05.05, N- rrgd BAHC r19.05.05, airtest 02.06.05, frd Marana-Honolulu 08.06.05, F-cvtd as of 20.10.05, sHKG 07.11.05 white, sCGN 13.06.06 is white

PP-VPK – Varig – Frankfurt am Main FRA

PP-VPK – Varig on takeoff to Sao Paulo – Los Angeles LAX – November 2004

Photo Sam Chui

Line	C/N	mfd	model	Engines
525	**48518**	**11.92**	**MD-11P**	**PW**

N271WA McDonnell Douglas s23.01.93 LGB first flt, ILFC/World AW 08.03.93; Malaysian AS slsd s25.05.93; sZRH white, MAS tit/logo, s20.10.94 full MAS cs; Garuda slsd s5.95; s MAS basic, Garuda tit, logo; Malaysian AS slsd, s25.06.95; sHKG; ILFC/World AW ret s4.07.97; sPHX, hangared white. City Bird short term; is 15.09.97, small tit, ret World 25.09.97 at Newark, GYR-LAX 29.09.03, ILFC to WTC 30.08.10, lsd to World, still in svc 01.14 pax config, World ceased ops 26.03.14, frd Baltimore-Goodyear 30.03.14, frd GYR-Tupelo 06.11.14, wfu, Wilmington TC to Universal Asset Management 06.11.14, filed 07.11.14, canc 24.11.14

N271WA • Malaysia • Zürich Kloten ZRH • May 1993 Photo Kurt Roth

N271WA • City Bird • Brussels BRU • October 1997 Photo Olivier Lamoral

Line	C/N	mfd	model	Engines
526	**48550**	**11.92**	**MD-11F**	**GE**

N1760A American AL 11.02.93; frd DFW-Fort Worth AFW 04.01.00, TT 25531, 3955L; **N592FE** Federal Express 13.01.00; to Venice for F-conv, WTC 11.05.00, rrgd and F-cvtd by then, named "Joshua" until 2012, then named "Hope"

N1760A • American • Miami MIA • February 1998 via Eddy J. Gual

N592FE • FedEx / Federal Express "Joshua" • Anchorage ANC • July 2006 Photo Kevin Stokes

Line	C/N	mfd	model	Engines	
527	**48551**	**11.92**	**MD-11F**	**GE**	**N1761R** American AL 28.01.93; wfu 30.05.01, Tulsa 31.05.01, TT 29880, 4537 L; **N593FE** Federal Express 28.06.01; to Venice for F-conv 29.06.01, named "Anissa"

N1761R • American • London Heathrow LHR

Photo Frank de Koster

N593FE • FedEx Express • Beijing Capital PEK • October 2007

Photo Sébastien Charousset

Line	C/N	mfd	model	Engines
528	**48503**	**12.92**	**MD-11F**	**GE**

N9020U McDonnell Douglas; EI-CDM GPA ntu, s01.93 Long Beach full Garuda cs, wfu sMHV 31.03.93, s05.93, s10.93 Long Beach; **PK-GII** Garuda Indonesia 28.10.93; own IAC, BCC tfd 12.08.97, ret BCC 10.07.98, sMZJ 11.08.98 Garuda cs; **N538MD** Boeing CC ret 02.07.98; arr Hong Kong 17.08.98, Dillon Inc own 27.08.98, arr Zürich white 27.08.98, Garuda rudder. sHong Kong 13.11.98 engine runs, N-reg canc 25.11.98, depa 27.11.98 as PP-; **PP-VQG** Varig r15.01.99; s9.10.98 Hong Kong, PP-rgd Dillon Inc 15.01.99, sis 10.06.04, sRio 19.01.05 parts missing, overhaul, is, dam 16.06.06 Brasilia Airport, central wheels cslapsed on landing, wfu ar 07.06; **N725BC** Dillon Inc r22.10.07; frd GIG-VCE 23-24.10.07 for F-conv, canc 10.04.08 to VP-; **VP-BDR** Aeroflot Cargo 17.06.08; arr AMS 31.05.08 basic RG cs, primer cargo door, for painting, s12.06.08 fc, Dillon Inc, frd AMS-HEL 16.06.08 N-rgd, N-reg canc 17.06.08, frd HEL-SVO 05.07.08, sis SVO 07.07.08; Aeroflot nn s20.01.10; sHHN Aeroflot titl, s06.13 FRA, undergoing checks prior return lessor, frd FRA-VCV 06.07.13 and str VCV, s23.10.14; **N382BC** Dillon Inc r06.02.15; Dillon Inc (Seattle WA) r06.02.15, marketed by Boeing for sale 03.15, still wfu VCV s24.10.15 VP-reg painted, N-reg canc 21.09.16 wfu VCV, s10.10.16

N9020U • Garuda Indonesia • stored at Mojave MHV • May 1993 via Eddy J. Gual

PP-VQG • Varig • Los Angeles LAX • April 2004 Photo Sam Chui

Line	C/N	mfd	model	Engines
529	**48512**	**12.92**	**MD-11F**	**GE**

OH-LGC Finnair 19.02.93; arr 20.2/Santa Claus cs end95,s 3.96 cartoon 'Moormins' cs, sNRT 12.12.01 white, new tail logo, Finnair AcF r23.12.03, last svc 16.10.08, frd to QPG 16.11.08 for F-conv, retd to Finnair AcF; **N512SU** WFBN 19.11.08; N-rgd 20.11.08, due for Aeroflot, ntu, canc 16.04.10; **OH-LGC** Finnair Cargo 23.04.10; re-del QPG-SIN-HEL white, tail logo, s02.05.10 now Finnair Cargo titl/fc, in svc 12.05.10; Nordic Global AL tfd s05.09.11; sis 05.09.11 white, s25.01.12, minor damage 20.03.12 Helsinki, started moving in hangar, hit door of hangar, sis 20.04.13 still white, AL ceased 31.05.15; **N512JN** Western Global AL tfd r29.07.15; M48512 LLC rgd, sOscada 18.10.15 white, seems optnl, frd to Tampa 18.11.15, s01.12.15 white, sMHV 22.05.16 white

OH-LGC Finnair • Beijing Capital PEK • January 2003 Photo Sam Chui

N512JN • Nordic Global Airlines • Nairobi Jomo Kenyatta NBO • December 2015 Photo Michel Huart

Line	C/N	mfd	model	Engines
530	**48552**	**12.92**	**MD-11F**	**GE**

N1762B American AL 25.02.93; wfu 12.10.01, Fort Worth, TT 35126, 4409 L, pkd Tulsa, arr Mojave 25.01.02, TT 35131, 4411 L, for storage, frd MHV-LAX 19.06.02, frd LAX-Venice 20.06.02 for F-conv; **N594FE** Federal Express 19.06.02; rr 24.07.02, ready for del. at VCE 29.11.02, f/f VCE 30.11.02 after F-conv, frd VCE-MEM 01.12.02, first revenue svc MEM-SEA 04.12.02, named "Derek"

N1762B • American • Miami MIA • 1999

Photo A.R. Rivera

N594FE • FedEx Express • Paris Charles de Gaulle CDG • August 2009

Photo Michel Saint-Félix

Line	C/N	mfd	model	Engines
531	**48553**	**01.93**	**MD-11F**	**GE**

N1763 American AL 11.03.93; wfu 4.09.01, Tulsa 6.09.01, TT 34614, 4322 L; **N595FE** Federal Express 27.09.01; sVenice 07.10.01 for F-conv, rr 14.11.01, s14.02.02 Venice now F-cvtd, named "Katey"

N1763 • American • Miami MIA • May 2000

N595FE • FedEx Express • Anchorage ANC • July 2010

Photo Pierre Rohr

Line	C/N	mfd	model	Engines
532	**48532**	**01.93**	**MD-11P**	**PW**

N9093P McDonnell Douglas, lessor 05.10.93; to 'unannounced customer' sMojave white, no tit 05.93, s12.03.95 no engs white, s09.95; **HZ-HM7** Saudi Government s17.04.99; sWaco Saudi cs, via Shannon 27.08.99 fc, arr San Antonio for str by 06.02, s San Antonio 23.05.03 Saudia cs, titl/reg covered by tarpaulins, s18.08.04 now full Saudi cs, s05.03.05, frd IAD-EWR-LTN 10.11.05, sis Leipzig 09.12.05, GVA 26.03.06, LAX 05.08.06, s str Jeddah 03.08.11 no titles, s10.15

N9093P • stored at Mojave MHV • May 1993 Photo M. Vogel

HZ-HM7 • Saudi Arabian • Nice Côte d'Azur NCE • August 2006 Photo Sébastien Charousset

Line	C/N	mfd	model	Engines
533	**48538**	**01.93**	**MD-11F**	**PW**

D-AERZ LTU 13.03.93; ff 23.02.93, is 21.03.93, wfu 26.10.98 ; **HB-IWU** Swissair 27.10.98; acc flight 27.10.98 as D-, TT 24152, 5413 L, to HAM 30.10.98 ro 12.11.98 fc as HB- for temp str, frd to ZRH 03.02.99, str s20.02.99, is, Federal Express **N644FE** 2002/05 ntu, str s3.12.01 Zürich fc, arr Mojave 31.05.02, s7.06.02, s20.02.03 SR cs, s05.10.03 ex SR cs, s19.09.04; **N48WF** WFBN 14.01.05; sMHV 23.01.05 Swiss cs, frd MHV-ROW 19.05.05 UPS flt nr; **N281UP** UPS 17.05.05; rr res 05.07.05, rr 25.08.05, F-cvtd as of 23.01.06 by SASCO, Singapore QPG, frd to HKG 03.02.06 white, blue Swiss belly, sis SYD 06.04.06 fnc

D-AERZ • LTU • Munich MUC • May 1993

Photo Schneider Herwart

HB-IWU • Swissair • stored at Mojave MHV • October 2002

Photo P.Van Oostrum

Line	C/N	mfd	model	Engines
534	**48431**	**02.93**	**MD-11F**	**GE**

I-DUPB Alitalia 30.04.93; named "Pietro Mascagni"; str FCO 12.03, arr Csogne CGN 08.03.04 no titles for str;
N431LT WFBN r10.06.04; sCGN 14.06.04 ex Alitalia cs, frd CGN-Singapore XSP 14-15.06.04 for conversion;
D-ALCQ Lufthansa Cargo r22.11.04; F-cvtd by 11.04, in svc 26.11.04, orange WOW-sticker; crashed on landing 27.07.10 Riyadh, Saudi Arabia 0(2), TT 73200, 10,075 L, canc 15.09.10

I-DUPB • Alitalia "Pietro Mascagni" • Milan Malpensa MXP • April 1995

D-ALCQ • Lufthansa Cargo • Frankfurt FRA • July 2010

Photo Alex Saffe

Line	C/N	mfd	model	Engines
535	**48554**	**02.93**	**MD-11F**	**GE**

N1764B American AL 25.03.93; wfu 01.09.00 Tulsa TT 31598, 3993 L; **N596FE** Federal Express 27.09.00; frd to Venice 28.09.00 for F-conv, rr 30.10.00 ny F-cvtd, FSB 05.03.01, frd VCE-MEM 05.03.01 after F-conv, first revenue svc MEM-ORD 13.03.01, named "Peyton"

N596FE • FedEx / Federal Express • Anchorage ANC • July 2010

Photo Pierre Rohr

N596FE • FedEx Express "Peyton" • Taipei TPE • June 2012

Photo Chi Lam Wong

Line	C/N	mfd	model	Engines
536	**48479**	**02.93**	**MD-11F**	**PW**

N808DE Victoria MD-11 Tr 22.06.93; wfu s29.06.93 Mojave Delta NTU/WTC; Delta AL r10.93; s19.10.99 97/99 nc, frd ATL-Goodyear 20.05.03 for str, fc, s28.03.04, s30.01.05 basic cs, s13.08.05 TIMCO ramp pkd, s30.04.06; **N523FE** Federal Express 15.10.04; frd GYR-Singapore QPG 04-07.05.06 for F-conv basic DL cs, rr res 19.06.06, rr 08.08.06, F-cvtd as of 07.09.06, sis fc 24.02.07, named "David"

N808DE • Delta • April 1994

N808DE • in basic Delta colors • Anchorage ANC on May 4th, 2006 en route to Singapore QPG for Freighter conversion for FedEx   Photo R. Shaw via Chris Witt

Line	C/N	mfd	model	Engines
537	**48596**	**03.93**	**MD-11F**	**GE**

N1765B American AL 30.03.93; wfu 13.10.01 (last AA MD-11 rev svc), frd to Ft Worth 15.10.01 TT 34892, 4357 L, Tulsa 17.01.02, arr Mojave 31.01.02, TT 34899, 4360 L, depa 04.06.02 to NAP for F-conv; **N597FE** Federal Express 04.06.02; rr 09.07.02, f/f NAP 29.11.02 after F-conv, frd NAP-MEM 30.11.02 still in basic AA cs, first revenue svc 03.12.02 MEM-SEA, named "Corbin"

N597FE • FedEx operating in ex American c/s • Frankfurt am Main FRA

Photo M.Baltes

N597FE – FedEx Express "Corbin" – Paris Charles de Gaulle CDG – October 2010

Photo Jacques Guillem

Line	C/N	mfd	model	Engines
538	**48480**	**03.93**	**MD-11F**	**PW**

N809DE Victoria MD-11 Tr 22.06.93; wfu s29.06.93 Mojave, no engs, taped Delta NTU/WTC; Delta AL r10.93; frd ATL-Goodyear 03.05.03, s23.05.03 fc, s28.03.04, s30.01.05 basic cs; **N524FE** Federal Express 15.10.04; s24.07.05 moved to TIMCO ramp still DL cs, frd ANC-SIN 01-03.10.05 basic DL cs no titl, for F-conv by SASCO, rr res 02.11.05, rr 14.12.05, sSIN 07.02.06 to be frd to Naples for F-conv, F-cvtd as of 22.09.06, frd LAX-PDX 20.09.06 for painting, first revenue svc 04.10.06 PDX-MEM, named "Nana" frd MEM-VCV 12.09.14 for str, s wfu 17.11.15

N809DE • Delta • parked at Mojave MHV • May 1993

N809DE • Delta Air Lines • Amsterdam Schiphol AMS • October 2000

Photo Wil Teunissen

Line	C/N	mfd	model	Engines
539	**48519**	**03.93**	**MD-11P**	**PW**

N273WA ILFC/World/Garuda 23.04.93; sZRH 25.05.93 Gar tit/logo; World AW ret s31.07.93; sCDG full cs; Malaysian AS slsd s18.10.94; sfc; Garuda slsd s05.95; s MAS basic, Gar tit, logo/ret World by 07.97; City Bird slsd 25.07.97; wfu 23.02.98, ret World; Garuda slsd s03.03.98; sIAD fc; Monarch AL slsd 14.05.98; del TPE-ANC-MAN 14-15.05, sMAN 19.05 white, tit+tail logo, is 21.05, due ret 01.11.98 but wfu 14.08.98, replaced by 48743; World AW ret 14.08.98; sSaudi Arabian old tit/tail 29.03.99, to MAN 28.04.99, titl removed 30.04.99, Monarch lsd, is 01.05.99, wfu 08.05.99, ret World, sATH 27.06.99 World cs white tail, s21.07.99 OST fc, frd BWI-GYR 19.07.03 -COS 22.07.03, ILFC to WTC 28.09.10, frd Baltimore-GYR 29.02.12 for str, frd GYR-TPE 18.05.12, presum ret in svc, last (military pax) flight arr EWR 23.10.13, frd Baltimore-Goodyear 04.11.13, s07.03.14 no engines, WTC sold to Bank of Utah 14.03.14, filed 27.03.14, r21.04.14, broken up 10.14

N273WA • City Bird "Seagull" • Zürich Kloten ZRH • September 1997

N273WA • Monarch • Manchester MAN • June 1998

Line	C/N	mfd	model	Engines
540	**48597**	**03.93**	**MD-11F**	**GE**

N1766A American AL 14.05.93; wfu 11.10.01, Fort Worth 15.10.01 TT 33633, 4190 L, Tulsa 17.01.02, arr Mojave 26.01.02 TT 33638, 4193 L, depa 03.06.02 for F-conv; **N598FE** Federal Express 03.06.02; rr 09.07.02, is 07.11.02 MEM-SEA basic AA cs following F-conv, sis 03.12.02 KIX in svc; named "Kate"

N1766A • American • Miami MIA

N598FE • FedEx, basic AA c/s • Memphis MEM • November 2002

Line	C/N	mfd	model	Engines
541	**48520**	**04.93**	**MD-11F**	**PW**

N9134D McDonnell Douglas; sMojave 4.93, ar 09.93; **B-2175** China Eastern AL 20.12.93; ILFC/World CANC, arr Venice 21.08.03 for F-conv, sis CDG 03.01.04 as freighter; China Cargo AL lsd 01.05; basic ChE cs, ret to China Eastern, Celestial Avtn Trading by 02.11; **N953AR** Sky Lease Cargo r03.02.11; WFBN bt 31.01.11, rgd, frd PVG-MIA 01-03.03.11, sis MIA 19.03.11 full cs, WFBN, Trustee, sold AFS Investments XV LLC 18.06.14, r18.06.14, lsd to Sky Lease 1 Inc, s wfu MIA 30.12.15 no engines but cowlings still attached, s09.02.17 all parts removed including nose, center and main landing gear, ready to be scrapped

B-2175 • China Eastern • Beijing Capital PEK • January 2003

Photo Sam Chui

N953AR • Sky Lease Cargo • Miami MIA • March 2013

Photo Jannik Femerling

Line	C/N	mfd	model	Engines
542	**48565**	**04.93**	**MD-11F**	**PW**

N810DE Victoria MD-11 Tr 22.06.93; wfu Delta NTU/WTC, sMojave 19.01.94 coming out storage; Delta AL 01.03.94; sMHV 07.03, LAX 08.03.94 full cs, wfu, frd ATL-GYR 07.04.03, s12.04.03 fc, s28.03.04, frd to LAX 03.12.04, s16.12.04 hangared, basic cs, for maint.; **N525FE** Federal Express 15.10.04; rr res 20.01.05, rr 17.03.05, s FedEx hangar 27.06.05 LAX still DL basic cs, arr 24.09.05 Mojave full FedEx cs for maint. still pax interior, used at MHV for anti missile tests (terrorist countermeasures), airtest 06.10.05, 14.10.05, 08.11.05, 10.11.05, s01.03.06 fc, depa 02.03.06 to LAX, F-cvtd by SASCO as of 14.12.06, named "McKinnon"

N810DE • Delta Air Lines • Amsterdam Schiphol AMS

Photo Frank de Koster

N525FE • FedEx Express • Anchorage ANC • August 2007

Photo Michael S.Prophet

Line	C/N	mfd	model	Engines
543	**48566**	**04.93**	**MD-11F**	**PW**

N811DE Victoria MD-11 Tr 22.06.93; wfu sMojave 29.06.93 all white, coming out of storage s19.01.94/ Delta NTU/WTC; Delta AL 03.94; dd estimated, wfu by 12.03, s str Montreal YMX 03.04 full onc, s13.05.05, Delta ret lessor 09.05, still at YMX 09.05, s30.12.05, WTC to BoNYTC 27.12.05, UPS 27.12.05, rgd 23.03.06; **N292UP** UPS 27.12.05; frd YMX-ROW 23.03.06 for str till F-cvtd, rr 05.10.06, F-cvtd as of 12.12.07, s12.01.17 ICN with new Worldwide Services titles

N811DE • Delta • Frankfurt am Main FRA

N811DE • Delta Air Lines • Manchester MAN

Photo Frank de Koster

Line	C/N	mfd	model	Engines
544	**48533**	**05.93**	**MD-11P**	**PW**

N9020Z McDonnell Douglas, lessor 23.12.93; GPA NTU s Long Beach 25.06.93 primer, no reg, no tail/nr 4/s 25.09.93 Garuda cs/to 'unannounced customert', sMojave 29.03.94 brown primer, s12.03.95 metallic, Garuda rudder, no engs, s09.95; **HZ-HM8** Saudi Government s17.02.99; sWaco Saudi cs, sLHR 2.07.99; **HZ-AFA1** Saudi Government rr s11.06.01; sCDG, LHR 26.06.01 full Saudi Arabian AL nc, sHAM pkd 05.10.05 fc, reg taped over, plastic sheeting over engines, arr ZRH 23.12.05 for maint, s16.05.06 no engines, titles painted over, HAM s23.06.06; **HZ-AFAS** Saudi Government rr s01.10.07; sHAM blue belly, golden cheatl, s06.11.07 first test flight HAM, sis STN 06.05.08, sJeddah 01.09.10 'dusty condition', str, s03.08.11 str, s10.15

HZ-AFA1 • Saudi Arabian • Paris Charles de Gaulle CDG • June 2001

HZ-AFAS • Saudi Government • Geneva GVA • April 2008

Photo Alex Saffe

Line	C/N	mfd	model	Engines
545	**48549**	**05.93**	**MD-11F**	**GE**

N609FE Federal Express 30.06.93; own WTC; named "Scott"

N609FE • Federal Express "Scott" • Norman Y. Mineta San José SJC

Photo Frank de Koster

N609FE • FedEx Express "Scott" • Dubai DXB • December 2010

Photo Guy Viselé

Line	C/N	mfd	model	Engines
546	**48470**	**05.93**	**MD-11F**	**PW**

B-152 China AL 30.06.93; Mandarin AL tfd s03.94; **B-18151** China AL ret s02.04.99; China AL old reg s07.03.99, sBKK 06.12.99 still Mandarin fc; **N579FE** Federal Express 30.07.01; bt Trust No N579FE/N580FE, sDubai 02.08.01 basic Mandarin cs, FedEx Corp bt 20.12.01, frd MEM-VCV 21.02.12 pkd, frd VCV-HNL 06.11.12 to prepare for ret in svc, sis mid 12.12, frd MEM-VCV 26.12.13 for storage but due ret in svc in 2014, still str s23.10.14, s wfu 16.09.15, s17.11.16

B-152 • Mandarin Airlines • Brussels BRU • February 1999

N579FE • FedEx Express • Sydney SYD • October 2004

Photo Sam Chui

Line	C/N	mfd	model	Engines
547	**48406**	**06.93**	**MD-11F**	**GE**

N9166X McDonnell Douglas; sLGB 30.07.93, 23.10.93; **PP-VPL** Varig 30.12.93; Compass Rose Leasing, Boeing AHC 28.12.01, ret Boeing 01.04.02 after lse, frd Rio GIG-Victorville 28.06.02, also repo ret BAHC 1.07.02, sVictorville 12.07.02 basic Varig cs, old reg PP-VPL; **N254UP** UPS 17.07.02; rBoeing 01.07.02, for F-conv, rUPS 17.07.02, cvtd F as of 07.11.02, nc s30.04.06

PP-VPL • Varig • Frankfurt am Main FRA • May 1996 Photo Marco Dotti

N254UP • UPS • Sydney SYD • April 2006 Photo Sam Chui

Line	C/N	mfd	model	Engines
548	**48504**	**06.93**	**MD-11F**	**GE**

N9020Q McDonnell Douglas; GPA EI-CDN NTU/sLGB 02.10.93, primer 25.10.93 with reg; **PK-GIJ** Garuda 01.12.93; own KTA, BCC tfd 12.08.97; **N539MD** Boeing CC ret 05.07.98; own Akash 8.98; **PP-VQH** Varig r4.11.98; PP-rgd Akash 4.11.98, sLHR 12.12.98 fc, is, presum wfu ar 07.06; **N702BC** Akash Inc r22.06.07; at Venice for F-cvtd, F-cvtd as of 22.02.08; **VP-BDQ** Aeroflot Cargo s26.06.08; sis HHN fc; Aeroflot nn s31.01.10; sHHN Aeroflot titl, frd FRA-VCV 16.08.13 ret lessor, s str 23.10.14, Akash Inc (Seattle WA) r06.02.15, marketed by Boeing for sale 03.15, still wfu VCV s24.10.15 VP-reg painted, N-reg canc 21.09.16 wfu VCV, s10.10.16

PP-VQH • Varig Brasil • London Heathrow LHR • December 1999 — Photo Richard Vandervord

VP-BDQ • Aeroflot • Frankfurt–Hahn HHN • March 2013 — Photo Wil Teunissen

Line	C/N	mfd	model	Engines
549	**48504**	**06.93**	**MD-11F**	**GE**

N606FE Federal Express 28.07.93; own WTC, named "Charles & Teresa"; center landing gear failure on landing at EWR 05.10.99, repaired few weeks later

N606FE • Federal Express • Hong Kong Kai Tak HKG • December 1996 Photo Marco Dotti

N606FE • FedEx Express • Toronto Lester B. Pearson YYZ coming in for runway 05 • July 2013 Photo Simon De Rudder

Line	C/N	mfd	model	Engines
550	**48598**	**07.93**	**MD-11F**	**GE**

N1767A American AL 24.09.93; is 27.09, wfu 10.10.01, Fort Worth 15.10.01, Tulsa 02.11.01 for maint, TT 32316, 4001 L; **N599FE** Federal Express 12.12.01; rr 17.01.02, F-cvtd, f/f NAP 08.07.02 after F-conv, frd NAP-BGR-PDX 08-09.07.02 for painting, later named "Mariana"

N1767A • American • Miami MIA • December 1993 via Eddy J.Gual

N599FE • FedEx Express "Mariana" • Narita NRT on approach to runway 16R • July 2011 Photo Kentaro Iemoto

Line	C/N	mfd	model	Engines
551	**48603**	**07.93**	**MD-11F**	**GE**

N610FE Federal Express 25.08.93; WTC r10.93, named "Marisa"

N610FE • Federal Express • Memphis MEM • August 1997

N610FE • FedEx Express • lining-up on Runway 16R at Narita International NRT • October 2009 Photo Kentaro Iemoto

Line	C/N	mfd	model	Engines
552	**48571**	**08.93**	**MD-11F**	**PW**

N91566 McDonnell Douglas; 1093/sLGB 04.09.93; **JA8580** Japan AL 05.11.93; own DiL, ChIL, SBC, NL 30.11.93/ frd WA-Tokyo 02-03.01.94, is 01.04, dam 14.06.98 Manila overshot on landing, KL-DL-SBC-NL r25.05.99, JAL 29.05.02, wfu 25.08.02, canc 10.09.02; **N272UP** UPS 10.09.02; bt BAHC 10.09.02, frd NRT-Marana MZJ 13.09.02 white, to be cvtd via Boeing, UPS 17.01.03, sMZJ 27.01.03 white not yet cvtd, s13.03.03 white, sSingapore QPG 14.04.03 white for F-conv, cvtd as of 21.08.03, sis CGN 22.09.03 nc

N91599 • JAL Japan Airlines without "J Bird" title on the tail engine • Long Beach LGB • September 1993 — via Kevin Stokes

N272UP • UPS • Sydney SYD • September 2006 — Photo Sam Chui

Line	C/N	mfd	model	Engines
553	**48604**	**08.93**	**MD-11F**	**GE**

N611FE Federal Express 22.09.93; Potomac Capital Investment Corp bt 29.09.93 and lsd back, named "Cory", crash landed 31.07.97 Newark NJ 0(5) at 01:35 a.m. destroyed by fire/WTC r09.93, canc 16.07.12 ; TT 13040, 2951 L

N611FE • Federal Express "Cory"

Photo Michel Saint-Félix

N611FE • vFedEx/Federal Express "Cory" • Bangkok BKK • November 1996

Photo Freek Blokzijl

Line	C/N	mfd	model	Engines
554	**48439**	**09.93**	**MD-11F**	**GE**

PP-VPM Varig 30.12.93; sLong Beach 04.09.93, Compass Rose Leasing II to BCC 28.12.01, still lsd to Varig, ret BCC, arr Victorville 26.04.02 ex Varig cs, offic retd 30.04.02 N-rgd; **N253UP** UPS 10.05.02; sVictorville 03.05.02 N-rgd, F-cvtd as of 18.09.02

PP-VPM • Varig • Amsterdam Schiphol AMS • September 1998

N253UP • United Parcel Service • Sydney SYD • July 2005

Photo Sam Chui

Line	C/N	mfd	model	Engines
555	**48605**	**09.93**	**MD-11F**	**GE**

N612FE Federal Express 30.09.93; WTC r08.10.93, named "Alyssa"

N612FE • Federal Express • Hong Kong Kai Tak HKG • November 1996

Collection Jacques Guillem

N612FE • FedEx Express "Alyssa" • June 2007

via Karsten Madr

Line	C/N	mfd	model	Engines
556	**48572**	**10.93**	**MD-11F**	**PW**

N90187 McDonnell Douglas; s09.10.93 Long Beach; **JA8581** Japan AL 08.12.93; r09.12 FSL+ 3 others, frd WA-Tokyo 02-03.01.94/is 01.04.94, SL-FGL-MLJ-NL r16.08.99, wfu 12.07.02, testfl 25.07.02 white, canc 30.07.02; **N271UP** UPS r01.08.02; bt and cvtd via Boeing bt 30.07.02 BAHC, rgd 02.08.02, BCC 14.08.02, BAHC 30.09.02, UPS 03.01.03, sMarana "still" str 27.01.03 white, frd to Honolulu 25.02.03, F-cvtd as of 10.07.03, nc

JA8581 • JAL Japan Airlines • Shanghai Hongqiao SHA • May 1999 Photo Richard Vandervord

Note the "Fairy Pitta" bird motif and name on the fuselage and winglet as well as the "We support Unicef" title and emblem above the passenger windows on the rear fuselage.

N271UP • UPS • Seoul-Incheon ICN • October 2016 Photo Martin Fenner

Line	C/N	mfd	model	Engines
557	**48555**	**10.93**	**MD-11P**	**GE**

PH-KCA KLM ff 03.11.93, del 07.12.93; arr AMS 09.12.93, named "Amy Johnson", KLM to ILFC 05.02, r17.01.03, lsd back by KLM, nc sis 17.03.04, wfu 30.08.14, frd AMS-Crestview CEW 22.09.14 bcs, canc 26.09.14 wfu, sCrestview 16.10.16 stripped no engines, doors etc. but standing on u/c

PH-KCA • KLM "Amy Johnson" • Amsterdam Schiphol AMS • April 2003

PH-KCA • KLM "Amy Johnson" • Amsterdam Schiphol AMS • August 2007

Photo Frank de Koster

Line	C/N	mfd	model	Engines
558	**48471**	**11.93**	**MD-11F**	**PW**

B-153 China AL 11.12.93; Mandarin AL tfd s7.11.95; **B-18152** China AL tfd s13.11.98; sHong Kong fc 13.11.98, old reg s11.04.99, rr s25.06.99 Tokyo; **N580FE** Federal Express 30.07.01; bt Trust No N579FE/N580FE, frd TPE-DXB-VCE 02-03.08.01 in ex China cs, for F-conv, s02.02.02 still China AL cs, being F-cvtd, FedEx r05.02.02 (as F), named "Ashton" wfu 08.05.15, frd Ont-Victorville 08.05.15, wfu

B-153 • China Airlines • Amsterdam Schiphol AMS

Photo Frank de Koster

B-153 • Mandarin Airlines • Hong Kong Kai Tak HKG • December 1996

Photo Marco Dotti

Line	C/N	mfd	model	Engines
559	**48573**	**11.93**	**MD-11F**	**PW**

N90187 McDonnell Douglas; s31.10.93 Long Beach, s22.01.94; **JA8582** Japan AL 05.04.94; frd LGB-NRT 05-06.04.94, r05.04.94, is 01.06.94, s26.12.03 new csors (first MD-11 with new JAL cs), in svc 27.12.03, seen in svc PVG 26.09.04, last JAL svc 12.10.04 HKG-NRT, canc 02.11.04; **N279UP** UPS 02.11.04; BAHC 02.11.04, bt UPS 16.11.04, cvtd via Boeing, frd NRT-GYR 09.11.04, bt UPS, frd GYR-HNL 03.03.05, F-cvtd in Singapore as of 29.06.05, dd 09.07.05 white, sis 11.06.06 CGN still white

JA8582 • JAL Japan Airlines with "Red-Crowned Crane" bird motif and name on the fuselage and winglet • Amsterdam Schiphol AMS

JA8582 • JAL Japan Airlines • Zürich Kloten ZRH • June 2004 via Nicholas Scherrer

Line	C/N	mfd	model	Engines
560	**48600**	**12.93**	**MD-11F**	**PW**

N90178 McDonnell Douglas; s30.03.94 Long Beach, primer, s 03.07.94 'experimental' tit, sYuma 08.10.94 primer, s10.95 Douglas titles, used for tests, s01.04.96 Long Beach/ reg seen 27.05.96 thought other/nw AC; **N9017S** McDonnell Douglas rr s01.05.96; sLGB; **N813DE** Delta AL 15.10.96; sis 30.10.96, s31.01.02 ATL first MD-11 in 2000 nnc, wfu by 12.03, sGoodyear 13.12.03 fc, s28.03.04, s30.01.05 basic DL cs, s13.08.05, frd GYR-LAX 01.02.06 basic DL nnc; **N526FE** Federal Express 15.10.04; rr res 24.04.06, rrgd 10.07.06, cvtd, sQPG 19.07.06, sis SIN 27.07.06 fc; crash landed 23.03.09 Tokyo NRT 2(i), rolled on back after bouncing on landing in gusty wind conditions, TT 40767, 7131 L; canc 04.09.12

N813DE • Delta • Paris Charles de Gaulle CDG • March 2002

N526FE • FedEx Express • Narita NRT • March 2009

Photo Kentaro Iemoto

Line	C/N	mfd	model	Engines
561	**48556**	**01.94**	**MD-11P**	**GE**

PH-KCB KLM 01.03.94; s22.01.94 Long Beach metal, frd LGB-AMS 01-02.03.94 metal, is 26.30.94, named "Maria Montessori", nc sXiamen 30.10.04 after overh, sAMS 07.11.04, sis 10.12.13, hangared 01.14, overhaul, ret in svc 13.02.14, YYZ-AMS and wfu 26.10.14, back up aircraft for 11.11.14 farewell flights (but not used), ferry to Crestview FL 08.12.14, canc 12.12.14 wfu , s16.10.16 stripped no engines, doors, major front section missing etc. but standing on u/c

PH-KCB • KLM "Maria Montessori " • Amsterdam Schiphol AMS
Photo Frank de Koster

PH-KCB • KLM "Maria Montessori " • Amsterdam Schiphol AMS • May 2005
Photo Frank de Koster

PH-KCB • KLM "Maria Montessori " • Amsterdam Schiphol AMS • November 11th, 2014
Photo Michael S. Prophet

Line	C/N	mfd	model	Engines
562	**48601**	**02.94**	**MD-11F**	**PW**

N6202S McDonnell Douglas; s metallic 22.01.94, 20.02 yellow primer, s03.07.94 Long Beach; **N812DE** Delta AL 08.04.96; in full "Atlanta 1996" markings, used to cslect the Olympic flame from ATH 26.04.96, s str Goodyear 28.07.03 fc, s13.12.03, s28.03.04, s30.01.05 basic cs, s13.08.05; **N527FE** Federal Express 15.10.04; frd GYR-Singapore 27-31.03.06 for F-conv at SASCO, rr res 20.04.06, rrgd 16.06.06, F-cvtd by 04.08.06, named "Zariah", frd MEM-VCV 05.01.15, str, s10.10.16

N812DE • Delta Air Lines "The Centennial Spirit" in special Atlanta '96 Olympic games c/s • September 1996

N527FE • FedEx Express • Anchorage ANC • August 2007

Photo Michael S. Prophet

Line	C/N	mfd	model	Engines
563	**48633**	**02.94**	**MD-11F**	**PW**

N274WA ILFC/World AW Cargo 31.03.94; to Zurich 18.11.94; MASKargo lsd 20.11.94; white,tit/s29.11.94 Dubai is/sOsaka 01.98 MASKargo white, tit+taillogo; World AW ret s14.09.97; s14.09.97 on wet lease for FedEx all white; MASKargo lsd s01.98; sOkaka tit, taillogo; World AW ret 26.09.98; replaced by 48631 at LHR, s San Bernardino 30.03.99 (World), sOstend 18.10.99 World, MAS Kargo titl still visible, sHKG 04.10.05 first Air Canada Cargo svc to Hong Kong, titles, frd JFK-GYR 28.02.12 for str, s27.03.12, frd GYR-VCV 05.10.12; **N68093** Federal Express 16.10.12; r25.10.12 rr 08.11.12, purchased for parts, s wfu VCV 24.10.13, s10.10.16

N274WA • MASkargo • Amsterdam Schiphol AMS • November 1994 via Frank de Koster

N274WA • World with "operated for Air Canada" titles • Frankfurt am Main FRA • August 2005

Line	C/N	mfd	model	Engines
564	**48513**	**03.94**	**MD-11F**	**GE**

OH-LGD Finnair 01.04.94; Finnair tried to postpone delivery for 1 year, to 03.95, still del 04.94, Finnair AcF r23.12.03, last svc 05.05.09, s05.09.09 basic cs, no engines, Aeroflot Cargo due 07.09 presum ntu, s 09.02.10 str, at QPG 28.02.10 fc, to be F-cvtd, VQ-BFH Aeroflot due 10 but presum ntu, also repo to fly charters Summer 2010, s08.08.10 HEL with engines again no titl, basic Finnair cs, frd HEL-QPG 09.10 for F-conversion, **N513AY** WFBN 20.09.10; r29.09.10, bt ex Finnair Aircraft Finance, canc 04.01.11; **OH-LGD** Finnair Cargo 04.01.11; frd QPG-HEL 25-26.01.11 white, F-cvtd, pkd since, awaits new Nordic Global AL late 2011; Nordic Global AL tfd 04.08.11; first service 04.08.11, sHEL 06.08.11 all white in svc, s04.02.12 white, s20.02.12 OST now large stickers, sis CNF 17.05.15 white, AL ceased 31.05.15; **N513SN** Western Global AL tfd r29.07.15; M48513 LLC rgd, s wfu Oscada 18.10.15, white, small Nordic Global AL titles, missing engines, bagged u/c, lsd to West Global, arr Fort Myers 13.03.16, s16.04.16 white

OH-LGD • Finnair • Tenerife Sur Reina Sofia TFS • February 1999

OH-LGD • Nordic Global Airlines • Liège LGG • October 2014

Photo Jean-Marie Hanon

Line	C/N	mfd	model	Engines
565	**48581**	**03.94**	**MD-11F**	**GE**

I-DUPC Alitalia 05.05.94; str FCO 12.03, frd to CGN 21.04.04, str basic AZ cs; **N581LT** WFBN 09.06.04; depa CGN 02.08.04 for F-conv, sF-cvtd and flying SIN 22.12.04 LH fc; **D-ALCR** Lufthansa Cargo 21.12.04; sSing QPG 23.11.04 rrgd, cvtd by SASCO, WFBN N-reg canc 21.12.04, WOW sticker, frd FRA-ORD-MEX-VCV for storage 10-11.01.10, frd VCV-FRA 06.05.10 ret in svc, frd FRA-VCV 14.08.14 wfu, s str 24.10.15, canc 04.12.15; **N581JN** Western Global AL 30.12.15; filed 31.12.15, Mobility Air LLC 30.12.15, for Western Global lse, frd VCV-Oscada 20.03.16, frd Oscada-Fort Meyers 06.01.17

I-DUPC • Alitalia "Vincenzo Bellini" • Hong Kong Kai Tak HKG • November 1995

D-ALCR • Lufthansa Cargo climbing out on a go-around while attempting to land on runway 07R • Frankfurt am Main FRA • June 2007 Photo Simon De Rudder

Line	C/N	mfd	model	Engines
566	**48574**	**04.94**	**MD-11F**	**PW**

JA8583 Japan AL 12.08.94; frd LGB-NRT 12-13.08, r23.08.94 NiL, DL, SBC, CL, is 04.09.94, KL-DL-SBC-NL r25.05.99, JAL bt 14.08.02, wfu 7.11.02, airtest white 18.11.02 NRT, canc 25.11.02; **N273UP** UPS 10.01.03; bt and cvtd via Boeing, N-rgd 25.11.02 BAHC, frd to Marana white by 31.12.02, BAHC to UPS 10.01.03, cvtd to -F as of 23.09.03

JA8583 • JAL Japan Airlines with "Golden Eagle" bird motif and name on the fuselage and winglet • Amsterdam Schiphol AMS • June 2011 Photo Frank de Koster

N273UP • UPS • February 2011 Collection Jacques Guillem

Line	C/N	mfd	model	Engines
567	**48630**	**05.94**	**MD-11F**	**GE**

I-DUPD Alitalia 10.06.94; sGVA 10.10.98 Team Alitalia tit, last AZ pax MD-11 flight MIA-MXP 01.12.03, str FCO 12.03; **N630LT** WFBN 09.06.04; frd FCO-Csogne 08.05.04; **D-ALCS** Lufthansa Cargo r19.01.05; sSingapore QPG 23.11.04 rrgd, cvtd by SASCO, WFBN N-reg canc 18.01.05, WOW sticker, in svc 23.01.05, arr VCV 20.07.09 for str, frd VCV-Xiamen 02.07.10, frd to Frankfurt 11.08.10 after C-check, wfu 07.01.15, frd ORD-VCV 07.01.15 wfu, reg canc 04.12.15; **N630SN** Western Global AL 30.12.15; filed 31.12.15, Mobility Air LLC 30.12.15, for Western Global lse, frd VCV-Oscada 22.03.16, s pkd 22.08.16 no regi, LH bcs

I-DUPD • Alitalia "Gaetano Donizetti" • Manchester MAN • May 2003 Photo Richard Vandervord

D-ALCS • Lufthansa Cargo • Chicago ORD • February 2007 Photo Guy Viselé

Line	C/N	mfd	model	Engines
568	**48575**	**06.94**	**MD-11F**	**PW**

JA8584 Japan AL 13.09.94; frd LGB-NRT 13-14.9, KoL + 5 others 16.09.94, is 3.10.94, KL,SL,O,SL,NL r29.03.98, JAL Cap + 5 others, r15.10.02 opb JAL, JAL bt 14.03.03, wfu 05.05.03, r/o NRT 15.05.03 white, canc 22.05.03; **N274UP** UPS 22.05.03; bt and cvtd via Boeing, N-rgd repaint 19.05.03, BAHC bt 22.05.03, frd NRT-Tucson-Goodyear 28.05.03 with Boeing callsign, s str 28.07.03 white, s04.10.03, UPS bt 07.10.03, frd GYR-Honolulu 10.12.03, cvtd to F by 04.05.04

JA8584 • JAL Japan Airlines with "Okinawa" bird motif and name on the fuselage and winglet • Hong Kong Kai Tak • November 1995

N274UP • UPS • December 2006 via Karsten Madr

Line	C/N	mfd	model	Engines
569	**48557**	**05.94**	**MD-11P**	**GE**

PH-KCC KLM del 24.06.94; rgd 23.06, arr AMS 25.06.94 in primer, named "Marie Curie", wfu 27.04.13 pkd AMS stored in hangar, s27.02.14 no titles/logos, frd to San Bernardino SBD 07.04.14, canc 11.04.14 wfu, s23.06.14 no titles, s wfu 16.09.15 no engines, s16.10.16

PH-KCC • KLM soon after delivery with "Aanvallen" sticker • Amsterdam Schiphol AMS • July 1994

PH-KCC • KLM "Marie Curie" • Quito Mariscal Sucre UIO • November 2006

Photo Sam Chui

Line	C/N	mfd	model	Engines
570	**48542**	**07.94**	**MD-11F**	**GE**

B-16101 EVA Air 18.08.94; s03.07.94 Long Beach, frd LB-Taipei 23-24.08.94, is 30.08.94, s27.10.03 Naples, new still unpainted F-door installed, sis LHR 26.11.03; **OH-NGA** Nordic Global AL 27.05.12; TPE-HEL white B-rgd, in svc 29.06.12 white, small titles, temp replacing OH-LGD on C-check, wfu 25.03.15 EBB-DFW, frd DFW-MIA 26.03.15; **N542KD** Western Global AL 21.04.15; M48542 LLC ret/N-rgd 21.04.15, white, slsd to FedEx, fis 01.12.15; damaged 03.06.16 at CKY during flight LGG-CKY-LOS-NBO, frd CKY-MXP 29.09.16 for repairs

B-16101 • Eva Air • Taipei TPE • August 2002 — Photo Sam Chui

B-16101 • Eva Air Cargo • Los Angeles LAX • October 2011 — Photo Sam Chui

Line	C/N	mfd	model	Engines
571	**48539**	**06.94**	**MD-11F**	**PW**

HB-IWN Swissair 29.07.94; is21.08, Swissair Asia s09.04.95 nc, Federal Express **N645FE** 2002-05 ntu; Swiss AL nn 31.03.02; s ZRH 17.03.02 basic SR cs, Swiss titl, Bandung/Crossair r31.03.02, s str ZRH 24.04.04 basic Swissair cs no tit; **PP-VTP** Varig 02.07.04; frd ZRH-GIG 02.07.04, s29.07.04 LIS fc, tfd to VRG Linhas Aéreas ar 07.06, continues to be op as Varig, sGRU 22.08.06; **N287UP** UPS 22.01.07; bt ex WFBN 22.01.07, sJNB 01.07 full RG cs, N-reg, presum on ferry, F-cvtd as of 18.06.07, sHKG 27.06.07 is white

HB-IWN • Swissair • September 1994 • Zürich Kloten ZRH Photo Stefan Höllering

HB-IWN • Swiss • Swissair Asia colors (with Asia winglets) after the bankruptcy • Zürich Kloten ZRH Photo Pierre Rohr

Line	C/N	mfd	model	Engines
572	**48543**	**07.94**	**MD-11F**	**GE**

B-16102 EVA Air 13.09.94; s19.09.94 Taipei, s04.98 ANK Joint Service add. inscription is, sis LHR 28.08.03 F-cvtd; **N7821B** WFBN 23.08.07; frd TPE-Macau-Shanghai 29.08.07; **B-2178** Shanghai AL 29.08.07; China Cargo AL r01.06.11; sKIX 14.07.11 still Shanghai AC cs, frd PVG--MHV 02-03.05.13, s25.01.14 (Western Global AL due 2013 app ntu), frd MHV-Oscada 07.06.14; **N543JN** Western Global AL lsd by10.14; frd Oscada-Lakeland 23.10.14 as such, depa 17.11.14, sis white ATL 14.12.14, sORD 21.03.15 white, sLGG 06.06.15, wetlsd to Allied Air (Nigeria) by 11.07.15, sSJU 12.01.16 white, sMEM 20.04.16

B-16102 • Eva Air Cargo • London Heathrow LHR • January 2007 Photo Richard Vandervord

B-2178 • Shanghai Airlines Cargo • Hong Kong Chek Lap Kok HKG • April 2011 Photo Chi Lam Wong

Line	C/N	mfd	model	Engines
573	**48558**	**08.94**	**MD-11P**	**GE**

PH-KCD KLM 16.09.94; WTC r16.09.94, named "Florence Nightingale"; wfu 24.01.14, s31.01.14 AMS covered in plastic, ret in svc 03.02.14, sis 01.03.14, wfu 26.10.14, used for farewell flights 11.11.14, ferried to LAX-Mojave, USA 11-12.01.15 wfu, s01.10.15

PH-KCD • KLM "Florence Nightingale" • Amsterdam Schiphol AMS

Photo Frank de Koster

PH-KCD • KLM "Florence Nightingale" with special Douglas Aviation History decal • Amsterdam Schiphol AMS • November 11, 2014

Photo Michael S.Prophet

Line	C/N	mfd	model	Engines
574	**48576**	**09.94**	**MD-11F**	**PW**

JA8585 Japan AL 05.04.95; s19.03.95 LGB, frd NRT 05-06.04, is 23.04.95, DioL + 3 r20.04.95, JAL r02.05.02, wfu 28.05.02, canc 18.06.02 to Boeing; **N270UP** UPS r18.06.02; rgd Boeing for F-conv, bt and cvtd via Boeing, frd NRT-Marana 24.06.02 white, BAHC to BCC 14.08.02, to BAHC 30.09.02, UPS 01.11.02, sMarana 27.01.03 white, s13.03.03, frd to Honolulu 12.05.03 being F-cvtd, sis CGN 17.07.03 nc

JA8585 • JAL Japan Airlines with "Hodgson's Hawk Eagle" bird motif and name on the fuselage and winglet • Hong Kong Kai Tak HKG • February 1996

N270UP • UPS • Sydney SYD • October 2005

Photo Sam Chui

Line	C/N	mfd	model	Engines
575	**48559**	**09.94**	**MD-11P**	**GE**

N91566 McDonnell Douglas; pkd 08.10.94 Yuma, primer, KLM sticker; **PH-KCE** KLM 18.11.94; s26.10 primer, arr 19.11 KLM tail, named "Audrey Hepburn", s24.12.04 nc, s06.10.14 add '95 Years' sticker, wfu on last KLM and pax scheduled MD-11 flight YUL-AMS 26.10.14, s30.10.14 logos, regi and stickers removed, still with KLM bcs and tail logo and temp reg for ferry to LAX and then Mojave on 17.11.14, canc 21.11.14. s by 03.01.15 engines and parts missing, s01.10.15

PH-KCE • KLM "Audrey Hepburn" with special 'The world is just a click away' decal • Amsterdam Schiphol AMS • September 2004 Photo Frank de Koster

PH-KCE • KLM "Audrey Hepburn" with special '95 Years' decal • October 2014 Photo Simon De Rudder

Line	C/N	mfd	model	Engines
576	**48415**	**10.94**	**MD-11F**	**GE**

N103EV EVA Air 30.11.94; rFSBU 11.94, xMit, FSN N-reg canc 10.06.99; **B-16103** EVA AW rr 28.05.99; s29.05.99, sis 11.10.03 pax, s08.09.04 KUL now F-cvtd; **N103EV** AFS r23.05.05; **B-2176** Shanghai AL 23.05.05; arr Shanghai PVG fc 11.06.05, ret to EVA AW, ret to lessor by 07.06.11; **N304MS** WFBN 07.06.11; Celestial Avtn Trading 29 to WFBN 07.06.11, sTPE 24.10.11 white no engines, at Eva hangars, s23.02.12 nr 2 engine and vertical stabilizer missing, s14.07.12 white, flying TPE (testflight) acc to photocap, AFS Investments XV LLC 10.01.13, r23.01.13, frd GIG-MHV 26.05.14; **N415JN** Western Global AL lsd 11.08.14; reg res 18.12.13, rr 22.08.14, frd MHV-Lakeland 27.09.14, s20.10.14 Lakeland white, AFS Inv. to M48415 LLC 13.07.15 lse continues, slsd to FedEx 12.15, damaged 17.09.15 Oscada MI, fire in cargo hold, 3 injuries, but app repaired as slsd to FedEx 12.15

B-16103 • EVA Air • Frankfurt am Main FRA — via Karsten Madrian

B-2176 • Shanghai Airlines Cargo • Hong Kong Chek Lap Kok HKG • January 2011 — Photo Chi Lam Wong

Line	C/N	mfd	model	Engines
577	**48616**	**11.94**	**MD-11F**	**PW**

PH-MCP Martinair Holland 22.12.94; s26.10.94 LBG fc, del 02.02. as F, AMS 03.12, ctd to CF 20.12.94, to Stansted 22.12 for h/o, is 24.12.94, last MP MD-11 pax season summer 2006 (only MD-11 not with big new "Martinair Cargo" titles), not converted back to pax since, wfu due 08.07.16 as final MP MD-11, frd MIA-MHV 09.07.16

PH-MCP • Martinair with special "40 years in the air" decal • Amsterdam Schiphol AMS
Photo Frank de Koster

PH-MCP • Martinair • Amsterdam Schiphol AMS • November 2005
Photo Frank de Koster

Line	C/N	mfd	model	Engines
578	**48560**	**11.94**	**MD-11P**	**GE**

PH-KCF KLM 17.12.94; arr AMS primer, named "Annie Romein", op first AMS-MEM flight 27.06.95 temporarily named "Elvis I", sXiamen 10.01.05 just repainted, AMS 16.01.05 nc, last svc 28.10.12, s17.11.12 Amsterdam no titles, frd to Victorville 26.11.12 for part out, canc 04.01.13, s wfu 05.03.14

PH-KCF • KLM "Annie Romein" • Amsterdam Schiphol AMS | Photo Frank de Koster

PH-KCF • KLM "Annie Romein" touching down runway 18R • Amsterdam Schiphol AMS • January 2012 | Photo Simon De Rudder

Line	C/N	mfd	model	Engines
579	**48631**	**12.94**	**MD-11F**	**PW**

N275WA ILFC/World AW 02.03.95; World s03.95 pax EWR-Mexico; Garuda slsd 04.95; Hadj, sZRH 05.95 white,Garuda tit + logo, due ret 06.95; MAS Kargo slsd s09.07.95; sAMS; World AW ret s03.06.96; sPHX, World tit applied,still MAS ch; Philippine AL slsd 17.09.96; MAS slsd s13.02.98; Osaka, titles; Garuda slsd 22.02.98; sPhoenix 19.02 Malaysian, Garuda tit appl 22.2/ret 5.98?; World AW ret 05.98; wlsd Monarch 16-19.06.98 whilst N273WA was on maint; MASKargo lsd 26.09.98; replacing 48633 at LHR, sDXB 28.05.99 still MAS K.; World AW ret s11.03.00; sManston 11.03.00 white/Garuda tit/tail, slsd Garuda 26.01-26.02.01, 09.03-09.04.01; World AW cvtd s27.06.02; dep Venice after F-cvtn, sYYZ 26.06.05 add Air Canada titl, sis OST 03.12, frd BWI-GYR 02.07.12 for str, ret to ILFC, sGYR 02.11.12 being parted out, Unical Aviation bt 14.11.12 r12.12.12, s01.12.12 World fcs, s wfu 10.13, canc 30.01.14

N275WA • MASkargo • Amsterdam Schiphol AMS • 1995 Photo Frank de Koster

N275WA • MASkargo • Ostend OST • November 1999 Photo P. Van Damme

Line	C/N	mfd	model	Engines
580	**48544**	**01.95**	**MD-11F**	**GE**

N105EV EVA Air 30.03.95; rFSBU, dam 28.11.01 Taipei hard landing, sis 28.12.01 ANC-Atlanta, canc 29.11.06; **B-2177** Shanghai AL 29.11.06; sFRA fc 15.01.07, s10.09.11 still fcs; China Cargo AL r01.06.11; **N216SC** Celestial Aviation Trading 17 Ltd 28.05.13; frd PVG-Mobile BFM 24-25.05.13, Celestial to WFBN 28.05.13, frd to Marana 07.06.13, WFBN to AFS Investments 57 LLC 20.06.13, filed 03.07.13, r01.08.13, NAS Investments 9 LLC 14.08.13, Keidann Air LLC 14.08.13, M48544 LLC 27.09.13, r29.10.13, frd MZJ-MHV 02.10.13, s str 01.10.15; **N544KD**; rr res 05.01.15, presum ntu, s str old reg 01.10.15, s12.10.16

N105EV • Eva Air Cargo • Ostend OST • November 1999 Photo P. Van Damme

B-2177 • Shanghai Airlines Cargo on final runway 07R • Frankfurt am Main FRA • June 2007 Photo Simon De Rudder

Line	C/N	mfd	model	Engines
581	**48617**	**01.95**	**MD-11F**	**PW**

PH-MCR Martinair Holland 30.03.95; arr 31.03.95, sis AMS 03.06 with "Martinair Cargo" titles on new csours, wfu 21.03.15, marketed by KLM as for sale by 02.06.15, s07.15 AMS inside hangar, frd AMS-MHV 06-07.09.15, wfu, canc 17.09.15, s12.10.16

PH-MCR • Martinair named "Frits" after Frits Pederson (Finance Director of Martinair) • Amsterdam Schiphol AMS

Photo Frank de Koster

PH-MCR • Martinair Cargo • Miami MIA • March 2013

Photo Jannik Femerling

Line	C/N	mfd	model	Engines
582	**48632**	**02.95**	**MD-11CF**	**PW**

N276WA ILFC/World AW 28.03.95; LGB s11.03.95 white, frd to Jak 30.03.95; Garuda slsd s05.95; sZRH, white,-tit & logo; MAS Kargo slsd s11.08.95; sAMS; Garuda slsd s27.04.96; sZRH, MAS cheatl Gar tit; World AW ret s31.05.96; sPHX,Gar tit,still MAS ch; Philippine AL slsd s09.96; sMEL; MAS Kargo slsd s08.97; sFRA, white, tit&logo; STAF lsd s13.08.98; sMIA titles/tail cs, s22.11.98 MIA fc but using World flightnr, s09.11.99 MIA with STAF, sAtlanta 12.02.00 overhaul, no tit, s17.06.00 Ostend is full STAF cs still; World AW ret 02.00; slsd Garuda 26.01-26.02.01, 09.03-09.04.01, cvtd to Freighter in 2003, operated inaugural Etihad Cargo service Abu Dhabi-OST 06.04.10 in World fc, ILFC to WTC 14.09.10, lsd to WO, sis OST 08.04.12, frd DOV-GYR 12.04.12 for str, frd GYR-VCV 09.10.12, WTC to ILFC 16.10.12, to FedEx 16.10.12; **N68092** Federal Express 16.10.12; r25.10.12 rr 09.11.12, purchased for parts, s wfu VCV 24.10.13, s10.10.16

N276WA • STAF • Miami MIA • September 1998

N276WA • World Cargo • Frankfurt am Main FRA • February 2008

Photo Julian Klein

Line	C/N	mfd	model	Engines
583	**48577**	**03.95**	**MD-11F**	**PW**

JA8586 Japan AL 11.04.95; s19.03.95 LGB, frd NRT 11-12.04, is 23.04, wfu 13.07.04, testfl 29.07.04 white, JA-reg canc 04.08.04; **N278UP** UPS 04.08.04; bt and cvtd via Boeing, frd NRT-GYR 10.08.04, s15.08.04 white no titl, s11.10.04, BAHC to UPS 18.10.04, F-cvtd as of 18.03.05, sANC 28.04.05, s06.08.05 KIX still white, s02.02.06 HKG fc

JA8586 • JAL Japan Airlines with "White Stork" bird motif and name on the fuselage and winglet Photo Bernard Crocoll

N278UP • UPS white • Cologne Bonn CGN • July 2005

Line	C/N	mfd	model	Engines
584	**48618**	**03.95**	**MD-11F**	**PW**

PH-MCS Martinair Holland 03.04.95; arr 04.04, is 09.04, new csours s02.06 with Martinair Cargo titles, wfu 28.03.15, pkd AMS (Schiphol east), marketed by KLM as for sale by 02.06.15, s07.15 AMS inside hangar, frd AMS-VCV 01.04.16 wfu, canc 11.04.16; **N68089** Federal Express 08.04.16; r12.04.16, wfu, s23.05.16 VCV, for spares

PH-MCS • Martinair • Amsterdam Schiphol AMS

Photo Frank de Koster

PH-MCS • Martinair Cargo • Miami MIA • March 2013

Photo Jannik Femerling

Line	C/N	mfd	model	Engines
585	**48561**	**04.95**	**MD-11P**	**GE**

PH-KCG KLM 12.05.95; named "Maria Callas", sAMS pkd 15.11.12, presum standby, titles/logos removed by 25.12.12 awaits disposal, frd to Victorville 18.04.13 (after returning on 15.04.13 to AMS) for part-out, canc 24.05.13 pwfu, s14.11.14 stripped no engines, doors etc. but standing on u/c

PH-KCG • KLM "Maria Callas" with special 'The world is just a click away' decal • Amsterdam Schiphol AMS • April 2004 Photo Frank de Koster

PH-KCG • KLM "Maria Callas" just newly painted • Amsterdam Schiphol AMS • October 2011 Photo Wil Teunissen

Line	C/N	mfd	model	Engines
586	**48629**	**05.95**	**MD-11F**	**PW**

PH-MCT Martinair Holland 23.05.95; is 24.05.95 bringing Soccer champion Ajax to Amsterdam, Malc Fin Two r21.03.03, opb MP, sis oc 24.02.06, nc 02.04.06, sis 20.01.13 but frd to Orlando SFB 09.03.13, ret to MALC Fin Two, repo to be brup and canc 18.03.13 but see below; **N956AR** Sky Lease Cargo 09.05.13; WFBN 22.04.13, r23.04.13, Sky Lease I LLC r05.06.13, frd SFB-MIA 29.06.13, s str MIA 06.12.13 MP bcs, no engines, s15.01.15 wfu, s06.12.15 on trestles derelict, s23.07.16 broken up in large sections

PH-MCT • Martinair • Amsterdam Schiphol AMS • April 2005 Photo Frank de Koster

PH-MCT • Martinair Cargo • Amsterdam Schiphol AMS • November 2011 Photo Frank de Koster

Line	C/N	mfd	model	Engines
587	**48545**	**05.95**	**MD-11F**	**GE**

B-16106 EVA Air 22.06.95; **N106BV** WFBN 14.05.08; **B-2179** Shanghai AL s02.06.08; China Cargo AL r01.06.11; sSIN 05.08.11 still full Shanghai cs, sHKG 01.09.11 now China Cargo AL cs, wfu mid 08.13 pkd Shanghai PVG 08.13, frd PVG-MHV 16-17.11.13, s25.01.14; **N545JN** Western Global AL lsd 15.08.14; Neff Air LLC N-rgd by 08.14, M48545 LLC (Miami FL) 15.08.14, lsd to WGA, frd MHV-Oscada 17.08.14, s pkd 24.08.14 China Cargo cs, wlsd to TAMPA by 02.05.15, sLGG 06.06.15 white, presum ret from TAMPA to Western Global, Allied Air Cargo slsd 06.15, aircraft held in Harare, Zimbabwe 14.02.16 after a dead body was found on board in the air conditioning vault, released and frd to Waterkloof 19.02.16 , s30.11.16 DFW with large billboard Western Global titles

B-16106 • Eva Air Cargo • Brussels BRU • September 2007 Photo Jean-Marie Hanon

N545JN • Western Global • Liège LGG • February 2017 Photo Michel Huart

Line	C/N	mfd	model	Engines
588	**48578**	**06.95**	**MD-11F**	**PW**

JA8587 Japan AL 28.06.95; frd 28-29.6,r30.06 DiL,is 14.07.95, KL-DL-NL-FSL-CF-NTT r25.05.99, JAL Cap + 5 others, r15.10.02 opb JAL, Mitsui SGL+5 others 01.10.03, opb JAL, JAL r07.01.04 ex lse, wfu 03.05.04, testfl NRT 17.05.04, canc 24.05.04; **N277UP** UPS r24.05.04; bt and cvtd via Boeing r24.05.04, frd NRT-Goodyear 28.05.04 for str, UPS 07.06.04, frd to Honolulu 10.06.04, cvtd to F as of 19.10.04, frd SIN-HKG 02.11.04, sis PHL 18.12.04 white no titl, nose gear cslapsed and ran off runway on take off 06.06.16 Seoul ICN 0(4), presum WO.

JA8587 • JAL Japan Airlines with "Pryer's Woodpecker" bird motif and name on the fuselage and winglet • London Heathrow LHR • February 2001 Photo Richard Vandervord

N277UP • UPS • Hartsfield–Jackson Atlanta ATL • July 2010 Photo Kevin Stokes

Line	C/N	mfd	model	Engines
589	**48546**	**07.95**	**MD-11F**	**GE**

B-16107 EVA Air 30.08.95; sLGB 05.07.95 fc; **OH-NGB** Nordic Global 01.11.12; in svc 26.11.12, sis 05.02.13 white, small sticker, frd STN-Oscoda 25-26.03.15; **N546JN** Western Global AL r26.06.15; M48546 LLC, Miami r26.06.15, frd Oscada-ROW 04.10.15, slsd to FedEx, fis 01.12.15, frd ONT-MHV 24.12.16

B-16107 • Eva Air Cargo • Anchorage ANC • August 2011 Photo Wil Teunissen

OH-NGB • Nordic Global Airlines • Lusaka LUN • March 2015 Photo Benoît Denet

Line	C/N	mfd	model	Engines
590	**48743**	**08.95**	**MD-11ER**	**PW**

N6203D Dynair; s17.10.95 DynAir PHX, primer, operator/owner status unk; **N277WA** World AW s30.11.95; sPHX fc; N6203D MdD s09.02.96; for testflights 'Experimental' tit, sPHX 25.02.96; **N277WA** World AW r3.96; sMDFC-Knox; Philippine AL lsd 24.06.96; sSYD fc 26.06; Garuda Indonesia lsd s05.98; s white, titles/logos, added 02.12; VASP lsd s03.07.98; sSeattle fc ntu?; Air Afrique lsd s8.08.98; sJFK, cs; Monarch AL lsd 14.08.98; World AW ret 03.11.98, s03.11.98 LAS; sis 27.03.99 LAX arabic-like tail logo, sCambridge 11.03.00 white/Garuda tit-tail logo, El Al cs s17.08.00 EWR, Garuda slsd 26.1-26.02.01, 09.03-09.04.01, sis Sofia 14.09.10 full old cs, pax conf, last svc 11-12.01.12, arr MIA, s all white 02.02.12, frd MIA-GYR 26.04.12 for onward str, repo 07.12 to be broken up, World ret to MDFC-Knoxville Company, sold to Unical Aviation Inc 20.12.12, r11.12.12, wfu, s wfu GYR 16.10.12, s01.12.12 white, s30.01.15, canc 26.08.15 wfu

N277WA • Philippines • Hong Kong Kai Tak HKG • December 1996 Photo Marco Dotti

N277WA • Monarch • Manchester MAN • September 1998

Line	C/N	mfd	model	Engines
591	**48562**	**07.95**	**MD-11P**	**GE**

PH-KCH KLM 31.08.95; arr AMS primer 01.09.95, sXiamen 24.01.06 nc, wfu 02.07.12 Delhi-AMS, dep 30.07.12 to Victorville, to be scrapped, s09.12 engines missing (empty cowlings), s09.10.12 many parts missing, s14.03.13 stripped no engines, doors etc. but standing on u/c, s wfu 05.03.14, broken up 07.14

PH-KCH • KLM "Anna Pavlova" • Amsterdam Schiphol AMS • August 2005 Photo Frank de Koster

PH-KCH • first MD-11 to leave the KL fleet, seen on July 30, 2012 at 9:45 a.m. leaving AMS to VCV via KEF Photo Cornelis Boersma

Line	C/N	mfd	model	Engines
592	**48744**	**09.95**	**MD-11F**	**GE**

PP-SPK VASP 17.11.95; sLGB 06.11.95, named "Kasato Maru", renamed "Luis Eduardo Magalhaes", sis LAX 27.04.99, repossessed 25.04.00, own Golden Gate Leasing Ltd by 10.00, s str Sao Paulo 14.10.00 no tit; **N797BA** RGL-3 Corp 29.09.00; to be F-cvtd by SASCO ann 04.01, sRGL-3 Corp s str Victorville 03.04.01 basic VASP cs; **N251UP** UPS 30.04.01; rr 03.07.01, sPaya Lebar 01.09.01 F-cvtd, on ST Aerospace Ramp fc, sis 05.11.01 Louisville KY, sis CGN 26.03.03 old csours

PP-SPK • VASP named "Kasato Maru" • Zürich Kloten ZRH

Photo Wil Teunissen

N251UP • UPS • Hong Kong Chek Lap Kok HKG • December 2005

Photo Mark Tang

Line	C/N	mfd	model	Engines
593	**48563**	**09.95**	**MD-11P**	**GE**

PH-KCI KLM 10.11.95; arr AMS 11.11.95 primer, KLM logo on rudder; **PP-SPM** VASP lsd 15.12.95; del fc/due ret 12.98; **PH-KCI** KLM ret 21.08.98; arr AMS as PP-SPM VASP cs, KLM to ILFC 05.02, r17.01.03 and lsd back, first KL MD-11 in nc, s17.01.04 MIA, last svc 16.09.12, wfu 17.09.12, frd to VCV 15.10.12, canc 22.10.12 ret lessor, many parts and engines missing by 12.13, s wfu 05.03.14, broken up 07.14

PH-KCI • VASP • Amsterdam Schiphol AMS • December 1995 Photo W. Wenot

PH-KCI • KLM "Moeder Teresa" • Caracas Maiquetía Simón Bolívar CCS • February 1999 Photo M.Rose

Line	C/N	mfd	model	Engines
594	**48747**	**10.95**	**MD-11F**	**GE**

N616FE Federal Express 30.11.95; r11.95 MDFC, del via LAX and YVR 30.11.95, named "Shanita"; first revenue svc YVR-MEM 02.12.95; to FedEx 05.12.07, later named "Terra"

N616FE • FedEx Express "Terra" • Seoul-Incheon ICN • January 2016 Photo Martin Fenner

Line	C/N	mfd	model	Engines
595	**48748**	**11.95**	**MD-11F**	**GE**

N617FE Federal Express 08.12.95; sLGB 06 & 12.11.95, own MDFC, del via LAX and YVR 03-07.12.95, first revenue svc YVR-MEM 08.12.95, named "Travis", to FedEx 12.12.07

N617FE • FedEx / Federal Express • Paris Charles de Gaulle CDG • July 1996 Photo Jacques Guillem

Line	C/N	mfd	model	Engines
596	**48745**	**12.95**	**MD-11F**	**GE**

PP-SPL VASP s20.01.96; sLGB 07.12.95/sSao 20.01/GGL r26.01.96, repossessed 25.04.00, s str Victorville 17.08.00 basic cs, PP-reg canc 22.08.00; **N798BA** RGL-3 Corp 29.09.00; sVictorville 25.12.00 now N-painted; **N250UP** UPS 14.03.01; at SASCO for F-conv by 04.00, rr 10.05.01, due complete 09.01, sPaya Lebar 01.09.01 F-cvtd, full cs, at ST Aerospace's ramp, frd to Hong Kong 01.10.01, sANC 04.10.01, first UPS MD-11

N250UP • United Parcel Service • Anchorage ANC • July 2003 Photo Sam Chui

N250UP • UPS • Cologne Bonn CGN • August 2014 Photo Rainer Bexten

Line	C/N	mfd	model	Engines
597	**48746**	**01.96**	**MD-11ER**	**PW**

N9020Q McDonnell Douglas s15.01.96; sPHX World cs, s26.02.96; **N278WA** World AW r03.96; sMDFC-Memph; Philippine AL lsd s02.10.96; sLHR; El Al lsd s13.07.98; El Al lsd s13.07.98 ORD partial cs/tit, Avianca Comombia lsd 10.12.98-17.01.99 for daily svc between BOG-JFK, white/tit; World AW ret early 99; Monarch lsd 08.05.99 El Al cheatl/Air Asia logo, ret 28.05.99, depa MAN by 31.05.99 for DFW, TransAer s28.07.99 white, sManston 11.03.00 Garuda tit-tail, sDXB 02.06.00 World fc, sIAH 08.11.00 add Sonair tit for IAH-Luanda twice-weekly, sATL 22.07.01, sLuanda 02.03, sSan Antonio 22.03.04, frd MIA-ANC-XSP 10-11.01.12 for cargo conversion, sVCV 19.05.12, frd QPG-HNL-VCV 12.06.12 for storage, cvtd to freighter 06.12, s22.11.12 pkd, frd VCV--CGK 05-09.04.13, N-reg canc 17.04.13; **Z-BAM** AV Cargo 17.04.13; frd CGK-NBO 02.05.13, in svc to Liege, sis 01.07.13 fcs; **Z-GAB** Global Africa Aviation s06.10.14; frd BKO-LGG 06.10.14, sNRT 29.10.14 white, sOST 20.12.14

N278WA • EL AL • Los Angeles LAX • June 1998 Photo Michael Carter

N278WA • Air Asia • Jeddah JED • 1999 Photo Benoît Denet

N278WA • World with latest titles and motif adopted by SonAir of Angola • Houston IAH • February 2008 Photo Tim Bryan

Line	C/N	mfd	model	Engines	
598	**48746**	**01.96**	**MD-11F**	**GE**	Saudia ntu; MD Federal Holding Co. rgd; **N613FE** Federal Express 12.03.96; frd LAX-YVR 12.03.96, is 13.03.96 YVR-MEM; own FedEx 31.03.03, named "Krista"

N613FE • FedEx / Federal Express "Krista" • May 1996 via Ruben Husberg

N613FE • FedEx Express "Krista" • Narita NRT • September 2013 Photo Alec Wilson

Line	C/N	mfd	model	Engines
599	**48579**	**02.96**	**MD-11F**	**PW**

JA8588 Japan AL 03.04.96; is 21.04.96, rDiL,NL,NL,CL,CIL,CB r05.04.95, KL-DL-SBC,NTT-NL-CL r25.05.99, JAL Cap + 5 others, r15.10.02 opb JAL, JAL bt 04.04.03, sNRT 14.10.03 white; **N276UP** UPS 17.12.03; bt and cvtd via Boeing, BAHC r21.10.03, frd NRT-TUS-GYR 27.10.03 still JA-rgd, rrgd and airtest GYR 09.12.03, s13.12.03, r04.02.04, still str GYR s28.03.04 white, frd to Honolulu 31.03.04, F-cvtd as of 20.08.04

JA8588 • JAL Japan Airlines with "White Tailed Eagle" bird motif and name on the fuselage and winglet • Hong Kong Kai Tak HKG • December 1996 Photo Marco Dotti

N276UP • UPS • Sydney SYD • November 2005 Photo Sam Chui

Line	C/N	mfd	model	Engines
600	**48766**	**03.96**	**MD-11P**	**GE**

N6203U McDonnell Douglas; s24.10.96 LGB primer; **OO-CTB** City Bird 09.12.96; sLGB fc 11.11.96, s04.12.96 LGB test fligh, opf Star Europe 15.12.96, ret BRU 26.03.97, is 27.03.97, wfu 30.04.01, ret BCC, frd to Abbotsford 3.05.01, OO-reg canc 9.05.01; **P4-BDL** BCC rr s19.01.02; sAbbotsford rrgd, full CityBird cs 19.01.02, sVictorville 28.02.02 fc, arr Rome FCO 19.03.02 for F-conv, s Victorville 02.10.02 own MDDC, s15.01.03; **OH-LGF** Finnair 26.03.04; frd VCV-BFL 01.04.04 for Finnair P4-rgd, arr HEL 04.04.04 white OH-rgd, BoeCC r31.05.04, i.s. 01.06.04, sis 08.06.06 in Moomin cs, last svc BKK-HEL 23.12.09, frd HEL-QPG 27.01.10 for str; **N783BC** MDD Dakota Leasing Inc ret r01.02.10; canc 01.06.10; **EI-EMS** Cargoitalia lsd 04.06.10; frd XSP-MSP 04.06.10 fc, F-cvtd, EI-rgd Boeing Capital Leasing r02.06.10, AL ceased 21.12.11, arr FRA 21.12.11 pkd, frd FRA-BGR-VCV 30-31.03.12; **N460BC** McDonnell Douglas Dakota Leasing r18.09.12; s str VCV 16.10.12, s wfu 23.10.14, s24.10.15 still painted EI-rgd, N-reg canc 21.09.16, wfu VCV, s10.10.16

OO-CTB • City Bird "Albatros" • Brussels BRU • September 2000 Photo Wil Teunissen

OH-LGF • Finnair "Official airline of Santa Claus" • Beijing PEK • January 2006 Photo Sam Chui

Line	C/N	mfd	model	Engines
601	**48768**	**04.96**	**MD-11F**	**GE**

N9134D McDonnell Douglas; **PP-SFA** VASP 26.06.96; s01.04.96, 27.05.96 LBG fc/rGGL 22.07.96 as PP-SPN NTU, sis 26.03.00, repossessed 25.04.00, to RGL-3 Corp 29.09.00, s Sao Paulo 17.11.00 no engs, testflight 27.03.01, to Victorville 11.04.01, plain blue tail no tit; **N252UP** UPS 07.06.01; N-rgd 25.05.01 RGL-3, UPS bt 07.06.01, sVictorville 17.05.01 N-rgd, ny F-conv, str, sPaya Lebar 1.09.01 bare metal, to be cvtd, dd 16.11.01 to UPS, s11.12.04 oc, s11.06.05 nc

PP-SFA • VASP • Miami MIA • August 1996

N252UP • UPS • Warsaw Chopin WAW • March 2014

Photo Robert Szymczak

Line	C/N	mfd	model	Engines
602	**48767**	**05.96**	**MD-11F**	**GE**

N615FE MDD s27.05.96 LGB, own MDDE r06.96, del Federal Express 26.06.96 via LAX and YVR; named "Youhei"; FedEx r18.04.03

N615FE • FedEx / Federal Express • Memphis MEM • November 1999

N615FE • FedEx Express "Youhei" • Narita NRT • December 2009

Photo Kentaro Iemoto

Line	C/N	mfd	model	Engines
603	**48769**	**06.96**	**MD-11F**	**GE**

N9166N sMDD LGB 08.96, **PP-SFD** VASP 27.11.96; named "Nossa Senhora Aparecida", sis 24.03.00, repossessed 25.04.00, str s17.08.00 Victorville basic cs; **N799BA** RGL-3 Corp 29.09.00; sVictorville 25.12.00 now N-painted, canc 18.05.01; **PP-VQX** Varig 18.05.01; sLHR 20.05.01 is, FRA 2.06.01, Varig r26.06.01, s str Rio de Janeiro GIG 14.04.05 fc no engines, undergoing maintenance, s04.10.05 no engines, no u/c, undergoing maint.; **PT-MSJ** TAM 29.03.07; frd GIG-GRU 29.03.07 fc, final TAM MD-11 svc 13.12.08; **N746BC** RGL-3 Corp ret r06.01.09; **N573FE** Federal Express 06.07.09; F-conv due 17.11.08-17.03.09, Ethiopian Cargo 01.09 ntu, cvtd to freighter by 07.09, frd VCE-XSP 08-09.07.09 basic TAM cs, rr 03.09.09, due in svc 11.09, sis 06.04.10 full FedEx cs, named "Tom"

N9166N • Long Beach LGB prior painting and delivery to VASP • August 1996

PT-MSJ • TAM Linhas Aéreas "The Magic Red Carpet" • Milan Malpensa MXP • April 2008

Photo Paolo Maggiolo

Line	C/N	mfd	model	Engines
604	**48754**	**07.96**	**MD-11F**	**GE**

N618FE Federal Express 22.08.96; rDoL 08.96, MDFH, FedEx 30.03.03, named "Justin", dam 25.01.13 Denver after tail strike on landing, frd DEN-LAX 04.02.13 for repairs, testfl 27.04.13, ret in svc 30.04.13

N618FE • FedEx / Federal Express • Paris Charles de Gaulle CDG • August 1998

N618FE • FedEx Express "Justin" • Narita NRT • April 2009 Photo Kentaro Iemoto

Line	C/N	mfd	model	Engines
605	**48623**	**08.96**	**MD-11P**	**PW**

N814DE Delta AL 14.09.96; frd ATL-Goodyear 21.05.03 for str, s fc 28.03.04, s30.01.05 basic cs, s30.04.06; **N528FE** Federal Express 15.10.04; frd GYR-LAX-HNL-GUM-QPG 02-05.09.06 for F-conv, rr 04.12.06, F-cvtd as of 04.01.07, frd QPG-SIN 06.01.07 after F-conv, first revenue svc SIN-HKG 21.01.07 and HKG-ANC-MEM 22.01.07, named "Trinity"

N814DE • Delta • London Gatwick LGW

Photo Frank de Koster

N528FE • FedEx Express • Anchorage ANC • October 2012

Photo James Rowson

Line	C/N	mfd	model	Engines
606	**48757**	**09.96**	**MD-11F**	**PW**

PH-MCU McDonnell Douglas, s19.09.96 LGB test flight, Martinair 01.10.96; named "Prinses Maxima", s27.05.03 special floral-themed livery, available for sale repo 11.15 TT 87000, 16000 L, wfu 01.07.16, frd AMS-MIA-VCV 01-02.07.16; **N68091** Federal Express r13.07.16, pwfu

PH-MCU • Martinair Cargo "Prinses Maxima" • Amsterdam Schiphol AMS • March 2007 Photo Frank de Koster

PH-MCU • Martinair Cargo "Prinses Maxima" • Amsterdam Schiphol AMS • January 2013 Photo Michael S.Prophet

Line	C/N	mfd	model	Engines
607	**48770**	**10.96**	**MD-11F**	**GE**

N619FE Federal Express 14.11.96; r MDAFNC 11.96, named "Joey", FedEx 31.03.03, later named "Lyndon"

N619FE • FedEx / Federal Express via Karsten Madr

N619FE • FedEx Express • Frankfurt am Main FRA • May 2010 Photo Pawel Kierzkowski

Line	C/N	mfd	model	Engines
608	**48753**	**11.96**	**MD-11F**	**GE**

PK-GIK Garuda 19.12.96; **PP-VQI** Varig 11.09.98; own BCC, arr Rio 18.09.98 white, MDFC Lakewood Comp r26.09.98, due wfu early 08.05 for maintenance, s towed to Varig ramp 05.09.05, stripped by 10.10.05, s07.10.05 OH-rrgd but PP-reg reapplied for ferry; **OH-LGG** Finnair 11.11.05; sVCV 20.10.05 as OH-LGG, Finnair tail, frd VCV-HEL 11-12.11.05, MDFC-Lakewood Company r16.01.06, deconverted ex MD-11ER (central tanks removed), sKIZ 19.01.06 fc, sKIX 24.11.07 Santa Claus cs, opf FC Barcelona for the USA tour 29.07-09.08.09, last AY MD-11 svc 22.02.10 DEL-HEL, charter 02.03.10 (YVR), frd HEL-Singapore QPG 24.03.10; **N785BC** MDFC-Lakewood Co ret/BCC r31.03.10; r31.03.10, F-cvtd by 09.10, MDFZC-Lakewood Company 15.09.10; **N625FE** Federal Express r28.09.10; frd KIX-ANC 30.11.10 after F-conv, rr 07.12.10, sis fc 13.03.11, named "Robyn"

PK-GIK • Garuda Indonesia • Roma Leonardo da Vinci Fiumicino FCO • January 1997 Photo Aldo Bidini

PP-VQI • Varig Brasil • Amsterdam Schiphol AMS • August 2005 Photo Frank de Koster

Line	C/N	mfd	model	Engines
609	**48773**	**12.96**	**MD-11F**	**GE**

N90187 McDonnell Douglas 16.01.97; 01.97 sLGB primer; **HZ-ANA** Saudi Arabian Cargo 24.12.97; del delayed, sLGB 10.97, s22.11.97 Marana, frd 24-26.12.97, last service 09.04.14 KRT-RUH, wfu Jeddah s10.14, s10.15

HZ-ANA • Saudi Arabian Cargo • Brussels BRU • May 2008 Photo Benoît Denet

Line	C/N	mfd	model	Engines
610	**48774**	**01.97**	**MD-11F**	**PW**

JA8589 Japan AL 03.03.97; r04.03.97, SCL Lotus & 5 others, r07.03.97, JAL bt 06.03.03, wfu 05.07.03, repaint white and rrgd 19.07.03; **N275UP** UPS 25.07.03; bt BAHC 25.07.03, and cvtd via Boeing, frd to Goodyear 31.07.03, airtest 11.11.03, UPS 14.11.03, sGYR 13.12.03 white str, frd to Honolulu 18.02.04 for F-cvtd, F-cvtd at SASCO as of 28.06.04, s flying HKG 12.07.04 white

JA8589 • JAL Japan Airlines with "Rock Ptarmigan" bird motif and name on the fuselage and winglet • Narita NRT • November 2002 Photo Sam Chui

Line	C/N	mfd	model	Engines	
611	**48540**	**02.97**	**MD-11F**	**PW**	**HB-IWO** Swissair 11.03.97; is 04.04.97, Federal Express N646FE 2002/05 ntu; Swiss AL nn 31.03.02; Bandung/ Crossair r31.03.02, s str ZRH 24.01.04 ex Swiss cs; **PP-VTK** Varig 10.05.04; arr GIG 10.05.04 ex Swiss cs, sis LHR 10.06.04, MUC 01.04.06, tfd to VRG Linhas Aéreas ar 07.06, continues to be op as Varig, sis FRA 10.12.06; **N288UP** UPS 27.02.07; frd N-rgd GIG-JNB-QPG 28.02-01.03.07 for F-conv, F-cvtd as of 13.07.07, sSapporo CTS 22.07.07 white is, SYD 05.08.07, s13.12.16 new style titles

HB-IWO • Swiss in former Swissair livery • Malabo SSG (Equatorial Guinea) • April 2002

Photo Pierre Rohr

PP-VTK • Varig Brasil • Paris Charles de Gaulle CDG • October 2005

Photo Christian Volpati

Line	C/N	mfd	model	Engines
612	**48564**	**03.97**	**MD-11P**	**GE**

PH-KCK KLM 25.04.97; sLGB in primer, named "Christine Teszler", later named ""Ingrid Bergman", s09.12.07 last MD-11 in ncs, due wfu 27.10.13, s04.11.13 bcs, frd AMS-VCV 02.12.13, canc 09.12.13 wfu, s04.14 engines and parts missing

PH-KCK • KLM "Ingrid Bergman" • Amsterdam AMS

PH-KCK • KLM "Ingrid Bergman" • Quito Mariscal Sucre UIO • December 2009 via Nicholas Scherrer

Line	C/N	mfd	model	Engines
613	**48755**	**04.97**	**MD-11F**	**GE**

PK-GIL Garuda 24.05.97; due mid 97,sLGB 24.04.97 fc, sMarana 06.07.98 str Gar cs, PP-SFO VASP res 22.09.98, ntu; **PP-VQJ** Varig 29.10.99; res 19.10.99, arr Rio GIG 29.10.99 fc, sis 13.11.99, MDFC Carson Comp r01.12.99; **PT-MSH** TAM 02.02.07; being prepared; white, red winglets by 15.12.06, fc sis 24.01.07 GIG, old reg, frd to GRU 02.02.07, is 03.02.07; **N730BC** MDFC Carson Co ret r17.11.08; cvtd due 17.03.09, Aeroflot Cargo ntu; **N572FE** Federal Express 04.06.09; frd VCE-DXB-XSP 04-05.06.09 basic TAM cs, rr 20.07.09, due in svc 09.09, named "Masaki"

PP-VQJ • Varig Brasil • Los Angeles LAX • March 2004 Photo Sam Chui

PT-MSH • TAM Linhas Aéreas "The Magic Red Carpet" • Milan Malpensa MXP • February 2008 Photo Paolo Maggiolo

Line	C/N	mfd	model	Engines
614	**48634**	**05.97**	**MD-11F**	**PW**

HB-IWP sLGB 29.04.97 no engs, Swissair 11.07.97; is 06.08.97; Swiss AL nn 31.03.02; Bandung/Crossair r31.03.02, arr Mojave 16.06.03 white by 17.06.03, N647FE Federal Express 02/05 ntu; **N38WF** WFBN 23.06.03; s str Mojave 30.06.04 still HB-rgd, frd Mojave-Zurich 10.09.04 white, s20.12.04, for F-conv at SASCO Singapore in 2005 ntu, repo 25.01.05 being prepared for return to Mojave for str; **N280UP** UPS 24.02.05; frd ZRH-Louisville UPS fltnr, offic still N38WF but external reg N280UP, to ROW 27.02.05, presum still not F-cvtd, s02.04.05 white, offic rrgd 29.08.05 and F-cvtd by 09.05, s white HKG 15.12.05, sis fc 27.04.06

HB-IWP • Swissair • Long Beach LGB • June 1997

N280UP • UPS • Sydney SYD • July 2006

Photo Sam Chui

Line	C/N	mfd	model	Engines
615	**48758**	**06.97**	**MD-11F**	**GE**

PK-GIM Garuda s24.04.97 on prod line, s10.97 Long Beach fc, del 01.11.97; sis 27.10 Melbourne, sMarana 06.07.98 Gar cs, PP-SFP VASP res 22.09.98, ntu; **PP-VQK** Varig 14.11.99; reg res 19.10.99, del Marana-Sao Paulo 14.11.99, McDonnell Douglas Indonesia Leasing Inc r01.12.99, sFRA 21.02.04 nc, sRio de Janeiro GIG 14.03.05 repo st but sis 22.03.05; **PT-MSI** TAM s18.02.07; sis GIG, frd GRU-Venice 20.08.08 for freighter conv; **N742BC** Aeroflot Cargo due 20.08.08; McDonnell Douglas Corp, to McDonnell Douglas Indonesia Leasing 22.08.08, r05.09.08, Aeroflot Cargo due/ntu, canc 29.01.09; **ET-AML** Ethiopian AL Cargo 31.01.09; frd VCE-ADD 31.01.09 fc, repo as -ERF, last svc repo 06.06.13, but photos is exist 2014 and 03.03.15, pkd Addis Ababa presum late 04.2015, frd ADD--VCV 01-02.08.15 white, partial ET rudder; **N546BC** BCC Equipment Leasing ret r23.12.15, sVCV 30.07.16 pkd, canc 20.10.16 wfu

PP-VQK • Varig Brasil • Los Angeles LAX • April 2005

Photo Sam Chui

ET-AML • Ethiopian Cargo • Liège LGG • January 2010

Photo Jean-Marie Hanon

Line	C/N	mfd	model	Engines
616	**48775**	**07.97**	**MD-11F**	**GE**

HZ-ANB Saudi Arabian Cargo 30.12.97; s24.04.97 on production line, s06.07.97 fc, s10.97 str, del delayed/sMarana 22.11.97, frd 30-31.12.97, damaged Khartoum 09.06.09, repo frd back to Jeddah and 'retired' ar 2009-10, but last svc 29.06.14 KRT-JED, wfu Jeddah s10.14, s10.15

HZ-ANB • Saudi Arabian Cargo • Brussels BRU • May 2008 — Photo Benoît Denet

Line	C/N	mfd	model	Engines
617	**48776**	**08.97**	**MD-11F**	**GE**

N90178 McDonnell Douglas s26.08.97 LBG; **HZ-ANC** Saudi Arabian Cargo 31.12.97; s10.98 LGB str, del delayed, s22.11.97 Marana, frd 31.12-01.01.98, last service 26.06.14 BOM-RUH, wfu Jeddah s10.14, s10.15

HZ-ANC • Saudi Arabian Cargo • Amsterdam Schiphol AMS • March 2013 — Photo Michael S.Prophet

Line	C/N	mfd	model	Engines
618	**48777**	**09.97**	**MD-11F**	**GE**

N9166N McDonnell Douglas s14.12.97; **HZ-AND** Saudi Arabian Cargo 09.01.98; due 11.97, sLGB 23.08.97 fc, del delayed, s22.11.97 Marana, s10.98 LGB, last svc 15.04.14 RUH-JED, Jeddah s10.14, s10.15

N9166N • Saudi Arabian Cargo • stored pending delivery at Marana Pinal Airpark MZJ • November 1997 via Nicholas Scherrer

HZ-AND • Saudi Arabian Cargo • Brussels BRU • April 2010 Photo Guy Viselé

Line	C/N	mfd	model	Engines
619	**48778**	**10.97**	**MD-11F**	**GE**

B-16108 EVA AW 19.11.97; sLGB 06.07.97,10.97, EVA sold to Aircastle 12.11 lsd back, frd LAX-VCV 25.10.14, s wfu 16.09.15, s17.11.16

B-16108 • EVA Air Cargo • Brussels BRU • March 2007

Photo Guy Viselé

Line	C/N	mfd	model	Engines
620	**48778**	**11.97**	**MD-11F**	**GE**

B-16109 EVA AW 22.12.97; sLGB 10.97, sis 11.01.98 LHR, EVA sold to Aircastle 12.11 lsd back, wfu 08.01.15, frd LAX-VCV 08.01.15

B-16109 • EVA Air Cargo • Ostend OST • November 1999

Photo P.Van Damme

Line	C/N	mfd	model	Engines
621	**48541**	**12.97**	**MD-11F**	**PW**

HB-IWQ Swissair 22.12.97; allocated option JAPL, sLGB 12.11.97 fc, is 13.01.98, Federal Express N648FE 2002/05 ntu; Swiss AL nn 31.03.02; Bandung/Crossair r31.03.02, wfu sZRH 24.03.04, s24.04.04 hybrid fc, no engines, s10.06.04 white, due for F-conv at SASCO Singapore in 2005; **PP-VTU** Varig 15.09.04; sLIS 13.10.04 Star Alliance cs, Southern Winds ntu; **N284UP** UPS 20.01.06; bt ex WFBN, F-cvtd by 12.06.06, sHKG 11.07.06 white/grey, s08.03.07

HB-IWQ • Swiss • Tel Aviv Ben Gurion TLV

Photo M.Baltes

PP-VTU • Varig Brasil in Star Alliance livery • Los Angeles LAX • December 2005

Photo Sam Chui

Line	C/N	mfd	model	Engines
622	**48624**	**01.98**	**MD-11F**	**PW**

N815DE Delta AL 20.02.98; s str Goodyear GYR 16.08.03, s28.03.04 fc, s30.01.05 basic cs, s30.04.06 no engines; **N529FE** Federal Express 15.10.04; s12.10.06 HNL frd to SIN for F-conv in basic DL cs, rr res 31.10.06, rr 13.12.06, F-cvtd as of 13.02.07, ferried SIN-SFS 28.02.07, op first rev service SFS-HKG 28.02.07

N815DE • ex Delta Air Lines • Phoenix Goodyear GYR • December 2005 Photo Sam Chui

N529FE • FedEx Express • Paris Charles de Gaulle CDG • August 2009 Photo Jacques Guillem

Line	C/N	mfd	model	Engines
623	**48756**	**02.98**	**MD-11F**	**PW**

OO-CTS City Bird/Sabena s14.02.98 and 19.03.98 LGB in full SN cs; r16.03.98 own CBSA PL, is 15.04.98, wfu 28.02.01; City Bird ret 01.03.01; frd to Zurich 01.03.01, Chateauroux 06.03.01, Victorville 27.03.01 fc, OO-reg canc 03.04.01, s29.07.01 str white no vis reg; **P4-TKA** CBSA PL rr 09.01; str VCV, id s28.10.01 white, s08.11.01, s28.02.02; **N279WA** World AW 22.05.02; CBSA Partners LLC rgd 15.05.02, testfl VCV 19.05.02, lsd to World AW 5.02, sis 3.08.02 Nüremberg fc, op military charter, sVCV 02.10.02; sVCV 16.11.02 as N279WA, sis BKK 21.11.02, sis FRA 27.02.04, cvtd to *F as of 17.10.06, sMXP 29.10.06 nc, frd Leipzig-VCV 31.03.12 for str, s16.10.12; **Z-BPL** AV Cargo 09.13; frd VCV-CGK 19-20.07.13 for repaint, N-reg canc 05.08.13, s19.08.13 fcs, sLGG 16.02.14 optnl, named "Hannah Mai", sis 21.10.14 white; **Z-GAC** Global Africa Aviation slsd 10.14; s30.12.14 OST white optnl, sLGG 04.07.15, s str VCV 17.11.16 (not flown since 15.10.16); **N640BC** CBSA Partners LLC rgd 03.01.17

OO-CTS • Sabena • Long Beach LGB • March 1998 Photo M.Carter

Z-BPL • AV Cargo "Hannah Mai" • Freetown Lungi FNA • February 2014 Photo Benoît Denet

Line	C/N	mfd	model	Engines
624	**48780**	**02.98**	**MD-11F**	**GE**

OO-CTC City Bird/Sabena 16.04.98; final passenger MD-11 aircraft, is 04.05.98, op last SN MD-11 svc CKY-BRU 28.02.01, wfu BRU 01.03.01; City Bird ret 01.03.01; wfu for Citybird 05.03.01, frd to VCV 24.03.01 full SN cs, OO-reg canc 29.03.01, s29.07.01 full SN cs str; **P4-SWM** CBSA PL rr s17.10.01; sVCV white no tit, id s08.11.01; **P4-TKB** CBSA PL rr s08.11.01; **P4-SWM** BCC rr s15.12.01; frd Victorville-Rome 15-16.12.01, own BCC by 08.02, sGoodrich/Everett 17.10.02 white, s01.11.02, s10.01.03 now full Finnair cs, s31.01.03 now OH-LGE on nosewheel door; **OH-LGE** Finnair 21.02.03; frd Everett-Helsinki 21-22.02.03, own CBSA P LLC r17.03.03, wfu 09.03.09, sHEL 27.03.09 basic cs no titles; **N588BC** CBSA Partners LLC ret r17.04.09; canc 25.08.09; **ET-AND** Ethiopian AL Cargo 25.08.09; in svc 18.09.09 after F-conversion at Singapore QPG, wfu 02.02.2015 pkd Addis Ababa, frd ADD-VCV 18-19.07.15 mostly white, partial tail cs, due to be broken up; **N588BC** CBSA Partners LLC ret r04.08.15, sVCV 30.07.16 pkd, N-reg canc 21.09.16 wfu VCV, s17.11.16

The last passenger MD-11 built … OO-CTC • Sabena with City Bird, Swissair and Sabena 75th 1928-1998 anniversary stickers • Brussels BRU • January 1999

ET-AND • Ethiopian Cargo • Brussels BRU • April 2011

Photo Sébastien Charousset

Line	C/N	mfd	model	Engines	
625	**48781**	**04.98**	**MD-11F**	**GE**	**N9020Q** McDonnell Douglas s24.04.98 in full LH cs; frd 25-26.06.98 LGB-FRA as such; **D-ALCA** Lufthansa Cargo 25.06.98; rr 26.06, is 30.06.98

N9020Q • Lufthansa Cargo • Long Beach LGB • June 1998

D-ALCA • Lufthansa Cargo • Sharjah SHJ • November 2009

Photo Guy Viselé

Line	C/N	mfd	model	Engines
626	**48782**	**05.98**	**MD-11F**	**GE**

N9166N McDonnell Douglas; frd LGB-FRA 25-26.06.98 N-rgd, rr 26.06.98; **D-ALCB** Lufthansa Cargo 25.06.98

D-ALCB • Lufthansa Cargo • Sharjah SHJ • December 2003 Photo Richard Vandervord

D-ALCB • Lufthansa Cargo • Frankfurt am Main FRA • August 2013 Photo Richard Vandervord

Line	C/N	mfd	model	Engines
627	**48783**	**06.98**	**MD-11F**	**GE**

D-ALCC Lufthansa Cargo 13.08.98; sLGB 28.06.98 fc, s30.08.11 add ULD Container/100 Year Air Cargo titles, last svc as such 24.12.12, in svc standard cs 26.01.13, in svc 05.02.13 add 'Aktion Deutschland Hilft' sticker

D-ALCC • Lufthansa Cargo • Long Beach LGB • June 1998

On August 19, 1911, the first German all-cargo flight with a single-engine "Harlan" was operated from Berlin to Frankfurt/Oder. For the 100th anniversary, this MD-11F received a special livery to demonstrate the long history of air freight.

D-ALCC • Lufthansa Cargo • Frankfurt am Main FRA • September 2012

Photo Frank de Koster

Line	C/N	mfd	model	Engines
628	**48784**	**07.98**	**MD-11F**	**GE**

D-ALCD Lufthansa Cargo 17.09.98; sLGB 28.06.98 fc

D-ALCD • Lufthansa Cargo • Long Beach LGB • June 1998

D-ALCD • Lufthansa Cargo • Nairobi Jomo Kenyatta NBO • February 2016

Photo Michel Huart

Line	C/N	mfd	model	Engines
629	**48785**	**08.98**	**MD-11F**	**GE**

D-ALCE Lufthansa Cargo 22.10.98; sLGB 08.08.98 fc, s07.08.03 Helsinki new Wow cs, frd FRA-Leipzig LEJ 19.03.09 for storage, ret to FRA 17.10.09, ret in svc 21.11.09, recertified 08.12.09, damaged 24.11.13 Sao Paulo VCP struck its tail on landing, subst. damaged, repaired, named 'Marhaba Turkey" at IST 15.10.14

D-ALCE • Lufthansa Cargo WOW livery • Frankfurt am Main FRA • July 2005 Photo Sébastien Charousset

D-ALCE • Lufthansa Cargo • Frankfurt am Main FRA • May 2014 Photo Frank de Koster

Line	C/N	mfd	model	Engines
630	**48786**	**08.98**	**MD-11F**	**GE**

B-16110 EVA AW 14.10.98; frd LAX-VCV 30.01.14, s str 27.01.15, s16.03.15 bcs engines taped, s04.08.16

B-16110 • Eva Air Cargo • Los Angeles LAX • March 2004 Photo Sam Chui

Line	C/N	mfd	model	Engines
631	**48787**	**09.98**	**MD-11F**	**GE**

B-16111 EVA AW 12.11.98; sLGB 08.10.98 fc, frd LAX-VCV 12.08.13 for str, s27.10.13 str no engines, s04.01.14 white, s 08.14 most parts like doors, cargo door missing, s23.10.14

B-16111 • Eva Air Cargo • Brussels BRU • August 2007 Photo Jean-Marie Hanon

Line	C/N	mfd	model	Engines
632	**48788**	**10.98**	**MD-11F**	**PW**

PH-MCW Martinair 20.11.98; sLGB 08.10.98 fc, sAMS 27.02.05 nc, sAMS 18.09.14 named "Martin Schröder", available for sale available 06.16 repo 11.15 TT 75000, 15000 L, wfu 05.03.16, frd MIA-Mojave 06.03.16, canc 14.03.16, wfu

PH-MCW • Martinair Cargo • Amsterdam Schiphol

Photo Frank de Koster

PH-MCW • Martinair Cargo • Nairobi Jomo Kenyatta NBO • January 2016

Photo Michel Huart

Line	C/N	mfd	model	Engines
633	**48789**	**12.98**	**MD-11F**	**GE**

N90178 McDonnell Douglas; sLGB 28.11.98 fc as **B-16112**, sKingman AZ 20.04.99 fc, s08.06.99 rrgd as N-; B-16112 EVA AW 29.07.99; sTPE 22.02.14 Eva bcs no titles, frd LAX-San Bernardino 03.03.14 for str, s05.15 engine(s) missing but good cond bcs, s wfu 16.09.15 no engines, s16.10.16

B-16112 • Eva Air Cargo • Taipei TPE • July 2012 Photo Mark Tang

Line	C/N	mfd	model	Engines
634	**48790**	**01.99**	**MD-11F**	**GE**

N9020Q McDonnell Douglas; sLGB 12.02.99 fc, tailplane being fitted as B-, s26.04.99 LB N-rgd; **B-16113** EVA AW 26.08.99; sis 01.09.99 SIN, frd 26.03.09 LAX-VCV for storage, frd VCV-LAX-TPE 08.05.10 after str, wfu 23.03.15 TPE-LAX as final Eva MD-11 service, frd LAX-San Bernardino 23.03.15, s wfu 16.09.15 no engines, s16.10.16, s05.02.17 most parts removed including engines, doors, etc. but still standing on undercarriage

B-16113 • Eva Air Cargo • Anchorage ANC • August 2007 Photo Michael S.Prophet

Line	C/N	mfd	model	Engines
635	**48791**	**03.99**	**MD-11F**	**PW**

N620FE Federal Express 30.03.99; sLGB 24.02.99 fc, to LAX 25.03.99 already, SSB&TC 29.03.99, frd LAX-YVR 31.03.99, frd YVR-MEM 01.04.99, first revenue svc MEM-OAK 03.04.99, named "Grady", USB r19.08.05

N620FE • FedEx Express "Grady" • on shoft final for Runway 34L at Narita NRT • September 2009 Photo Kentaro Iemoto

Line	C/N	mfd	model	Engines
636	**48792**	**04.99**	**MD-11F**	**PW**

N621FE Federal Express 28.05.99; sLGB 03.04.99 fc named "Connor", TT 10, 15 L at del, SSB&TC 28.05.99, USB r15.08.05

N621FE • FedEx Express • Anchorage ANC • August 2011 Photo Wil Teunissen

Line	C/N	mfd	model	Engines
637	**48798**	**07.99**	**MD-11F**	**GE**

D-ALCF Lufthansa Cargo 27.08.99; sLGB 13.07.99, named 'Marhaba Egypt' on 16.10.16

D-ALCF • Lufthansa Cargo • Johannesburg O. R. Tambo JNB • September 2010 Photo Richard Vandervord

Line	C/N	mfd	model	Engines
638	**48794**	**05.99**	**MD-11F**	**PW**

N623FE Federal Express 28.06.99; sLGB 29.05.99 fc named "Meghan", sLAX 23.06.99, TT 14, 15 L at del, del LAX-YVR-MEM 29-30.06.99, SSB&TC r29.06.99, first revenue svc MEM-LAX 01.07.99, USB r15.08.05

N623FE • FedEx Express "Meghan" • Dubai DXB • February 2008 Photo Benoît Denet

Line	C/N	mfd	model	Engines
639	**48799**	**08.99**	**MD-11F**	**GE**

D-ALCG Lufthansa Cargo 12.10.99; wfu 22.12.15, frd FRA-VCV 01.02.15 for str, named "Konnichiwa Japan", s20.02.16

D-ALCG • Lufthansa Cargo • Johannesburg O. R. Tambo JNB • September 2010 Photo Richard Vandervord

Line	C/N	mfd	model	Engines
640	**48801**	**10.99**	**MD-11F**	**GE**

D-ALCH Lufthansa Cargo 24.11.99; sis 15.06.15 'Buenos dias México' add titles, s12.15 special "Step by step. Giving children a future – cargohumancare.com" livery to support a special humanitarian and medical aid project which was founded by employees of Lufthansa Cargo in 2004

D-ALCH • Lufthansa Cargo • Frankfurt am Main FRA • August 2013 Photo Jannik Femerling

Line	C/N	mfd	model	Engines
641	**48800**	**11.99**	**MD-11F**	**GE**

D-ALCI Lufthansa Cargo 27.01.00; sLGB 04.12.99 fc

D-ALCI • Lufthansa Cargo • Frankfurt am Main FRA • August 2013 Photo Jannik Femerling

Line	C/N	mfd	model	Engines
642	**48802**	**01.00**	**MD-11F**	**GE**

D-ALCJ Lufthansa Cargo 23.03.00; sis Delhi 18.03.15 christened 'Namaste India' at ceremony

D-ALCJ • Lufthansa Cargo • Frankfurt am Main FRA • November 2012 Photo Jannik Femerling

Line	C/N	mfd	model	Engines
643	**48803**	**02.00**	**MD-11F**	**GE**

N9166N Boeing; sLGB 10.04.00 fc; **D-ALCK** Lufthansa Cargo 31.05.00

D-ALCK • Lufthansa Cargo • Frankfurt am Main FRA • August 2013 Photo Jannik Femerling

Line	C/N	mfd	model	Engines
644	**48804**	**04.00**	**MD-11F**	**GE**

D-ALCL Lufthansa Cargo 24.08.00; sLGB 25.04.00 fc, frd FRA-VCV 26.04.16, wfu

D-ALCL • Lufthansa Cargo with WOW sticker • Frankfurt am Main FRA • July 2005 Photo Sébastien Charousset

Line	C/N	mfd	model	Engines
645	**48805**	**08.00**	**MD-11F**	**GE**

N90178 Boeing; sLGB 02.10.00, s13.11.00 primer/LH tail; **N9069R** Boeing rr; **D-ALCM** Lufthansa Cargo 22.02.01; sLGB 22.06.00 tail LH cs, final MD-11 delivery, s27.07.16 now named 'Buongiorno Italy', damaged 10.11.16 Buenos Aires EZE 0(2), left nosewheel came off on landing, lower fuselage damage, ferried EZE-VCV 24.01

D-ALCM • Lufthansa Cargo • Frankfurt am Main FRA • July 2014 Photo Jannik Femerling

Line	C/N	mfd	model	Engines
646	**48806**	**10.00**	**MD-11F**	**GE**

D-ALCN Lufthansa Cargo 25.01.01; last MD-11, ro 14.09.00

The last MD-11 built … D-ALCN • Lufthansa Cargo • Frankfurt am Main FRA • March 2009 Photo Frank de Koster

MD-11 Registration Cross Reference

Reg	Line	c/n
9M-TGP	459	48444
9M-TGQ	463	48446
9M-TGR	502	48485
9M-TGS	509	48486
B-150	518	48468
B-151	519	48469
B-152	546	48470
B-153	558	48471
B-16101	570	48542
B-16102	572	48543
B-16103	576	48415
B-16106	587	48545
B-16107	589	48546
B-16108	619	48778
B-16109	620	48779
B-16110	630	48786
B-16111	631	48787
B-16112	633	48789
B-16113	634	48790
B-18151	546	48470
B-18152	558	48471
B-18272	519	48469
B-2170	475	48461
B-2171	461	48495
B-2172	496	48496
B-2173	512	48497
B-2174	522	48498
B-2175	541	48520
B-2176	576	48415
B-2177	580	48544
B-2178	572	48543
B-2179	587	48545
D-AERB	484	48484
D-AERW	502	48485
D-AERX	509	48486
D-AERZ	533	48538
D-ALCA	625	48781
D-ALCB	626	48782
D-ALCC	627	48783
D-ALCD	628	48784
D-ALCE	629	48785
D-ALCF	637	48798
D-ALCG	639	48799
D-ALCH	640	48801
D-ALCI	641	48800
D-ALCJ	642	48802
D-ALCK	643	48803
D-ALCL	644	48804
D-ALCM	645	48805
D-ALCN	646	48806
D-ALCO	488	48413
D-ALCP	491	48414
D-ALCQ	534	48431
D-ALCR	565	48581
D-ALCS	567	48630
EI-CDI	486	48499
EI-CDJ	493	48500
EI-CDK	513	48501
EI-EMS	600	48766
EI-UPA	468	48426
EI-UPE	471	48427
EI-UPI	474	48428
EI-UPO	500	48429
EI-UPU	508	48430
ET-AML	615	48758
ET-AND	624	48780
HB-IWA	458	48443
HB-IWB	459	48444
HB-IWC	460	48445
HB-IWD	463	48446
HB-IWE	464	48447
HB-IWF	465	48448
HB-IWG	472	48452
HB-IWH	473	48453
HB-IWI	477	48454
HB-IWK	487	48455
HB-IWL	494	48456
HB-IWM	498	48457
HB-IWN	571	48539
HB-IWO	611	48540
HB-IWP	614	48634
HB-IWQ	621	48541
HB-IWR	484	48484
HB-IWS	502	48485
HB-IWT	509	48486
HB-IWU	533	48538
HL7371	456	48407
HL7372	457	48408
HL7373	490	48409
HL7374	495	48410
HL7375	516	48523
HS-TMD	466	48416
HS-TME	467	48417
HS-TMF	501	48418
HS-TMG	505	48451
HZ-AFA1	544	48533
HZ-AFAS	544	48533
HZ-ANA	609	48773
HZ-ANB	616	48775
HZ-ANC	617	48776
HZ-AND	618	48777
HZ-HM7	532	48532
HZ-HM8	544	48533
I-DUPA	468	48426
I-DUPB	534	48431
I-DUPC	565	48581
I-DUPD	567	48630
I-DUPE	471	48427
I-DUPI	474	48428
I-DUPO	500	48429
I-DUPU	508	48430
JA8580	552	48571
JA8581	556	48572
JA8582	559	48573
JA8583	566	48574
JA8584	568	48575
JA8585	574	48576
JA8586	583	48577
JA8587	588	48578
JA8588	599	48579
JA8589	610	48774
N103EV	576	48415
N105EV	580	48544
N106BV	587	48545
N111MD	447	48401
N15WF	509	48486
N1750B	450	48419
N1751A	451	48420
N1752K	452	48421
N1753	469	48487
N1754	492	48489
N1755	499	48490
N1756	503	48491
N1757A	462	48505
N1758B	504	48527
N1759	482	48481
N1760A	526	48550
N1761R	527	48551
N1762B	530	48552
N1763	531	48553
N1764B	535	48554
N1765B	537	48596
N1766A	540	48597
N1767A	550	48598
N1768D	483	48436
N211MD	448	48402
N216AW	474	48428
N216SC	580	48544
N250UP	596	48745
N251UP	592	48744
N252UP	601	48768

N253UP	554	48439
N254UP	547	48406
N255UP	523	48404
N256UP	524	48405
N257UP	505	48451
N258UP	466	48416
N259UP	467	48417
N260UP	501	48418
N269WA	479	48450
N270UP	574	48576
N270WA	455	48449
N271UP	556	48572
N271WA	525	48518
N272UP	552	48571
N272WA	506	48437
N273UP	566	48574
N273WA	539	48519
N274UP	568	48575
N274WA	563	48633
N275UP	610	48774
N275WA	579	48631
N276UP	599	48579
N276WA	582	48632
N277UP	588	48578
N277WA	590	48743
N278UP	583	48577
N278WA	597	48746
N279UP	559	48573
N279WA	623	48756
N280UP	614	48634
N280WA	449	48458
N281UP	533	48538
N282UP	472	48452
N283UP	484	48484
N284UP	621	48541
N285UP	498	48457
N286UP	473	48453
N287UP	571	48539
N288UP	611	48540
N289UP	487	48455
N290UP	494	48456
N291UP	511	48477
N292UP	543	48566
N293UP	481	48473
N294UP	480	48472
N295UP	489	48475
N296UP	485	48474
N30051	480	48472
N30075	485	48474
N311MD	449	48458
N37WF	473	48453
N380BC	520	48502
N380WA	456	48407
N381WA	516	48523
N382BC	528	48503
N382WA	453	48411
N383BC	548	48504
N383WA	454	48412
N384WA	478	48435
N38WF	614	48634
N411MD	450	48419
N411SN	453	48411
N412SN	454	48412
N413LT	488	48413
N414LT	491	48414
N415JN	576	48415
N431LT	534	48431
N435KD	478	48435
N460BC	600	48766
N485LS	493	48500
N489GX	449	48458
N48WF	533	48538
N499HE	486	48499
N501FR	513	48501
N510MD	452	48421
N511MD	451	48420
N512JN	529	48512
N512SU	529	48512
N513AY	564	48513
N513SN	564	48513
N514MD	453	48411
N521FE	514	48478
N522FE	510	48476
N523FE	536	48479
N524FE	538	48480
N525FE	542	48565
N526FE	560	48600
N527FE	562	48601
N528FE	605	48623
N529FE	622	48624
N538MD	528	48503
N539MD	548	48504
N540MD	520	48502
N542KD	570	48542
N543JN	572	48543
N545BC	624	48780
N545JN	587	48545
N546BC	615	48758
N546JN	589	48546
N572FE	613	48755
N573FE	603	48769
N574FE	486	48499
N575FE	493	48500
N575SH	495	48410
N576FE	513	48501
N577FE	519	48469
N578FE	449	48458
N579FE	546	48470
N580FE	558	48471
N581FE	450	48419
N581JN	565	48581
N581LT	565	48581
N582FE	451	48420
N583FE	452	48421
N584FE	483	48436
N585FE	482	48481
N586FE	469	48487
N587FE	492	48489
N588BC	624	48780
N588FE	499	48490
N589FE	503	48491
N590FE	462	48505
N591FE	504	48527
N592FE	526	48550
N593FE	527	48551
N594FE	530	48552
N595FE	531	48553
N596FE	535	48554
N597FE	537	48596
N598FE	540	48597
N599FE	550	48598
N601FE	447	48401
N602FE	448	48402
N603FE	470	48459
N604FE	497	48460
N605FE	515	48514
N6069R	645	48805
N606FE	549	48504
N607FE	517	48547
N608FE	521	48548
N609FE	545	48549
N610FE	551	48603
N611FE	553	48604
N612FE	555	48605
N613FE	598	48749
N614FE	507	48528
N615FE	602	48767
N616FE	594	48747
N617FE	595	48748
N618FE	604	48754
N619FE	607	48770
N6202D	557	48555
N6202S	562	48601
N6203D	590	48743
N6203U	592	48744
N6203U	600	48766
N620FE	635	48791
N621FE	636	48792
N623FE	638	48794
N624FE	458	48443
N625FE	459	48444
N625FE	608	48753
N626FE	460	48445
N627FE	463	48446
N628FE	464	48447
N630LT	567	48630
N630SN	567	48630
N631FE	477	48454
N640BC	623	48756
N642FE	502	48485
N643FE	509	48486
N644FE	459	48444

N645FE	463	48446
N68089	584	48618
N68091	606	48757
N68092	582	48632
N68093	563	48633
N701GC	476	48434
N702BC	548	48504
N702GC	478	48435
N703GC	453	48411
N705GC	454	48412
N71WF	502	48485
N725BC	528	48503
N730BC	613	48755
N742BC	615	48758
N746BC	603	48769
N74WF	472	48452
N774BC	520	48502
N783BC	600	48766
N785BC	608	48753
N797BA	592	48744
N798BA	596	48745
N799BA	603	48769
N801DE	480	48472
N802DE	481	48473
N803DE	485	48474
N804DE	489	48475
N805DE	510	48476
N806DE	511	48477
N807DE	514	48478
N808DE	536	48479
N809DE	538	48480
N810DE	542	48565
N811DE	543	48566
N812DE	562	48601
N813DE	560	48600
N814DE	605	48623
N815DE	622	48624
N891DL	453	48411
N892DL	454	48412
N9012J	506	48437
N90178	560	48600
N90178	633	48789
N90187	577	48616
N90187	596	48745
N90187	596	48745
N90187	609	48773
N9020Q	597	48746
N9020Q	625	48781
N9020U	528	48503
N9020Z	468	48426
N9020Z	474	48428
N9020Z	544	48533
N9076Y	548	48504
N9093P	532	48532
N91078	617	48776
N9134D	601	48768
N91566	616	48775
N9166N	603	48769
N9166N	618	48777
N9166X	547	48406
N950AR	475	48461
N951AR	461	48495
N952AR	512	48497
N953AR	541	48520
N954AR	522	48498
N955AR	496	48496
N956AR	586	48629
N984AR	500	48429
N985AR	508	48430
N986AR	468	48426
N987AR	471	48427
N988AR	476	48434
N988PG	457	48408
OH-LGA	455	48449
OH-LGB	479	48450
OH-LGC	529	48512
OH-LGD	564	48513
OH-LGE	624	48780
OH-LGF	600	48766
OH-LGG	608	48753
OH-NGA	570	48542
OH-NGB	589	48546
OO-CTB	600	48766
OO-CTC	624	48780
OO-CTS	623	48756
P4-BDL	600	48766
P4-SWM	624	48780
P4-TKA	623	48756
P4-TKB	624	48780
PH-KCA	557	48555
PH-KCB	561	48556
PH-KCC	569	48557
PH-KCD	573	48558
PH-KCE	575	48559
PH-KCF	578	48560
PH-KCG	585	48561
PH-KCH	591	48562
PH-KCI	593	48563
PH-KCK	612	48564
PH-MCP	577	48616
PH-MCR	581	48617
PH-MCS	584	48618
PH-MCT	586	48629
PH-MCU	606	48757
PH-MCW	632	48788
PH-MCY	460	48445
PK-GIG	520	48502
PK-GIH	493	48500
PK-GII	528	48503
PK-GIJ	548	48504
PK-GIK	608	48753
PK-GIL	613	48755
PK-GIM	615	48758
PP-SFA	601	48768
PP-SFD	603	48769
PP-SOW	488	48413
PP-SOZ	491	48414
PP-SPD	453	48411
PP-SPE	454	48412
PP-SPK	592	48744
PP-SPL	596	48745
PP-SPM	593	48563
PP-VOP	476	48434
PP-VOQ	478	48435
PP-VPJ	523	48404
PP-VPK	524	48405
PP-VPL	547	48406
PP-VPM	554	48439
PP-VPN	486	48499
PP-VPO	493	48500
PP-VPP	513	48501
PP-VQF	520	48502
PP-VQG	528	48503
PP-VQH	548	48504
PP-VQI	608	48753
PP-VQJ	613	48755
PP-VQK	615	48758
PP-VQL	488	48413
PP-VQM	491	48414
PP-VQX	603	48769
PP-VTF	459	48444
PP-VTG	463	48446
PP-VTH	498	48457
PP-VTI	494	48456
PP-VTJ	487	48455
PP-VTK	611	48540
PP-VTP	571	48539
PP-VTU	473	48453
PP-VTU	621	48541
PR-LGD	457	48408
PR-LGE	495	48410
PT-MSH	613	48755
PT-MSI	615	48758
PT-MSJ	603	48769
V5-NMC	484	48484
V5-NMD	473	48453
VP-BDP	520	48502
VP-BDQ	548	48504
Z-BAM	597	48746
Z-BAV	457	48408
Z-BPL	623	48756
Z-BVT	495	48410
Z-GAA	495	48410
Z-GAB	597	48746
Z-GAC	623	48756

7 Traffic jam in the Monsoon

by Pierre Rohr

On this morning of the 26th of May 2001, I came as usual on the early flight from Geneva to Zürich to start my duty there. I was quite happy since, even after three years on the MD-11 at Swissair, today will be my first flight to Mumbai (BOM/VOMM).

Part of the daily routine was the meeting with the captain, collecting the papers at the dispatch, and if necessary, getting additional information from the dispatcher in conversation, and then meeting our cabin crew.

It soon became apparent that routine will not be the perfect word to describe the following days. It started with the captain, who I did not know before today: overweight and sweating profusely, even before starting duty. (During the trip, I noticed that his crew bag was about the weight of a dead cow, but I also noticed this was not the only reason of the sweat coming out from all parts of his body.)

The departure from routine continued at the dispatch office. They started by telling us that one runway in Mumbai was closed (14/32). In addition, taxiway N ("November") normally used to vacate runway 27 ("two-seven") was closed as well, requiring backtrack after landing, leading to delays due to longer runway occupancy time. Oh, and by the way, they also expect the first monsoon rains after the dry season, with strong gusty southerly winds. To be elaborate: pouring rain over five months of dust is more slippery than a mixture of slush, wet snow and ice. Add a crosswind of twenty knots gusting up to forty and you have the perfect ingredients for a possible diversion.

The rest of the preflight process ran smoothly and we got airborne on time. Our expected remaining fuel at Mumbai was twenty-five and a half tons. A quite unusual figure when ten is normal; ten tons covering a missed approach at destination, a diversion and then a final reserve of three and a half tons. Get down to those last three and a half tons and you're declaring an emergency.

The flight was comfortable, the captain not very talkative. Everything was quiet until our first contact with Mumbai upper sector.

In the cockpit at Shanghai Pudong in November 2000

We were cleared to descent to FL270, to proceed via our route to the BBB VOR overhead the field and to hold there. Starting your holding pattern at FL270 is never a good sign. You directly start looking at your fuel gauges, calculate how long? What if…?

The frequency was surprisingly quiet, with two or three other aircraft checking in, giving us an overly optimistic mental picture of the traffic situation. After almost an hour circling, we managed to get only 2000 feet down to FL250. I contacted the tower on box two; they were as communicative as my captain, but they did say to expect five knots of crosswind and light rain. Traffic seemed fairly light on his frequency as well. I asked him the reason for the long holding times. "Standby." Thirty seconds later, we got clearance to descent to FL140, giving us a real hope of a somewhat successful landing at the planned destination.

We still had suspicions about the tower controller, since the weather we got from our ACARS was definitely not as clement as the weather he gave us. On the other hand, as every house-trained pilot, we remained company-minded, with every intention of bringing our passengers to their destination. So we stayed over BBB and lost New Delhi (DEL/VIDP) as alternate (the furthest, requiring some sixteen tons at the start of the diversion, but a very good option, since it was a

Swissair station, and it was not yet affected by the monsoon). It left us with three possibilities: two airports in India, Hyderabad (HYD/VOHS), and Ahmedabad (AMD/VAAH), also affected by the monsoon, as well as Karachi (KHI/OPKC) in Pakistan which was rather politically incorrect given that we had about two-hundred Indian passengers on board.

We checked the fuel gauges. I also told the captain I would keep a constant listening watch on the tower frequency, and, if necessary, push a bit the controller to get some decent information, but some fellow pilots did that for me, courtesy of Singapore Airlines and British Airways. The first politely said they were performing a missed approach due to low visibility in heavy rain and out of limits crosswind. Speedbird got their landing clearance accompanied by a report of a five knot crosswind. They also ended up performing a missed approach but without the politeness, and called the controller a liar and a cheat, guilty of endangering air safety by giving wrong informations. It was a lovely treat to hear such nonstandard phraseology delivered with such a beautiful British accent. But it was now clear, our passengers would not reach their final destination in the near future.

After checking the weather situation, we asked for diversion to Hyderabad. The reply from Mumbai Upper Sector, even without a real British accent, was clear. "Oh no, no, sir, airport is closed. Too many aircraft, too many aircraft, taxiways blocked." "Huh. OK, what about Ahmedabad then?" The reply was the same as before, word for word.

Thirty minutes later, we performed a perfect touchdown (although by now nobody could care less!) at the politically incorrect airport of Karachi, after nine hours and forty-five minutes flying time instead of the planned seven hours fifteen, with just 5.7 tons of fuel on board, fifteen minutes of flying time shy of declaring an emergency.

The message from Zürich was clear and not unexpected. "Return to Mumbai." The first rainy front will be gone in three hours, they say. OK. No word about duty time, no word about the wind, which after verification on ACARS, will be exactly the same as it was an hour ago. Despite carefully studying our airport charts, I could not find any mention of a huge hairdryer driven by a 200,000 horse power engine to turn the iceskating park of Mumbai (also sometimes known as runway 09/27), into a proper landing facility for heavy aircraft.

Our reply to Zürich was not unexpected either. "No way!" We were unable to return to Mumbai in these conditions. The whole crew went quickly to an hotel to get the minimum required rest, while our passengers, not being allowed to leave the terminal, had a very uncomfortable night in comparison.

The next morning, we return to our brave MD-11 to prepare the flight to Mumbai. The captain looked like he just went under the shower in uniform. He was sweating even more than in Zürich. The temperature outside rising quickly to up to forty-six degrees so he wisely retired in the flight deck, in the hope that our poor APU will somewhat cool the aircraft, and its commander. I jumped out to help fuel the plane (no MD-11 qualified mechanics in Karachi), did the outside check, and then joined the station manager in his not-airconditioned car to do a real fully manual old-fashioned loadsheet. (The car was nicely parked in the sun and my sweating was close to reaching that of my captain, who was still retired in the cockpit. I am still wondering today what he did up there, since the cockpit

April 1998

preparation, for the captain, requires a maximum of five minutes, after which he is usually busy with some simple administrative jobs, and then around the aeroplane with other operational matters.) Finally we were done, all passengers on board, ready to go. Story finished…?

NOPE! Hardly two minutes before requiring start up, a cute little yellow light showed up on the overhead pannel: AGT LOW. Argh! We just lost one of our two extinguishing bottles for our tail-mounted engine and the APU. This was a no-go item. The situation was dramatically clear for me. The APU had been running for one and a half hours at maximum power with an outside temperature of forty-six degrees. An overheat in the tailcone area had led the overpressure valve to blow and discharge the extinguishing agent. I urge the captain to call our duty officer in Zürich to grant an exceptional authorisation to leave with just one bottle. We were so light, we could even offer to shut off engine number two just a few minutes after take-off and fly one-engine out to Mumbai. We really had to hurry to get this permission before the second bottle went the same way. And even as the thought was forming, bottle two blew. We had lost all extinguishing possibilities for the engine number two engine. We just had one back-up bottle left for the APU only. Now this poor device (sweating like us to deliver power and air conditioning to some 240 people) had almost no more fire protection in his overheated area. We had to keep a close look at the APU parameters.

This might actually seem like a detail, compared explaining to two-hundred exhausted Indians, they will have to deboard the plane for a second time in Pakistan. We had four Indian flight attendants on board to both New Delhi and Mumbai, but all four were afraid and hid in the cockpit.

So well, someone had to do it. I went bravely to the cabin and soon found myself facing thirty quite aggressive people standing in the galley, all wondering why exactly we could not go again. It took me more than twenty minutes to explain it could be more dangerous to fly than to stay. It was not easy, and I could really understand those poor people fearing for their lives.

Only then did the local Swissair operation explain to me the passengers could get a temporary forty-eight hour visa to leave the airport and be accommodated in hotels nearby! Why did not they tell me that the last evening? Still a wonder for me.

So is that where the story finished?! More or less, yes! Finally!

Our passengers left Karachi during the night on a specially chartered PIA Airbus A300. The Swissair Cargo flight from Basel to Hong Kong, operated by a Gemini Air Cargo DC-10 (another beautiful tri-jet!) took two mechanics and the spare parts along, and dropped them during the same night in Karachi. The next day, we left ferry

At São Paulo with HB-IWL

back to Zürich after some «easy sweat» flight preparation. We started the APU as late as possible before starting up our engines for an uneventful flight back home.

Upon our return to Zurich, we had a meeting in the chief pilot's office, with people from different operations centres, maintenance, dispatch, you name it. We then learnt that this story went quickly to Indian newpapers, saying that two-hundred Indians were threatened to death in Pakistan due to an unplanned landing of a Swissair MD-11 there. The embassies of Pakistan, India and Switzerland were on a top emergency level. All that while we were sweating under the Pakistani sun.

But to top it all, a girl from the planning office told me: "I don't understand why you didn't directly leave Karachi for Dubai instead of staying there?" What? This would have been THE solution! Why did she tell me that upon our return, quietly sitting in an office with tea and cookies, and not four days ago, that night when we landed in Karachi with 5.7 tons, and other things to think about, instead of reaching for an atlas and checking for our dream destination. The weather at Dubai was perfect, tons of hotels around, no political problems with our passengers, and no risk to skid our beautiful MD-11 out of a slippery runway while on overduty. Well, this is another unexplained wonder of life!

Today, I look back at this adventure with a smile, happy to have survived such an experience, to have learnt so much in such a short time! But I also look back at my six years flying the MD-11 for Swissair and Swiss International Airlines as a very intense and beautiful part of my flying career. Beside the very tragic loss of HB-IWF, I only have very good memories of the best-looking airplane I ever flew!

Photo Felix Gottwald